# Jesus, Qumran and the Vatican

# Jesus, Qumran and the Vatican

*Clarifications*

## Otto Betz and Rainer Riesner

SCM PRESS LTD

Translated by John Bowden from *Jesus, Qumran und der Vatikan. Klarstellungen*, third revised edition, published 1993 by Brunnen Verlag, Giessen and Herder Verlag, Freiburg im Breisgau.

© Brunnen Verlag 1993

Translation © John Bowden 1994

Maps by John Flower

334 02109 X

First British edition published 1994
by SCM Press Ltd,
26–30 Tottenham Road, London N1 4BZ

Phototypeset by Intype, London
and printed in Great Britain by
Biddles Ltd, Guildford and King's Lynn

# Contents

viii                        *Contents*

# Foreword

The Jewish scrolls which were discovered between 1947 and 1956 at Qumran near the north-western shore of the Dead Sea were the find of the century. This was perhaps the most important archaeological discovery ever for biblical scholarship. So it is understandable that from the start there was extraordinary interest in it, extending far beyond the church.

Two developments over the last five years have again stimulated the interest of a large public. First there was a great dispute over the publication of previously unpublished fragments from the scrolls. And then, since 1991, newspaper articles, reports in magazines, and indeed books have been appearing in close succession. Many of these publications claim to offer sensational disclosures and information about Qumran, Jesus and the earliest Christian community.

The present book is intended to provide some much-needed clarification of statements which have been propagated, sometimes in an irresponsible way. So our language is quite plain. Bluntness sometimes needs to be answered with bluntness. Qumran scholarship both scales the heights of academic activity and plumbs its depths. There are some matters about which one would prefer to keep silent, for the sake of those concerned, but in the end truth cannot be concealed.

We speak as scholars representing two different generations of Qumran scholarship. *Jesus, Qumran and the Vatican* is addressed to all interested readers and therefore does not presuppose any specialist knowledge, but in Chapters 3, 5 and 6 in particular the reader will be introduced to the difficulty of putting together, reading and understanding very fragmentary ancient texts. Here even the professionals may find some new proposals. Theological students who want to go more deeply into particular questions will find plenty of references to further literature in the notes. And interested readers who are not historians or theologians can pursue their study further through the bibliography at the end.

Chapters 3, 5-7 and 9 were written mainly by Otto Betz, and the rest by Rainer Riesner. However, each of us has read all the chapters of the book, so we are both responsible for it. We are delighted that this book documents a collaboration which began in the middle of the 1970s in the form of a relationship between doctoral student and supervisor. We would like to thank Professor James H.Charlesworth of Princeton Theological Seminary, Professor Heinz-Wolfgang Kuhn of the University of Munich and Carsten Peter Thiede of the German Institute in Paderborn for obtaining press-cuttings for us from both Germany and abroad. Rainer Straub provided us with important publishing information. We received great support in different ways from our assistants Ulrich Bauersfeld, Guido Heft and Tilmann Roth. Christoph Schilling and our wives Isolde Betz and Cornelia Riesner also read the proofs.

March 1993                                    Otto Betz and Rainer Riesner

Two editions sold out so quickly that it has proved possible each time only to correct a few mistakes and update some information. We are particularly grateful to Professor Joseph A. Fitzmyer SJ for his corrections which could be used in the English edition.

September 1993                              Otto Betz and Rainer Riesner

# 1

## Did the Vatican Suppress the Publication of the Qumran Scrolls?

*The Dead Sea Scrolls Deception* – Qumran: The find of the century – The editing of the Qumran writings – Top scholars and their personal crises – Warmed-up interpretations and controversies – Professors, television presenters and journalists

### *The Dead Sea Scrolls Deception*

One of the bestsellers of 1992 was *The Dead Sea Scrolls Deception*, by the journalists Michael Baigent and Richard Leigh.[1] The German translation, under the meretricious title *Verschlussache Jesus*, i.e 'the secret file on Jesus', appeared in September 1991 with a major advertising campaign, and within a month had begun to top the non-fiction bestseller lists, where it stayed for a year;[2] to date more than 400,000 copies have been sold in Germany alone. Unlike most theological books about Jesus and the early church, in this case one can certainly say that most of the copies bought were also read. The content of the book became an ongoing topic of private conversations and it was dealt with in countless lectures in parishes, colleges and academies. Anyone speaking on 'Jesus and the Qumran Scrolls' can still count on a full house.

These two authors have shown once more how one can achieve a sales success running into hundreds of thousands with a sense of what will catch on today, and with some journalistic skill. Baigent and Leigh combine three themes, each of which is in itself the ingredient of a bestseller. They promise new information about the Qumran scrolls, the uncovering of a conspiracy in the Vatican, and finally a revolution in our view of earliest Christianity. The book jacket of the German edition lures the reader on: 'In this book for the first time Michael Baigent and Richard Leigh disclose what explosive material has been suppressed – texts about the earliest Christians hitherto unknown...'

Their starting point is that the Gospels are fictitious accounts of the life of Jesus which are as late as the second century. In their view the Acts of the Apostles was not written to illuminate the beginnings of Christianity but to obscure them. So we must read precisely the opposite from Acts to what has previously been written. That would mean that the earliest Christians were not at all pious and peace-loving but part of the Jewish resistance movement against the occupying forces of Rome. Referring to as yet unpublished writings from Qumran, in their book Baigent and Leigh paint a real horror picture of the history of earliest Christianity. Thus they claim that whereas we know virtually nothing tangible about Jesus, the 'Teacher of Righteousness' in the Qumran texts denotes James the brother of the Lord. According to them he was a leader of the Jewish freedom movement in the first century CE. James lived in Qumran and was even elected a anti-High Priest there. The Jewish Sanhedrin, which had fallen into line with the occupying forces, attempted to suppress the rebels by force. In this connection, in particular a Jew called Saul, whom we know better under the name Paul, came to the fore. Paul alias Saul soon recognized that to make martyrs can only strengthen a rebel movement. It would be much more effective to destroy a powerful movement from within. Paul therefore feigned a conversion and consequently was able to slip into the innermost circle of the leadership. James even made him a kind of foreign minister. Paul was to recruit Jews for the messianic liberation struggle in the Diaspora, but he did something completely different. He falsified the execution of the revolutionary Jesus, turning it into an expiatory religious death, and elevated the rebellious Jew to the status of a divine being. With this new religion Paul succeeded in reassuring the Diaspora Jews and alienating the rebel movement. As the Romans wanted, they became good citizens and above all paid their taxes promptly.

However, James finally came under suspicion. Paul, the informal collaborator and official with a special church task, threatened to get away. But the Roman authorities knew what was going on. Anticipating the methods of modern security police they arranged a mock-arrest of Paul, which was made, highly effectively, in the temple of Jerusalem. Paul was put on trial publicly, and even underwent a mock-execution. In fact the Roman security forces gave him a new identity. So there would certainly be enough material for a further bestseller.

As we shall see, Baigent and Leigh write as public propagandists for the American professor Robert H.Eisenman. If his account of earliest Christianity were right, it would be alarming not only for the Catholic church but for Christianity generally. So we can understand why non-Christians react with satisfaction to *The Dead Sea Scrolls Deception* and it makes Christians feel insecure.

Many people ask whether Baigent and Leigh are not right in accusing Christian scholars of having suppressed Qumran texts. If the Qumran texts contain anything like what these two journalists claim, would not the Vatican really have an understandable motive for suppressing publication? So our first questions are: how were the Qumran scrolls discovered, and how does their publication come about? Is there any indication that important texts are still being withheld from the public?

## Qumran: The find of the century

According to the most probable version, Muhammad ed-Dhib, a young Bedouin of the Ta'amire tribe, discovered the first scrolls at the beginning of 1947.[3] He found them in a cave less than a mile from Khirbet Qumran (map 1). Qumran is near the north-west shore of the Dead Sea and has been known as ruins since the middle of the last century.[4] In April 1947, Metropolitan Athanasius Yeshua Samuel of the Syrian Orthodox Church in Jerusalem was offered some scrolls for sale. At about the same time a professor at the Hebrew University, Eliezer L.Sukenik, the father of the famous archaeologist and less successful politician Yigael Yadin, discovered the existence of the find. On 25 November 1947 the resolution to partition Palestine was passed in the United Nations with the narrowest of majorities, and serious Arab unrest followed.[5] Nevertheless, just four days after the UN decision Sukenik managed by devious ways to purchase some of the scrolls for the Hebrew University. These comprised an incomplete Isaiah scroll, a scroll with previously unknown songs

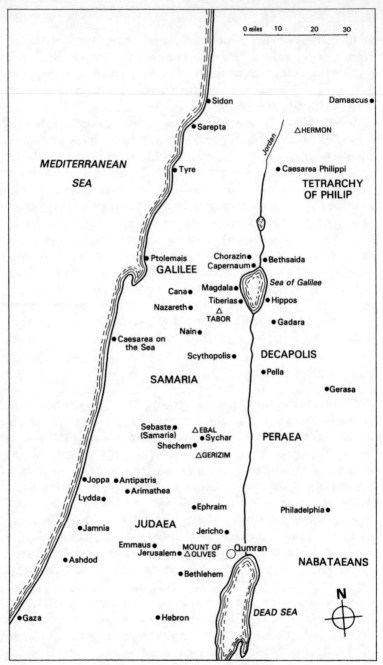

1 Palestine in the New Testament period

of thanksgiving, and a writing about the final war between the followers and the opponents of God, who are called 'sons of light' or 'sons of darkness'.

Four other scrolls came into the possession of the Metropolitan: a complete scroll of the prophet Isaiah, a commentary on the prophet Habakkuk, a handbook of instruction (consisting of two partial scrolls), and a further scroll which could not be opened immediately. This later proved to contain a considerably embellished retelling of Genesis. These texts were kept in St Mark's Monastery in the Christian quarter of the Old City of Jerusalem. In February 1948, Metropolitan Samuel approached the American School of Oriental Research in Jerusalem about the scrolls. The Institute's representative, John C.Trever, quickly recognized that the scrolls included one with the text of the prophet Isaiah which had to be earlier than any complete copies known previously. The American School was given permission by the bishop to photograph the scrolls. At this time Samuel was negotiating with the Hebrew University over the sale of the scrolls. However, contacts broke off with the end of the British Mandate and the proclamation of the State of Israel on 15 May 1948. Because of the uncertain situation the Metropolitan travelled – with the scrolls in his luggage – to Syria and then to the United States, but could not find any purchasers because of the horrendous price he was asking. Through a small advertisement in *The Wall Street Journal* and with the help of a middleman the scrolls were then secretly sold to Israel in July 1954 for $250,000. Prime Minister David Ben Gurion announced the purchase to the public in a radio broadcast in February 1955.

In November 1948, Gerald L.Harding, who was head of the Department of Antiquities in Jordan, had heard of the discoveries. After the end of the Israeli War of Independence, Jordan annexed the north-west shore of the Dead Sea. On 28 January 1949 an expedition under the Belgian officer P. Lippens of the UN and Colonel Ashton of the Arab Legion came upon the cave where the discoveries had been made. An archaeological excavation was made of the caves as early as February and March of that year. The French Dominican Fr Roland de Vaux, who was director of the famous 'École Biblique de Jérusalem', also went there. Under his leadership, scholars of this school among other things pro-

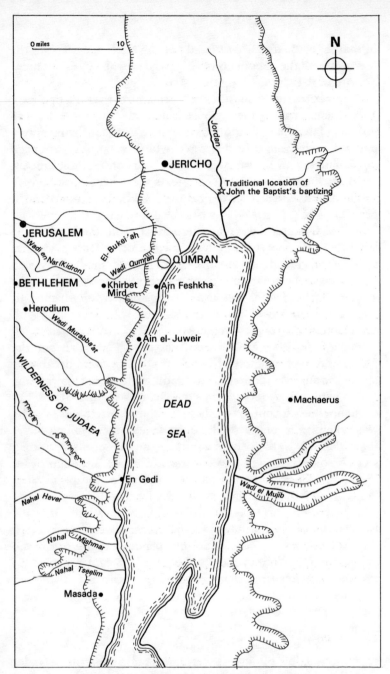

2 Finding-places of writings in the Wilderness of Judea

duced the Jerusalem Bible, which has a reputation world wide.[6]
The École Biblique is in East Jerusalem, which at that time
belonged to Jordan. Within that small country it was one of the
few competent institutions with enough experienced staff trained
in archaeology to deal with a project the size of which was now
emerging. From 1952 to 1956 the settlement of Khirbet Qumran
was excavated under the direction of Harding and De Vaux.
De Vaux gave an ongoing report of this in the internationally
respected journal *Revue Biblique*. In 1961 a provisional report
on the excavation was published, with numerous photographs
and plans.[7]

In 1952 Bedouins found another cave not far from Cave 1, but
this contained only a few fragmentary writings (Map 3). The
same year the archaeologists themselves tracked down Cave 3,
the chief contents of which were the famous copper scroll. Right
next to Khirbet Qumran the Bedouins then discovered a fourth
cave with a rich, though very fragmentary, content, and finally
two further hoards with a few scraps of writing (Caves 5 and 6).
In 1955 four further caves with writings were found by the
Ta'amire (Caves 7 to 10); in 1956 the Bedouins came upon a
hiding place rather more than a mile north of Qumran which
again contained some complete scrolls (Cave 11).

Thus so far eleven caves which contained scrolls are known
in the immediate neighbourhood of Qumran. These caves are
designated 1Q to 11Q to distinguish them from other hiding
places with scrolls on the west shore of the Dead Sea like Wadi
Muraba'at, Khirbet Mird, Naḥal Hever and Naḥal Tse'elim (map
2). In Qumran abbreviations the designation of the cave is
followed by the title of a writing, e.g. 1QH (H for *hodayot*,
Hebrew 'songs of praise'), 1QM (M for Hebrew *milḥamah*, 'war',
hence War Scroll). 1QS 3.6 is a reference to the sixth line in the
third column of the Community Rule (S stands for Hebrew *serek
ha-yaḥad* = 'Rule of the Congregation') from Cave 1.

## The editing of the Qumran writings

To begin with, the publication of the scrolls proceeded very
quickly in comparison to that of other archaeological discoveries.

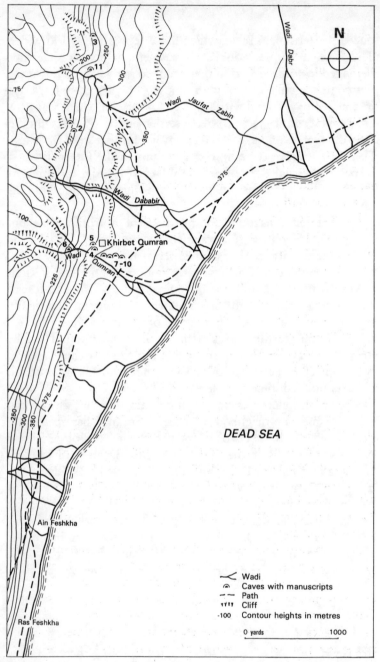

3 The surroundings of Qumran with caves 1-11

Scholars of the American School of Oriental Research published parts of the discovery as early as 1948.[8] By 1951 the photographs of three of the scrolls which at the time were still in the possession of the Syrian Metropolitan Samuel were also accessible to the public.[9] They are of very good quality for the time. The edition of the texts by the American scholars can also be regarded as valuable work in other respects. Only a little later came an Israeli publication. After the death of Professor Sukenik, in 1954 Nahman Avigad produced an edition of the scrolls in Jewish hands.[10] Sukenik himself had already published parts of the writings in 1948 and 1949.[11]

The fragmentary scrolls of Cave 4, which were being kept in the Rockefeller Museum in East Jerusalem under the supervision of the Jordan Department of Antiquities, were handed over to an international team of seven scholars for research and publication. This team was headed by Roland de Vaux, an Old Testament scholar and archaeologist with an international reputation, and consisted of scholars from different countries and with very different intellectual interests. The seven originally recruited in addition to Roland de Vaux included three more Catholics: Józef T.Milik from Poland, Jean Starcky from France and Patrick W. Skehan from the United States. Then there were three Protestant members, the Lutheran Claus-Hunno Hunziger of Germany and the Presbyterians Frank M.Cross of the United States and John Strugnell, also from the United States. The English atheist John M.Allegro, of whom we shall be hearing more shortly, was a further editor. So particularly in view of the inclusion of Allegro, it can hardly be said that this was a group of scholars obedient to the Vatican. That Hunzinger was soon replaced by Fr Maurice Baillet and Strugnell much later converted to Catholicism does not alter that fact.

The two authors of *The Dead Sea Scrolls Deception* are adept at stirring up the emotions of uninformed readers. Because the Dominicans were the order responsible for the Inquisition in the thirteenth century, they suggest to a public hungry for scandal that the same could be the case now. On that basis one might just as well accuse all present-day chemists, for example, of being charlatans just because their predecessors began as alchemists. Baigent and Leigh describe the École Biblique as an institution which since the Modernist dispute at the beginning of the twentieth century has had the task of suppressing the freedom of Catholic biblical scholarship. Anyone aware of the history of Catholic exegesis in our century will know that this is complete nonsense. Rather, the École Biblique stands at the head of those Catholic exegetes who called for a free application of historical-critical methods. Because of this attitude the founder of the École Biblique, Marie-Joseph Lagrange, encountered great difficulites and barely escaped condemnation by the church. More than once the school was threatened with closure.

To begin with, the team of scholars under Roland de Vaux also worked very quickly. In addition to a series of preliminary publications of texts, the Clarendon Press of Oxford started another series in which the final publications of the texts appeared. It is entitled 'Discoveries in the Judaean Desert'. The first volume appeared in 1955 with the discoveries from Cave 1.[12] In 1957 Józef T.Milik produced an informative interim report on the state of work.[13] All the discoveries from the so-called 'minor caves' (2-3Q, 6-10Q) were published in 1962[14] and the great Psalms Scroll from Cave 11 in 1965. This contains at the end some apocryphal psalms which were already known from the tradition of the Syrian church and which the Protestant Old Testament scholar Martin Noth had recognized as being originally Hebrew compositions.[15]

Work on the highly fragmentary texts from Cave 4 proved difficult. John M.Allegro published the texts entrusted to him in 1968,[16] but incurred vigorous criticism as his edition contained many mistakes – evidently because the editing had been done too rapidly and very carelessly. John Strugnell wrote a critical review of this edition on behalf of the rest of the scholars on the international team. It is not often that a review is almost as long as the book under review.[17] The judgment of the Würzburg New Testament scholar Karlheinz Müller was: 'In general, DJD V is the worst and most unreliable Qumran edition to be foisted on the reader since the beginning of the discoveries.'[18] By 1982 two further volumes with texts from 4Q had been added to the Oxford series.[19] A set of individual publications outside the series made further Qumran texts available. Thus as early as 1956 the paraphrase of Genesis from Cave 1, the so-called Genesis Apocryphon (1QGenAp) had been published in Israel,[20] and in 1977 Józef T.Milik in collaboration with Matthew Black published the fragments of the apocryphal book of Enoch found in Cave 4.[21] Material from Cave 11 includes a Targum (Aramaic translation) of the book of Job,[22] a copy of Leviticus in Old Hebrew script[23] and hymns for the sabbath sacrifice.[24] The publication in 1977 of the longest Qumran scroll, the so-called 'Temple Scroll', of more than eight metres, edited by Yigael Yadin, was particularly spectacular.[25]

The discovery of the 'Temple Scroll', which also comes from Cave 11, was an adventure in itself. An antique dealer in Bethlehem, Iskander Shahin (called Kando), kept this scroll hidden in a shoe box under floorboards in his house. As early as August 1960 Yigael Yadin had heard mention of it from an American clergyman whose name he never disclosed. Since then the view has been floated to the *Biblical Archaeology Review* that he was the Reverend Joe Uhrig, who brought the leader of the Moral Majority, Jerry Falwell, into the business of being a television evangelist.[26] When the Old City of Jerusalem and Bethlehem fell into Israeli hands during the Six Day War on 7 June 1967, Yadin had the Temple Scroll retrieved with the help of the Israeli Army intelligence.

By the time that the English original of *The Dead Sea Scrolls Deception* appeared in September 1991, about eighty per cent of the text of the Qumran discoveries had been published.[27] So it is highly misleading for the reader to be told on the book flap of the German edition that 'seventy-five per cent of the around 800 manuscripts written in Old Hebrew and Aramaic are being withheld from the public'. This percentage can be arrived at only if the Temple Scroll, more than eight metres long, is put on the same footing as a snippet the size of a postage stamp, which is all that is left of another scroll. The truth is that when Baigent and Leigh's book appeared in autumn 1991, only around twenty per cent of the texts were as yet unpublished, all of them from Cave 4 or Cave 11. This situation, around forty years after the discovery, can indeed be described in the words of the famous Oxford Qumran scholar Geza Vermes as 'the academic scandal *par excellence* of the twentieth century'.[28] But the reason for the delay over the publication of the rest of the manuscripts is not that there has been a Vatican plot.

## Top scholars and their personal crises

It has been slow work editing the discoveries from Cave 4 because
they are all in such a fragmentary state. Many fragments are not
much larger than a coin or a postage stamp. Putting such fragments
together in a way that makes sense is strenuous and demanding
work. Nevertheless, the difficulty of the textual material is not in
itself sufficient explanation of the delay in publishing the remaining texts. A further answer lies in the peculiarities of archaeology,
which still need to be noted today. Thus up until official publication a discovery is regarded as being virtually the personal
property of the excavator. So it is unfortunately not at all unusual
for the publication of even important discoveries to take decades.
Famous scholars have died during work on a publication and
taken irreplaceable knowledge with them to the grave. Thus
presumably Yigael Yadin knew the place where the cuneiform
archive of the Canaanite city of Hazor in North Galilee was
located. After his sudden death his successors can only hope to
discover it by expensive exploration.

The climate in archaeology has begun to change only in more
recent times. Scholars are increasingly demanding that important
discoveries should be made public immediately through photographs, especially when written material is involved. Those who
did the excavations still have the right of final publication. In their
edition of the texts they can then already take note of discussions
among their colleagues which have begun in the meantime. It is a
legitimate demand in keeping with an open democratic society
with its ideal of freedom of research that cultural objects should
be a universal intellectual possession of all humankind. So they
must be made available as quickly as possible, at least in printed
form, to all interested parties.

A further reason for delays in the editing of all the Qumran
texts was that some members of the Jerusalem research team
occupied regular professorial chairs at other universities and
could only work on the scrolls for a limited period in their
vacations. Thus Frank M.Cross of Harvard University did not
personally publish any of the Old Testament scrolls entrusted to
him. To explain this in terms of the dark authorities of the Vatican
is really absurd. It was with some hesitation that Cross and other

university professors began to entrust the task of editing to their own doctoral students. In this way the publications at least remained 'in the family'. But as more and more time elapsed before publication, some of the editors constantly supplied information on request to other colleagues about texts which interested them. The subterranean stacks of the Rockefeller Museum in no way resemble the notorious library in Umberto Eco's novel *The Name of the Rose*. One of the authors of the present book (R.Riesner) was shown unpublished texts on request, but was not allowed to work on them.

That Israeli scholars were not allowed to work on the discoveries in the Rockefeller Museum was a result of the political situation, in the face of which the editors, too, were of course powerless. Up to June 1967 East Jerusalem was under Jordanian rule and no Jewish scholars were allowed entry. Not everyone was aware of these political circumstances. Thus the Israeli Qumran scholar Shemaryahu Talmon tells the following story. At a congress in 1956 he was 'sharply attacked by a colleague on the way to lunch: "How come that you are there in Jerusalem and won't help the people [in the Rockefeller Museum to edit the texts]?" The poor man had never heard that Jerusalem was a divided city. And when I said to him, "Look, we'd love to but we can't," he said to me, "Then why don't you yourself go into the Old City?" After the Six Day War I sent him a telegram: "We followed your advice!".'[29]

In the Six Day War of 1967, in their onslaught from the north the Israelis also took the enormous, fortress-like Rockefeller Museum. There are dramatic shots of this by a cameraman who kept directly behind the front line. The Israeli Department of Antiquities, which soon afterwards moved into the Rockefeller Museum, did not at first change the composition and method of working of the international group of seven scholars in any way, in order to avoid adding yet one more to the problems of foreign policy which already existed. Thus for example an international press campaign was provoked by the excavations on the western and southern Temple walls (from 1968), which led to a condemnation of Israel by UNESCO. Here intervention by the Israeli authorities in the editing of the Qumran texts would have been quite justified. For in the meantime momentous personal crises had come about in the lives of some of the scholars involved.[30]

One finds serious human problems among top scholars more frequently than in other circles. Józef T.Milik had an alcohol problem, left the priesthood quite unexpectedly, and one day turned up in Beirut. Then he married and settled down again in Paris. This temporary lapse by Milik was particularly serious for the team, because he was virtually a genius at putting together even the tiniest fragments of text correctly.

John Strugnell also had an alcohol problem. It was a quite incomprehensible decision, and one which was also personally unfortunate, that after the death of Pierre Benoit, the successor of Roland de Vaux (who died in 1971), in 1987 he should have been appointed head of the team of editors. Most unfortunately Strugnell parted company with his wife and had to struggle with a serious nervous breakdown. He was not dismissed until 1990. However, this takes us far ahead of events.

Another scholar developed in an equally tragic way. In his publications John M. Allegro turned to increasingly abstract themes. In the German-language sphere, *Der Spiegel*[31] helped his work on the cult of the sacred mushroom[32] to become widely known. In it Allegro developed an obsession that Christianity, too, goes back to hallucinations produced by a particular kind of poisonous mushroom. It was almost a matter of course that the Qumran writings should have played a key role in Allegro's fantasies. Meanwhile the sex wave had begun in the West. It was in this context that Allegro rooted his later work *The Dead Sea Scrolls and the Christian Myth* (1979) with passages to match. One point which attracted his interest was the celibate life of the Qumran monks, and he illuminated this thoroughly. According to Magen Broshi, the Curator of the 'Shrine of the Book' in the Israel Museum, the index of this Allegro work reads like that of a sex handbook.[33]

## Warmed-up interpretations and controversies

In many cases the statements made in *The Dead Sea Scrolls Deception* are about controversies mainly fought out during the first ten years after texts from the Dead Sea Scrolls had been made

public, which are given something of a face-lift. At that time there
were three main questions: 1. How old are the Qumran writings?
2. To which Jewish group can they be attributed? 3. What is the
significance of their discovery for the understanding of the New
Testament and earliest Christianity? In this context we must leave
aside the fourth important question: what do the Qumran scrolls
teach us about the origin and tradition of the Old Testament?

As early as April 1948 the scholars of the American School of
Oriental Research dated the Isaiah manuscript which has been
preserved complete to the first century BCE, and announced this
in a press release.[34] That made this scroll around a thousand years
older than any other complete copy of the prophet Isaiah. Shortly
afterwards Professor Sukenik similarly stated that the manuscripts
were around two thousand years old. However, that same year
this dating came under criticism above all from the American
Jewish professor Solomon Zeitlin,[35] who to the end of his life
claimed that the scrolls were a mediaeval forgery. Zeitlin persisted
in his view with impressive stubbornness, but was fair enough to
allow opposite views to be expressed in the *Jewish Quarterly
Review* which he edited. Whereas at the beginning of the 1950s
some other scholars than Zeitlin still also argued for a late dating,
by the end of this decade the scholarly world was agreed on the
early dating.

Four different kinds of arguments led to this unanimous assessment. Comparisons of the script put the age of the manuscripts
between the third century BCE and the first century CE. The
neighbouring settlement of Qumran had been inhabited from the
second century BCE on and was evidently destroyed in 68 CE in
the Jewish war against the Romans. Allusions in various scrolls
can be connected with events between the second century BCE
and the first century CE. Finally, the radio carbon method, which
at that time was brand new, produced a dating for the linen
covering in which some of the scrolls had been wrapped of
between 200 BCE and 200 CE. This test was performed by
Willard F. Libby, who was later awarded the Nobel prize for the
process which he had developed.[36] Robert H. Eisenman then
fought a remarkable rearguard action over the question of dating
at the beginning of the 1990s (see p. 75 below).

Baigent and Leigh and Robert Eisenman, who stands behind them, also have spiritual ancestors for the theory that the Qumran scrolls were directly connected with Christianity, but they do not say much about them. Thus soon after the discovery of the scrolls the English scholar Jacob L.Teicher put forward the view that these were documents of the Ebionites, a Jewish-Christian sect.[37] It was Jewish scholars like Hans-Joachim Schoeps in particular who resolutely opposed this view.[38] Indeed so far the names of Jesus, James or even Paul have not been found in any of the scrolls to which Baigent and Leigh or Eisenman refer. Soon after the discovery of the scrolls the conviction became established in almost all scholarly circles that those who settled at Qumran and were the owners of the scrolls were members of the Jewish group called Essenes. We shall be going into this in detail later (Ch.3).

Millar Burrows, a member of the American School of Oriental Research team, wittily remarked that the Qumran scrolls were discovered twice, in Palestine in 1947 and in the United States in 1955.[39] Until then a large section of the American public had not paid very much attention to the scrolls. This changed all of a sudden in 1955 when the writer and critic Edmund Wilson published a long article in *The New Yorker*[40] which soon afterwards also appeared in somewhat extended form as a book.[41] Wilson put forward the theory that all the important Christian doctrines had really already been anticipated in Qumran, and that the predominantly Christian Qumran researchers were attempting to cover up this fact.

This claim by Wilson was already far-fetched in 1955, but that did not prevent the Unitarian minister A.Powell Davies from putting forward the view in an even cruder form.[42] Right from the beginning scholars had drawn attention to parallels in content and form between some Qumran writings and the New Testament. Among the 1500 (!) titles mentioned in a bibliography compiled by Christoph Burchard as early as 1957 there are quite a few works on this subject.[43] For example, from 1950 onwards the Protestant New Testament scholar Karl-Georg Kuhn wrote articles on Qumran and earliest Christianity.[44] In particular the French Jesuit and later Cardinal Jean Daniélou made similar comparisons.[45] Other Catholic authors like Georg Molin[46] and Kurt Schubert[47] saw relatively close connections between Qumran texts and the New Testament. So those who claim that the Catholic church in particular is attempting to keep new information under wraps can at best be excused on grounds of ignorance.

The American writer Edmund Wilson, mentioned above, based his article on remarks by the French scholar André Dupont-Sommer and popularized them.[48] He put forward the following view, albeit more cautiously than Wilson: some Qumran texts say that the 'Teacher of Righteousness', who is mentioned often, was crucified and his followers then expected his resurrection and return. John M.Allegro also published similar remarks,[49] but soon afterwards broke completely with the Jerusalem team of editors. In Manchester Allegro had gained access to the opened Copper Scroll from Cave 3 (3Q15) and published an unauthorized text shortly before the official edition.[50] It is the opposite of the truth when Baigent and Leigh write in connection with this: 'When they [the Jordanian authorities] at last consented, the cutting [of the Copper Scroll] was performed in Manchester under the auspices of John Allegro...'[51] Moreover Allegro organized an archaeological campaign, which was both unauthorized and unscientific, to find the treasure listed in the Copper Scroll. We have already mentioned earlier his most unfortunate edition of the Qumran texts officially entrusted to him. Subsequently a mocking comment from a colleague went the rounds about this scholar who operated as it were in such a breathless fashion: 'Piano, Allegro, piano!'

Allegro moved over from Near Eastern studies to theology in 1957.[52] He embarked on a series of sensational publications and even attempted to write plays.[53] The first performance of his play 'The Lively Oracles' was given in England in 1966. It begins with a university assistant opening the gummed-up parts of a Qumran scroll amidst clouds of steam. Her professor rushes in, reads the text quickly and exclaims, 'That will shake the Catholic church!' Professor Lanson alias John Allegro infers from the Aramaic scroll that Jesus did not call the disciple Peter *kaypha'* (rock), as the Gospel of Matthew reports (16.18), but only *gaypha'* (investigator). That is said to refute the whole of the papacy. But while the Catholic assistant loves her professor, she immediately confesses all to a priest. Through him the Vatican gets wind of the matter and middlemen attempt to convince the professor to read *kaypha'*, the rock, again. However, Lanson/Allegro stands firm. But when he wants to reveal the secret to a press conference, the safe in which he kept the Qumran scroll is empty. The professor protests, 'They are suppressing the words of Jesus...'

This whole action reads like the screenplay for *The Dead Sea Scrolls Deception*. The first advertisement for this work in Germany bore the slogan, 'The truth about early Christianity – suppressed by the Vatican'. It was announced that 'These documents (the unpublished Qumran texts) disclose that the beginnings of Christianity have been handed down falsely. Moreover there are passages of the New Testament which deviate perplexingly from the versions familiar to us.' Even the best-disposed readers could only understand this statement to mean that the unpublished fragments also include fragments of the New Testament, for the publication of which we are still waiting in vain. The advertisement ended with the words: 'New discoveries are to be expected which will shake the Roman Catholic church.' The person who is shaken more than anyone else is the critical observer, who begins to understand why some people think that all advertisements are lies. It might be mentioned in passing that this advertisement contained a cover of the book with Hebrew letters on it printed upside down. Perhaps that is the only way of reading from the Qumran texts what Baigent and Leigh discover in them!

On the positive side, the two copyist-authors must at least be credited with mentioning the names of Dupont-Sommer and Allegro in *The Dead Sea Scrolls Deception*. However, they still claim that Christian scholars would play down the parallels between Qumran and the New Testament.[54] What with Wilson in 1955 is merely shamelessness is in 1991 a quite malicious insinuation. The readers of Baigent and Leigh are not told that Allegro at any rate was honest enough to concede that his interpretations were not based on texts which had been preserved in their entirety, but on the extremely controversial filling in of gaps. Later (in Ch. 6) we shall again consider in more detail the specific method of basing rash assertions on something that is not contained in the text, in connection with the new book by Robert Eisenman and Michael Wise, *The Dead Sea Scrolls Uncovered* (1993).

*Professors, television presenters and journalists*

At a congress in Cambridge in 1979 one of the authors of this book (R.Riesner) had a memorable encounter with Professor Robert H.Eisenman of California State University. The subject of the meeting was the Synoptic question, i.e. the agreements and differences between the Gospels according to Matthew, Mark and Luke. When it was Eisenman's turn to speak, he embarked on a speech in which he sought to explain Christianity as a product of pyschological disturbances. Thereupon the chairman of the discussion, Professor William R.Farmer, asked him to stop. At that time no one could guess that Eisenman's great hour as a controversial Qumran scholar was still to come. In the first half of the 1980s, in two studies he put forward the theory which was then disseminated so effectively by Baigent and Leigh: it follows from the Qumran writings that the earliest Christians under the leadership of James the brother of the Lord were part of the Jewish resistance movement against Rome.[55] The scholarly world remained completely unimpressed by this. And Professor Geza Vermes, whom Baigent and Leigh are fond of calling on as a key witness to a conspiracy among the editors of the scrolls, remarked with gentle mockery: 'Perhaps readers who are less familiar with these things than the reviewer can cope better with Professor Eisenman's loaded arguments.'[56]

However, the professional world was soon to be laughing on the other side of its face. While hosts of Qumran scholars were racking their brains over individual consonants and publishing hundreds of articles in professional journals which would be read only by colleagues, Robert Eisenman began his publicity campaign. In letters to newspapers he darkly intimated that the delay in the publication of the 4Q fragments could be connected with Vatican influence.[57] However, he landed his most successful coup when he won over the journalists Michael Baigent and Richard Leigh as propagandists for his cause. The two journalists unscrupulously wrote down what Eisenman did not dare to assert in public for the sake of the last remnants of his academic reputation, following the slogan 'Once one's reputation is ruined, one can write what one likes.' In their books *The Holy Blood and the Holy Grail* (1983), and *The Messianic Legacy* (1986, both written with Henry Lincoln), they had claimed that physical descendants of Jesus are still alive in Europe today and that they are preparing to take over rule of the world. The fact that professional historians slated the book did not prevent *The Holy Blood and the Holy Grail* from becoming a bestseller.[58]

Baigent and Leigh enjoyed more than the support of Professor Eisenman in their most recent publishing success, *The Dead Sea Scrolls Deception*. In the acknowledgments in their book they thank 'Ann Evans, who co-instigated it and has now found a new vocation as medium for the restless shade of Jehan l'Ascuiz [a long-dead old French poet]'. In addition to this occult helper they also mention extremely earthly protection, 'Rod Collins... for fostering fiscal well-being and peace of mind.'[59] It would be illuminating to investigate the real interests behind the support for a book like *The Dead Sea Scrolls Deception*, which could have been a complete flop. The international advertising campaign which led to the great success of the book would hardly have been possible without considerable financial help.

The new outbreak of Qumran fever was also fuelled from elsewhere in German-speaking countries. During the heated debate over NATO and rearmament the German television journalist Franz Alt wrote a book *Frieden ist möglich. Die Politik der Bergpredigt* (Peace is Possible. The Politics of the Sermon on the Mount), which also sold very rapidly. In this book, which is strikingly uneven and thin even for a bestseller, Alt quotes hardly any texts from the Sermon on the Mount (Matthew 5-7), but does refer to the so-called 'Peace Gospel of the Essenes'.[60] This often somewhat unappetizing work is a forgery which Edmond B.Székely claimed to have discovered in the secret archives of the Vatican.[61] So it is only to be hoped that the articles by Franz Alt in the television magazine *Report* were better researched. Alt took over the view that Jesus survived the crucifixion[62] from his spiritual mentor, the former Catholic priest Karl Herbst.[63] Elmar R.Gruber and Holger Kersten also made the same claim, bringing the Essenes into it. However, their 1992 book *Das Jesus-Komplott* (The Jesus Plot), seemed to get submerged in the tumult around *The Dead Sea Scrolls Deception*. Similar remarks made three years earlier by Gerald Messadié in his work *L'homme qui devient Dieu* ('The Man who became God'; the German title was 'A Man

Named Jesus') seem to have been more successful. This novel appeared like the first fit of the shivers before the real new outbreak of Qumran fever. We shall also be making a critical investigation of the claims of these authors later (80ff.).

The nadir of sensational publications about Qumran so far is the claim of the Australian professor Barbara Thiering in her book *Jesus the Man* (1992, US title *Jesus and the Riddle of the Dead Sea Scrolls*). However, we shall not anticipate her detective story here, as we have devoted a later chapter to it (Ch.7). Other publishers are now jumping on the Qumran bandwagon. It is not surprising that Pinchas Lapide has taken the opportunity to produce a new book on this topic with his accustomed regularity: his *Paulus zwischen Damaskus und Qumran* (Paul between Damascus and Qumran) was published in February 1993. The same month Walter Verlag, hitherto known only for publishing the writings of Carl Gustav Jung, also joined in. The lawyer Paul F.Rudolf gave up his profession to devote his time to writing on religion. The result is a voluminous book of almost four hundred pages with the title 'Jesus and Qumran. Was the Nazarene an Essene?'.

Before we turn to a detailed critical discussion of sensational books on Qumran, in the next chapter we shall discuss the question whether there are still any unpublished Qumran texts. In it we shall see that few authors have argued so resolutely for the immediate publication of all the remaining Qumran texts as the American Jewish journalist Hershel Shanks. So he can be regarded as being above suspicion as a witness on the question whether the Vatican has hindered or even suppressed the publication of the Qumran writings. Shanks called Robert Eisenman's remarks to this effect 'hogwash'.[64] Such a remark can banish any suspicion that Professor Eisenman was not being criticized as a Qumran scholar but rather as a non-religious Jew.

Israeli specialists on Qumran who have now been entrusted with leading roles in preserving and editing the scrolls have been hardly less reticent in their remarks on Baigent and Leigh. Magen Broshi called *The Dead Sea Scrolls Deception* 'a stupid book',[65] and Shemaryahu Talmon found it 'indecent'.[66] If we wanted to regard the statements by the two scholars as self-interested, we would have to assume an additional plot between the Roman

Catholic church and the state of Israel. The Vatican and Israel would have had to conspire together to salvage the uniqueness of Christianity. It may be that some people will find such a conspiracy theory plausible if the State of Israel and the Holy See take up diplomatic relations in the foreseeable future. Now already the creed of some opponents of Christianity is, 'I believe because it's absurd!' Unfortunately this slogan has also become the scientific principle of the Qumran enthusiasts.

# 2

# Which Qumran Texts are Still Unpublished?

The fight for free access – Dramatic events in autumn 1991 – Qumran and the mass media – Qumran, the churches and specialist scholarship

## The fight for free access

Individual scholars have called time and again for more rapid publication of the rest of the Qumran texts. However, the interest of a wider public was first aroused by the commitment of Hershel Shanks, the editor of the bimonthly *Biblical Archaeology Review*, which appears in Washington with almost 200,000 (!) subscribers in the USA. Since 1985 articles on Qumran have appeared in almost every edition of this journal and its sister publication *Bible Review*.[1] With praiseworthy stubbornness Robert Eisenman also managed to get the question of the Qumran scrolls discussed even in the Israeli parliament, the Knesset.[2] Not least through the *Biblical Archaeology Review* it became known world wide that John Strugnell had given an anti-Jewish interview in Jerusalem on 28 October 1990 to the journalist Avi Katzman of the Israeli daily paper *Haaretz*.[3] The possibility cannot be ruled out that here Strugnell was falling into a well-laid trap.[4] Nevertheless, there was good reason for dismissing him in December 1990[5] and replacing him as chief editor with Emmanuel Tov of the Hebrew University. However, Strugnell continued in the team as an editor of texts. The Israeli Department of Antiquities had already appointed Professor Tov as deputy editor in November 1990. The episode of John Strugnell was not without its tragedy in that he was the first editor to invite Jewish scholars (Emmanuel Tov and Elisha Qimron) to collaborate in work on the unpublished Qumran scrolls.

Strugnell's dismissal was followed by important steps in the reorganization of publication.[6] Today Eugene Ulrich of the University of Notre Dame, USA, and Émile Puech of the École Biblique of Jerusalem are serving as senior editors. In addition the Israeli Department of Antiquities under ex-General Amir Drori has appointed a control group which is to ensure more rapid publication. It includes Professors Jonas C.Greenfield and Shemaryahu Talmon and the Curator of the Shrine of the Book (in the Israel Museum), Magen Broshi. Above all, a group of about fifty collaborators were appointed from the international community of scholars, half Jews and half non-Jews. However, the previous procedure was to be retained, namely that other scholars normally do not get to see the texts before official publication. Still, the positive demands made by the Israeli Department of Antiquities on the new editors also contained a condition that they should keep to set deadlines: the edition was to be completed by 1997.

Nevertheless, despite better planning, an edition of all the Qumran texts before the year 2000 seems uncertain. Encouraged by the energetic Hershel Shanks, Professor Ben-Zion Wacholder of the Hebrew Union College in Cincinnati therefore decided on a drastic step. From as early as the late 1950s there has been a concordance, a list of key words, of most of the unpublished discoveries from Cave 4.[7] In 1988 twenty-five (according to other accounts thirty) copies of this list were made public. The Institute for Ancient Judaism and Hellenistic Religion, in association with the Protestant Theological Faculty of Tübingen, under the direction of Professor Martin Hengel, was also able to secure a copy. Thus it was in principle possible, though laboriously, to recover Qumran texts from the concordance. The Tübingen Old Testament scholar Hans-Peter Rüger, who sadly died young, succeeded in restoring the Hebrew and Aramaic fragments of the book of Tobit for a critical edition of the text. One of the two authors of this book (O.Betz) also checked and enlarged a number of his academic articles with the help of this concordance.[8]

Professor Wacholder went still further. As he was already approaching seventy years of age, he was afraid that he would not live to see the final publication of the Qumran writings. So he had texts reconstructed systematically with the help of the computer. A first volume produced in this way apppeared at the beginning of September 1991.[9] According to the Göttingen Qumran specialist Hartmut Stegemann, who is working with the original documents in the Rockefeller Museum, around 98% of the reconstructions are correct.[10] However, again the names which appear in the fragments of the so-called Damascus Document published by Wacholder are not particularly favourable to Robert Eisenman's theories. These are not New Testament names but the names of Hasmonaean rulers of the second and first centuries BCE (see p.72 below). The 'computer coup' led the world press to debate vigorously whether such a step was morally permissible.[11] But after a few days the question settled itself, since within three months, between September and November 1991, events took place with bewildering speed.[12]

## Dramatic events in autumn 1991

In 1980 all the finds in the Rockefeller Museum had been put on microfilm on the initiative of the prominent patron Elizabeth Hay Bechtel so that they would be safe if hostilities broke out in the Middle East. Several sets of films were deposited secretly for safekeeping in various museums throughout the world. Following a dispute between Mrs Bechtel and the first Director of her foundation, The Ancient Biblical Manuscript Center, in Claremont, California, James A.Sanders, it transpired that while Sanders subscribed to the obligation to the Israeli Department of Antiquities, Mrs Bechtel did not. The Huntington Library in Los Angeles, which accepted the film from Mrs Bechtel, was thus not bound by the earlier agreements about secrecy. In the name of freedom of information and scholarship, on 22 September 1991 the new Director of the Huntington Library, William Moffett, announced that he would grant access to photographs of the material to all interested scholars. (In London, *The Times* had scooped the news the previous day.) Now a real, healthy 'scrolls fever' broke out in the USA. *The New York Times* reported it on its front page,[13] and the well-known Qumran scholar James H.Charlesworth of Princeton University was much in demand as a dialogue partner on television. CBS and Good Morning America vied for news. Moffett's announcement also found its way into German newspapers.[14]

Originally the Israeli Department of Antiquities wanted to take legal proceedings against the free access to the microfilms in the Huntington Library.[15] However, they very soon realized that there was virtually no prospect of winning their case. They were above all rightly afraid that the public would not accept further limitations on the freedom of scholarship. So on 27 October 1991 the Department abandoned any measures against the use of the photographs,[16] which today are also accessible in the Oxford Centre for Post-Graduate Studies (under Geza Vermes), in the Ancient Biblical Manuscript Center (at Claremont, California) and at the Hebrew Union College (Cincinnati, only in part).[17] This toing and froing gave the unfortunate impression that the real culprits were in the Israeli Department of Antiquities, though these were merely trying to protect the rights of scholars, about whose long-drawn out *modus operandi* they themselves were unhappy. The waves mounted high. Thus a well-known Israeli journalist complained to *The New York Times* that it was now extending its anti-Israel policy to the sphere of Qumran scholarship.[18]

As soon as it became clear that no legal steps stood in the way of free access to the documents,[19] on 19 November 1991 the Biblical Archaeology Society headed by Hershel Shanks published a two-volume facsimile edition of all the photographs so far unpublished, amounting to 1787 plates in all.[20] To decipher them, however, one often needs a good magnifying glass. It is expressly stated that the photographs in this edition do not come from the Huntington Library but were received by Robert H.Eisenman in 1989 and 1990; together with the well-known Gnostic scholar James M.Robinson he appears as editor. However, it emerges from the foreword that Robinson does not share Eisenman's special Qumran theories.[21] This publication, too, made a great stir in the world press.[22]

After that, though, came an interlude which was rather painful for scholarly ethics. A reconstruction of one of the most interesting and controversial Qumran texts was also published in the facsimile edition: this is a letter with the abbreviation 4QMMT

found in Cave 4 in six (fragmentary) copies. The published
reconstruction had emerged anonymously in a number of places
throughout the world;[23] work was also being done on it in senior
seminars in Tübingen. Today the brilliant Israeli scholar Elisha
Qimron claims it for himself. He also reckons that the premature
publication has lost him around $250,000 in royalties and fees.
Clearly historical scholarship pays well! Qimron secured a temporary injunction from a Jerusalem court[24] against the dissemination of the facsimile edition, though most copies had already
been sold. A second edition of this facsimile edition appeared in
1992 without the reconstructed text but with some improved
photographs in place of it. To this degree the purchasers of this
edition must be grateful to Professor Qimron for sparing their
eyes! However, the legal dispute goes on. Once Robert H.Eisen-
man, too, had been drawn into the accusation,[25] he distanced
himself from Hershel Shanks's actions.[26] Meanwhile Shanks had
put in a counter-accusation, but this was rejected by a Jerusalem
court in April 1993.[27] Qimron's financial demands were met with
a sum of just $43,000, but his copyright in the reconstruction of
the text was confirmed. Shanks is considering appealing against
this judgment, which is possibly a success for freedom of scholarship.[28] Elsewhere, too, the debate over the publication of the
scrolls is heating up. Thus a report went the rounds that two
Qumran scholars had engaged in fisticuffs at a congress in New
York in December 1992. The widely respected *Jerusalem Post* felt
constrained to issue an express denial.[29]

In the meantime, it has also become possible to purchase the
microfilms in the Huntington Library.[30] An official microfiche
edition was announced by the Israeli Department of Antiquities
for summer/autumn 1992,[31] and was available by June 1993.
Nevertheless, the monopoly over access to the Qumran scrolls
has been broken once for all, marking a new phase of research
into the Qumran texts. Here international scholarship has not
only the films and facsimile editions but also other valuable aids.
Thus – at last – there is an official list of all still unpublished texts
from 4Q and 11Q with information about the planned editors
and places of publication.[32] Furthermore, Stephen A.Reed is
working on a catalogue which will contain a brief description of
all the discoveries from the wilderness of Judaea and list the most

important literature.[33] A concordance has been edited by James H.Charlesworth.[34]

The answer to the question 'What Qumran texts are still unpublished?' must be, 'In principle, none'.[35] Anyone who understands Hebrew and Aramaic can take part in research into the last hitherto inaccessible Qumran writings. It is now possible to check the assertions of Baigent and Leigh and Eisenman about the relations between Qumran and earliest Christianity by the texts themselves.

A further publication by Robert H.Eisenman is occasion for that. In December 1992 (i.e. just in time for Christmas) a collection of fifty Qumran texts appeared in England under his editorship and that of Michael Wise, and after some delay it was also published in Germany in 1993. The title was *The Dead Sea Scrolls Uncovered*.[36] The editors' judgment is that 'the fifty documents it contains represent in our judgment the best of what exists,'[37] although they give no criteria for their selection. However, about fifty per cent of the texts had already previously been published elsewhere, though the reader can discover this only by looking closely at the notes at the end: there is no survey of all the preliminary work. Special importance is attached to the text 4Q448, a song of praise to King Jonathan (i.e. Alexander Jannaeus, 103-76 BCE), which is said to prove the pro- and not anti-Hasmonaean character of the Qumran group.[38] Although this is a spectacular reading by the Israeli manuscript expert Ada Yardeni,[39] her name is not mentioned. However, there must be the strongest suspicions about the whole reconstruction of the text. Geza Vermes concludes from a computer-enhanced reading that no king's name is mentioned at all and this text is a great hymn to the holy city of Jerusalem.[40]

A reading of the introduction of the work edited by Eisenman and Wise is somewhat painful.[41] The introduction is to some degree a modernized form of the War Scroll. In the midst of a host of academic sons of darkness there are only a few 'sons of light' who, under the leadership of Robert Eisenman (Melchizedek?), are waging war for the illumination of the world. He even goes so far as to assert that before he began his crusade in 1986 there were no more than fifteen to twenty Qumran scholars anywhere in the world.[42] Granted, Eisenman's theory that Jewish Christianity is directly descended from Qumran and that James the brother of the Lord is the 'Teacher of Righteousness' (Ch. 5) is not stated in so many words, but in the detailed introductions to the Qumran texts it is suggested to the reader with great verbosity on almost every other page.[43] At any rate there can be scientific discussions of many of the suggestions for reconstruction and translation, even if a number of them will not stand up to criticism (Ch. 6).

Without doubt the collaboration of Michael Wise, a specialist in Aramaic, is an advantage in the reconstructions and translations in the book. Nevertheless his role in the whole enterprise remains somewhat unclear. Wise began his academic career at the Conservative Evangelical Trinity Theological Seminary in Deerfield, Illinois, and then did his doctorate under the controversial Qumran scholar Norman Golb (see below, 52f.) on the Temple Scroll (11QTemple);[44] he is now Professor of Aramaic in the University of Chicago. Wise does not seem to share many of Eisenman's theories, but the degree to which he differs from him remains open.[45] According to a reliable source Eisenman prohibited Wise from referring to differences between them in the Preface to the edition of the texts. According to an article in *Time Magazine* Wise evidently also thinks possible an interpretation of the Qumran texts which supports a conservative theological view of earliest Christianity.[46] Not in the book itself, but only when asked, Eisenman conceded that the collection of Hebrew texts essentially comes from Wise, but that he himself wrote the commentary.[47] In *The Dead Sea Scrolls Uncovered* the differences of opinion between the editors have led to some confusion: what at the beginning of a commentary is presented as the only correct interpretation (Eisenman), appears at the end as no more than a possibility (Wise?).

## Qumran and the mass media

In their eagerness to read *The Dead Sea Scrolls Deception*, many people have clearly overlooked the fact that at least one essential connecting link in this detective story is missing. Baigent and Leigh claim that the hitherto unpublished Qumran texts speak of a revolutionary primitive Christianity. But the unpublished texts were secret – so secret that the two journalists have not even seen them. The conspirators maintained such a solid front that Baigent and Leigh evidently could not persuade any of them to give any indication of the approximate content. Nevertheless, in some miraculous way both of them know it. Anyone who is not susceptible to such miracle stories must simply note that contrary to the expectations aroused on the wrapper ('previously unknown texts about the earliest Christians'), Baigent and Leigh did not publish a single new Qumran document.

If we reflect once again on the chronicle of events in autumn 1991, one thing becomes clear: sometimes a few days decide whether a newly emerging intellectual trend can establish itself or remains a seven-day wonder. Had *The Dead Sea Scrolls Deception* appeared perhaps just a month later, it could hardly have attracted such extraordinary attention. It derived its explosive force from the fact that important texts were in fact still inaccessible when it came out – at the beginning of September. From the second half of September onwards, blow by blow news followed about the forcing of access to the scrolls for all interested scholars. These new developments would have stolen much publicity from a book which appeared only in October. But by that time *The Dead Sea Scrolls Deception* was already no.1 on the German non-fiction bestseller list. Despite all criticism, even in May 1993 it still had a top place there.

The astonishing success of the German edition of *The Dead Sea Scrolls Deception* is inexplicable without the powerful support of a variety of mass media. The illustrated magazine *Stern* made a special contribution with the title story 'The Acts of Jesus' in the first number of 1992, which the churches had pronounced the 'Year with the Bible'.[48] The title picture left no doubt about the thrust: Jesus hangs there nailed to a question mark. The occasion was the appearance of *The Dead Sea Scrolls Deception*. While the article inside rejected the main theories of Baigent and Leigh, it also disputed whether there was virtually any assured knowledge about Jesus. For Joachim Köhler, the author of the text in *Stern*, in addition to 'classics' like Rudolf Bultmann and Werner Georg Kümmel, modern research into Jesus is represented by the trio of Eugen Drewermann, Franz Alt and Pinchas Lapide. Whereas journals like *Die Zeit*[49] and *Frankfurter Allgemeine*

*Zeitung*[50] published critical reviews of *The Dead Sea Scrolls Deception* which can only be described as devastating, the Vatican plot theory found assent from the woman reviewer in *Süddeutsche Zeitung*.[51] A journalist on the *Frankfurter Rundschau*, who evidently found things rather too demanding, wrote a somewhat unedifying article on Christmas in which essentially he reported only Eisenman's theories.[52]

One might add a particularly crude example from Austria. 'Saturday. The Austrian Weekly for Entertaining Moments' surprised its readers with the front-page headline 'Did Jesus Christ live 200 Years Earlier?'. As was to be expected, the question was answered decisively in the affirmative by a manifest ignoramus who hid himself behind the initials G.S.[53] Compared with the remarks of this author, *The Dead Sea Scrolls Deception*, which formed the starting point of the article, was virtually a competent work of scholarship. Thus in *Samstag* one could read, 'Many parts of the [Qumran] writings are identical with the New Testament.'[54] Baigent and Leigh would never have dared to say that. And the article concludes: 'But Rome, at least under its present leadership, can hardly recognize such a "truth".' It is unnecessary to argue with such a statement. One could at most ask what kind of a book the author has read.

Television also played a very mixed role in the Qumran debate. Norddeutsche Rundfunk was quick off the mark and broadcast a programme 'The Dead Sea Scrolls' on 30 December 1991. If the German transmission is compared with the American version on which it was based, one can see considerable differences. The NDR version was expanded throughout to suggest Baigent and Leigh's plot theory, partly directly and partly under the surface.

On 7 June 1992 ZDF screened a film 'The Unknown Jesus', which was announced in a television magazine as the film of Baigent and Leigh's book.[55] However, nothing was further from the mind of the makers, Klaus Wölfle and Carsten P.Thiede of Bavarian Radio, than to provide publicity for *The Dead Sea Scrolls Deception*,[56] and one could have wished that the writer in the magazine had seen the film over which she misled the public.

Hubert Seipel's 'Jesus Thriller', shot under the auspices of the foreign affairs (!) department of ZDF, then offered – at peak viewing time – a skilfully staged presentation of Robert Eisenman's

theories (Dynamite: 'The Jesus Thriller. The Qumran Affair, or
Who was Jesus Really?', 24 June 1992). Michael Baigent was
given a lot of space to himself by Thomas Gottschalk on RTL
Plus. By contrast, it will have helped only a few people to see
things more clearly that on Radio Bavaria's Third Programme,
devoted to culture, the Israeli scholar Shemaryahu Talmon produced a devastating critique of *The Dead Sea Scrolls Deception*.[57]

The silence of the news magazine *Der Spiegel* remains remarkable. Granted, two articles about Qumran research have appeared
there recently,[58] but a critical review of *The Dead Sea Scrolls
Deception* has yet (up to the end of May 1993) to appear there,
although the book features on its own non-fiction bestseller list
week after week. One wonders about the reason for this restraint,
all the more so as the editor Rudolf Augstein himself acted as an
amateur historian with his book *Jesus-Menschensohn* (Jesus –
Son of Man),[59] and at an earlier date the *Spiegel* did not let
the fantasies of either Joel Carmichael[60] or John M.Allegro go
unnoticed. One can only speculate on the motives.

The scandal over *The Dead Sea Scrolls Deception* is good
reason once again to enquire into the morality of the mass media
and the responsibility of publishing houses. Thankfully, the
weekly *Die Zeit* published an interview with Robert Eisenman
from which a few sentences can be quoted here:

*Die Zeit*: You claim that the Qumran community is identical
with early Christianity.

*Eisenman*: That is my theory, just as Einstein had his theory of
relativity. One applies theories to the subject matter and sees
whether they fit. That's how science functions. I have put
forward the theory that the Teacher of Righteousness could
have been the leader of the earliest Christian community, and
this theory is admirably confirmed by the texts. I have never
claimed that it has been proved, but the other people don't have
such a theory.[61]

These remarks are a good illustration of Eisenman's way
of arguing, or better, agitating. Droemer Knaur, the German
publisher of the book by Baigent and Leigh, would have done
well to get an expert opinion on the original British edition.

Virtually every Qumran specialist, whether Jew, Christian or atheist, would have advised against publication. But a publisher's reader is quoted as saying: 'Even if the theory is wrong, the topic is right.'[62]

Evidently people think in very much the same way at Güt- ersloher Verlagshaus. In a publisher's statement, the planned publication of a German edition of Barbara Thiering's book *Jesus the Man* (see Chapter 7 below) is justified as follows: 'More important than the correctness of the results is that the topic should be approached from all sides...'[63] The publishers should have learned from the critique by the Jewish journalist Hershel Shanks which described Doubleday's[64] publication of Thiering's book as irresponsible because it not only attacked the foundations of Christianity but also made historical scholarship a caricature under the pretence of great learning.[65] It is with regret that one remembers that Bertelsmann, the group to which Gütersloh belongs, once counted the famous Tübingen biblical scholar Adolf Schlatter (1852-1938) among its authors.

It would be a magnificent gesture on the part of a German publisher, not least on grounds of historical truth, to produce a comprehensive translation of the Qumran writings and not just a selection to meet a hunger for sensation. In the 1950s there were quite substantial German collections of Qumran texts – remarkably, on the whole published by Catholic houses.[66] It looks as if with the decline in Christian faith, interest in historical truth is also receding. Or to put it another way: lack of faith is followed by historical folly.

## Qumran, the churches and specialist scholarship

*The Dead Sea Scrolls Deception* even made some impact on a number of Christian journals. *Publik-Forum*, the mouthpiece of critical Catholicism, essentially accepted the theory of a Vatican plot through its regular contributor Norbert Copray.[67] In the meantime, however, Copray has distanced himself from this view, though he has said about *The Dead Sea Scrolls Uncovered*: 'It offers all the Qumran discoveries for the first time with German translations...'[68] One wonders how an author who at least has had something to do with the material could write such nonsense.

Remarkably enough, the newsletter *Nachrichten aus Israel*, edited by Ludwig Schneider, which is read above all by many Protestant Christians, took the same line. As a 'book review' the news agency printed the key anti-Christian statements from the jacket,[69] supplemented by a commentary from an obscure source which not only wrongly presented Baigent and Leigh as editors of Qumran texts but again remarked that eighty per cent (!) of the discoveries 'were not available for publication'.[70]

Other church organs reacted in a markedly helpless way. Thus the *Deutsches Pfarrer-Blatt* took a year to publish a confused review. It appeared in the 'Miscellaneous' column and commented on Baigent and Leigh's remarks about Paul: 'But although this particular section again makes exciting reading, the probability that the authors are right is unfortunately extremely small.'[71] One can hardly believe one's eyes – but that is what is said. The review seems to regret that the authors are wrong in their estimation of the apostle. Unfortunately Paul did not collaborate confidentially with the Roman state security services to the mutual advantage of both church and empire. The *Deutsches Allgemeines Sonntagsblatt* also took a year to publish a detailed critique of *The Dead Sea Scrolls Deception*.[72]

So one can hardly blame ordinary church members when they write letters like this to church papers: 'The Word of God is to be preached and not imprisoned in archives. I find it incredible that the Catholic Bible School in Jerusalem should now already have been withholding the contents of the Qumran texts from a wide international public for more than thirty years. Doesn't the Catholic church trust its believers to interpret the texts of the Bible – and now also the Dead Sea Scrolls? That's what it sounds like. But as mature Christians we claim the right to know about these Essene accounts. Since, as is well known, the Holy Spirit blows where it wills, we can make up our own minds without being told what to think.'[73] As one can see, the suspicions aired by Baigent and Leigh have some influence.

Doubtless a lamentable neglect on the part of scholarship and the church public also paved the way or a work like *The Dead Sea Scrolls Deception*.[74] If one looks for relevant publications in the subject index of the 1992/3 German booksellers' *Books in Print* under the heading 'Essenes and Qumran' one finds only about twenty titles listed,[75] three of which are incomprehensible to non-specialists. Twelve titles come from esoteric publishing houses or take a similar line to *The Dead Sea Scrolls Deception*. Among other things we are offered 'The Essene Letter from the Year AD 40', a blatant forgery which appeared in a tenth edition as long ago as 1986.[76] Only three of the serious works on offer are also accessible to non-specialists, including two partial editions of texts. A new edition of the only general account of the discovery appeared in 1991 – evidently as a consequence of the new discussion about Qumran. However, this was a totally unchanged reprint (!) of two works from 1958 and 1960.[77] Given such a lack of information to a wider circle about such an important topic of biblical scholarship as the Dead Sea Scrolls, it is not surprising that a book like *The Dead Sea Scrolls Deception* should have been taken up with much curiosity but uncritically.

# 3

# Were the Qumran Writings Composed by Sadducees?

An unusual letter from Qumran – Zadokites and Sadducees –
Essenes, Pharisees and Sadducees in Flavius Josephus – The
festival calendar and the hallowing of the sabbath – Written
law and oral tradition – A split within the Jewish priesthood.

## *An unusual letter from Qumran*

Sensation-seeking outsiders like Baigent and Leigh are not the
only ones recently to have put in question the conviction, preserved
for so long that it seems almost unshakeable, that the texts from
the Dead Sea are a personal testimony from the sect of the Essenes,
which came into being before Christ. Professional scholars, too,
are expressing fundamental doubt about the previous consensus,
and a new generation of Qumran scholars is putting forward new
theories. These can be based on hitherto unknown texts, which
come from the reservoir of fragments from Cave 4 which is now
available. Such theories, published in technical journals and often
presented in a strictly academic way, are often complicated, and
difficult in language and subject-matter. They cannot be refuted
flatly and simply; they require to be treated in a scholarly rather
than a journalistic way. They usually point beyond the circle of
monastic Essenes familiar to us and the missionary activity of the
first Christians to other parties in the Judaism of the time. We
learn something about them from the New Testament and more
still from Flavius Josephus and the early writings of the rabbis:
they are the Sadducees, whose members were above all drawn
from the priestly nobility in Jerusalem; then the Pharisees, popular
among the people, strict in their observance of the law and

concerned with everyday practices; and finally the Zealots, who fought for God's honour and the purity of Israel.[1]

The thesis that the Qumran community must be regarded as a Sadducean foundation is particularly worth noting. This claims that the Essene theory needs to be revised, since the attitude to the regulations about sacrifice and cleanness in the Mosaic law represented by the Qumran writings corresponds with the doctrine of the Sadducees. So we should not in any way understand the pious people of Qumran as forerunners of Jesus and early Christianity. Rather, their texts illuminate the eventful history of Judaism before the destruction of Jerusalem (70 CE) and offer us some new knowledge about the different religious parties.

The author of the Sadducee thesis is Lawrence H. Schiffman, Professor of Hebrew Studies at New York University and a particularly competent representative of the second generation of Qumran scholars. He is regarded as an outstanding expert on the Hebrew language and rabbinic Judaism and is known less from headlines in the daily press than from his well-researched contributions to professional journals: for a long time now he has played a dominant part at Qumran conferences. His thesis about the Sadducees did not arise out of a desire for sensational novelty; rather, his pioneering work on a previously unpublished and unusual text from Cave 4 led him to it. This text is the so-called 'Letter of the Teacher of Righteousness' (4QMMT).[2] This document, composed of a number of fragments, had been known as such to the team of scholars working in the Rockefeller Museum from as early as 1955,[3] but it was only around thirty years later that the public was informed of its existence and approximate contents, at the International Congress for Biblical Archaeology held in Jerusalem in 1984.[4] Schiffman was able to get hold of a photocopy of this document and distribute it to friends.

There is still no official edition of 4QMMT. However, a makeshift translation of the document has been made and it has not only been studied thoroughly, especially by Schiffman, but also discussed at conferences, above all at Mogilany, near Krakow.[5] It is a lengthy letter, unfortunately full of gaps and difficult to read.[6] The opening with sender and address has not been preserved, but it can be seen from the document that it comes from priestly circles and is addressed to the high priest and his colleagues at the temple of Jerusalem. The author, who speaks in the first person plural for a group of like-minded people, is identified, in our view rightly, with the leader of the Qumran community, the 'Teacher of Righteousness'.

What is this letter about? And why could Schiffman put forward, specifically on the basis of this document, the theory that the fathers of the Qumran community must have been Sadducees? The recipients of the letter are reminded by around twenty precepts which are based above all on the law for priests in the biblical books of Exodus to Deuteronomy that the purity of Jerusalem and in particular of the temple is in danger; the priests are to guard against burdening the people with guilt (4QMMT B 12.26-27) and must see that they apply the law in the twenty cases discussed precisely along the guidelines offered here.

Here are some examples. The part of the peace offering which according to Lev.7.15 is due to the priests must be consumed on the day of the offering and may not be kept, say, until the morning of the next day (B 9-13).[7] Similarly, a priest who has become unclean during the preparation of the ashes of the red heifer and subsequently has taken the prescribed bath of immersion is completely clean only after sundown and therefore may not consume consecrated food before then (B13-16).[8] This interval is also to be observed strictly in the rites of purification for someone healed of leprosy (B59-67).

Furthermore, not only the flesh but also the skin of an animal slaughtered outside the city of Jerusalem is cultically unclean; so it may not be used for transporting wine or oil in the temple (B18-23).[9] Access to the temple is allowed only to Israelites, who then must be ritually pure and physically intact: foreigners, Moabites and Ammonites, but also handicapped people like the blind, the deaf and the mutilated, are to be excluded (B39-42).

Schiffman is regarded as an expert on the interpretation of the legal regulations in Qumran[10] and also on the later written instructions (*halakoth*) in the rabbinic law books of the Mishnah, Tosephta and two Talmuds. He noted that some of the regulations treated in the Qumran letter are also discussed in the Mishnah (which was completed around 180 CE), as instructions which are a matter of dispute between Sadducees and Pharisees.[11] Moreover such a controversy between Pharisees and Saducees is mentioned very rarely in the Mishnah, in which elsewhere the rabbinic sages argue amongst themselves. The attitude of the two groups is also surprising: the Pharisees adopt the more generous standpoint which is criticized in our Qumran letter 4QMMT and was evidently put forward by the priesthood in Jerusalem. By contrast the Saducees criticized in the Mishnah (*ṣadduqim*) had the precise view which is stressed by the 'Teacher of Righteousness' and his group. From this, Schiffman concludes that the authors of the letter 4QMMT found in the Qumran library must have been Sadducees, just like the Ṣaddukim mentioned later in the Mishnah.

## Zadokites and Sadducees

Schiffman's thesis came as a shock. The view had increasingly become established among Qumran scholars, both Christian and Jewish, that the pious people expressing themselves in the Qumran texts, who lived in the settlement of Qumran, were to be identified with the Essenes or at least associated with them. It is really difficult to connect this group of ideal Jews, which was thought of so highly by Josephus, Pliny the Elder and especially Philo, with the Saducees, who do not get a good write up either in the New Testament or in Josephus, far less among the rabbis. Nevertheless Schiffman is right to seek the origin of the Qumran movement in priestly circles; however, the term 'Saducees' must be used in a subtler way.

The 'Teacher of Righteousness' is explicitly termed a priest in the Habakkuk commentary (1QpHab 2.7f.), and the Qumran community was led by priests and ruled on priestly principles. However, this was the small group of those priests who had remained faithful, the 'sons of Zadok', those priests who kept the covenant of God and sought out God's will. The law of Moses had been revealed anew to them, and according to the Community Rule they were at the head of the community (1QS 2.19). The self-designation 'sons of Zadok' and the name 'Saducees' are derived from a Zadok who was priest at the time of David (II Samuel 15.24-37) and was therefore regarded as the ancestor of the regular 'Zadokite' or 'Saducean' priesthood (I Kings 1.22-

29; 2.5,13). In the Damascus Document he is revered as a revealer of the book of the Torah (instruction of Moses) which after Joshua was hidden in the ark of the covenant (CD 5.25).

The Zadokites of the Qumran community certainly corresponded in some important points to Josephus's Pharisees; here they differ from the Pharisees. The latter taught a twofold Torah: the book of Moses also included an oral tradition which was revealed, like the written one, on Mount Sinai and had been faithfully handed down to the present day. This is claimed at the beginning of the Mishnah tractate 'Sayings of the Fathers' (Aboth 1.1). However, an orally transmitted Torah is never mentioned in the Qumran texts. Josephus's Sadducees explicitly rejected it (*Jewish Antiquities* XIII, 297), as did Jesus (Mark 7.8f.). The author of our letter 4QMMT also refers only to the written Torah (B 77; C 10-12). However, he also indicates a serious conflict in the 'Sadducean' priesthood when he declares, 'We have parted company with the mass of the people', i.e. we reject the official doctrine. Here for the first time a tendency towards splitting is articulated in Judaism and thus a division within the priesthood begins.

This tendency is confirmed by the two great law books in Qumran, the Community Rule (1QS) and the Damascus Rule (CD). Anyone who wants to belong to the 'congregation' (Hebrew *yaḥad*) must 'separate from the congregation of the men of falsehood', 'under the authority of the sons of Zadok, the priests' (1QS 5.1f.,8). According to the Damascus Rule these sons of Zadok repented and left the land of Judah (CD 3.21-4.4). Conversion calls for turning away from the 'way of the people' and the official priesthood and applying oneself to the newly revealed Torah of Moses, to true obedience to the Law (1QS 5.8).

Such radicalism was remote from the politically committed, enlightened priesthood in Jerusalem. So conceptually we must distinguish between 'Zadokites' (Sons of Zadok, Hebrew *bᵉne ṣadoq) and Sadducees (Hebrew ṣadduqim, Greek Saddoukaioi*): the Zadokites wanted to be the true 'Sadducees', those who had remained loyal to the covenant of God and the Torah of Moses (and were ready to repent). For this reason they became a kind of real 'Pharisees' (Hebrew *pᵉrishim*, i.e. separated ones). According to 4QMMT they 'separated' (*parashnu*) themselves from the people on grounds of conscience (C7). According to Josephus this separation, i.e. the emigration of the Zadokites in spirit and in body and thus the formation of the Essenes, must have taken place in the time of the first Hasmonaean high priest Jonathan (152-134 BCE), since the Essenes are mentioned for the first time in this period (*Jewish Antiquities* XIII, 171-3).[12] Under the 'Teacher of Righteousness' this separation led to a spiritualization of the sanctuary and sacrificial worship in self-chosen exile, intensification of obedience to the law and the ideal of priestly purity, and in the Qumran settlement to a really un-Jewish, monastic way of living.

This sect (Josephus's Greek term is *hairesis*), whose priesthood Levites and laity also joined (Damascus Document 3.21-4.4), claimed to be the true people of God. Like Israel once on Sinai they wanted to prepare for the coming of God in the wilderness (cf. Ex.19.10-19) and therefore be 'a kingdom of priests and a holy people' (Ex.19.6). The Sinai tradition is the 'basic law' of Qumran.[13] The life of poverty and chastity ordained in the Community Rule (1QS) and confirmed by Philo, Josephus and Pliny is unique in Judaism, and quite different from the activity and theological aims of the Sadducees as we find them in the New Testament and the works of Josephus: they embody the priestly aristocracy, the rich upper classes in Jerusalem who were not always popular with the people.

These Sadducees could not separate off nor could they emigrate, either internally or externally. They had not only to perform sacrificial service in the temple, which was so important, but also to guide the people legally and politically. In so doing they had to collaborate with Greek (Seleucid) rulers, with the house of Herod and the Roman governors, and also to make compromises offensive to the Zadokites, who were loyal to covenant and law. These were regarded among the people as the 'pious, holy ones' – that is how Philo explains the name 'Essene'.[14] Josephus, who wrote above all for pagan readers, mentions the Jewish religious parties by names whose Hebrew equivalents we seek in vain in the Qumran writings – with perhaps one exception. In these writings no Sadducees (*ṣadduqim*), Pharisees (*pᵉrushim*) or Essenes are mentioned, unless the last word is to be derived from the Aramaic form *ḥasayya'*, which corresponds to the Hebrew *ḥasidim*, 'the pious' (see n.14). But what Josephus reports of the Essenes agrees very well with the ordinances of the Qumran texts for the Zadokites and the separated penitents in Israel, while in very few cases does it fit the Pharisees and Saduccees, whom he describes much more briefly.

## Essenes, Pharisees and Sadducees in Flavius Josephus

The Essenes also differ in important points from the Sadducees in Josephus' account. But in precisely these differences the Essenes correspond to the Dead Sea Scrolls and also to the characteristic statements in the letter 4QMMT.[15] A first criterion follows for Josephus from the question whether human fate is predestined by God or is dependent on our own free will. The Essenes believe in the omnipotence of 'destiny' (*heimarmene*), as Josephus seeks to explain to his readers with their Greek education (*Jewish Antiquities* XII, 172). He would have been more correct to speak of God's predestination (predetermination), as is done in the Community Rule of Qumran: 'From the God of Knowledge comes all that is and shall be. Before ever they (i.e. human beings) existed, he established their whole design, and when, as ordained for them, they come into being, it is in accord with his glorious design that they accomplish their task without change' (1QS 3.15f.). By contrast the Sadducees 'rule out destiny'. In their view we ourselves forge our fortunes and fare badly in life if we lack wisdom (*Jewish Antiquities* XIII, 3). The Pharisees stand between these two extremes, but closer to the Essenes.

That is also true of eschatology, the doctrine of the last things. The Sadducees deny the incorruptibility of the soul, or in Jewish terms the resurrection of the dead and the last judgment. In contrast to them the Essenes expect an existence in the beyond in light or in darkness and pain (*Jewish Antiquities* XVIII, 18). Accordingly the Community Rule promises the 'children of light' the eternal life of glory and threatens the godless with everlasting shame (1QS 4.2-14). The newly discovered letter of the 'Teacher of Righteousness' also speaks in a quite anti-Saducean way of the 'end of days'. Then everyone will experience the truth and be justified by God if they have acted rightly and well (4QMMT C 32f.).

A further point of distinction is belief in angels: the Sadducees do not share in it (Acts 23.8), while it plays an important role for the Essenes (*Jewish War* II, 142). This belief also appears in the Qumran texts. According to the War Scroll Michael and his angels bring about the decision in the Holy War (1QM 17.6-9). The liturgical worship of the community is modelled on the liturgy of the angels as shown by the sabbath songs of the Qumran community (4QShirShabb), which Carol Newsom[16] has edited.[17] The dualistic distinction between good and evil angels is character-istic of the Community Rule. The latter are led by Belial, the devil, who will seduce human beings to evil and thus bring them under his power (1QS 3.12-4.25). According to 4QMMT the recipient of the letter is to ask God to 'make firm his counsel and remove from him the evil plans and the counsel of Belial' (C30f.).

## The festival calendar and the hallowing of the sabbath

Such information from Josephus, the Qumran texts and also the letter 4QMMT does not justify our identifying the Qumran community with the Jewish religious party designated 'Sadducees' in the New Testament and in Josephus. Granted, both were led by priests and saw Zadok, David's priest, as their common ancestor. However, there was a split between the Zadokites who were loyal to the Torah and the more liberal Sadducees. This schism is not only indicated by the letter 4QMMT edited by Schiffman, who explains it by the strict attitude of the 'Teacher of Righteousness' over the cult and the holiness of the temple. The pollution of the temple is also similarly lamented in the Damascus Rule (CD 4.16-19). Josephus also stresses the 'differ-ence' (*diaphorotes*) and independence of the Essenes over temple sacrifice and ritual cleanness; they kept away from the common sanctuary and performed their rites of purification and sacrifice independently (*Jewish Antiquities* XVIII, 19).

This exclusiveness and independence of worship is also con-ditioned by the particular festal calendar of the Qumran com-munity. An explicit reference is made to the festivals of the solar calendar at the beginning of the letter 4QMMT. Only in the separate community led and given its theological stamp by the 'Teacher of Righteousness' was this calendar used – the group felt that it also applied in heaven. For in the Damascus Rule it is asserted that God has revealed to those who are faithful to his law 'hidden things in which all Israel had gone astray. He unfolded before them his holy sabbaths and his glorious feasts, and the desires of his will which a man must do in order to live' (CD 3.14f.). The fact that the cultic community had its own festival calendar excluded it from other groups.

Finally, the same applies to the particularly strict observance of the sabbath. Josephus says of the Essenes that they are fundamentally different from all other Jews in their observance of the sabbath, for this must be free of any activity (*Jewish War* II, 140). The particularly strict observance of the day of rest is fully confirmed in the Damascus document and laid down in individual regulations (CD 10.14 – 12.1).

## Written law and oral tradition

A brief word might be said here about the method of Lawrence Schiffman and others who rebel against the Qumran consensus: the concern to take note of differences and contradictions in the content of the Qumran texts and to demonstrate them above all from the fragments from Cave 4 which are finally coming into public view is justified. But this should not mislead us into overlooking the basic common features. Schiffman has shown very well that some of the regulations cited and described as disputed in the letter 4QMMT are also put forward in the Temple Scroll (11QMiqd) in the same rigorous formulation. This applies above all e.g. to the slaughter of sacrificial animals, the consumption of the peace offering or the offering of the fruits of trees in the fourth year to the priests. But Schiffman thinks that the Temple Scroll and the letter 4QMMT deviate considerably from the rest of the Qumran texts. First of all thematically, because the latter are not interested in the form of the temple and its sacrificial cult, and then in detail, above all as compared with the Damascus Document. However, at the present stage of Qumran work caution is called for here, since numerous fragments of the text have still to be evaluated.

The American Professor of Jewish Studies, Ben-Zion Wacholder, has only recently (see pp.24f.) reconstructed previously

unknown parts of the Damascus Rule from the concordance with
the help of the computer.[18] They demonstrate a more original and
much more extensive form of this work, which previously was
available to us only in two incomplete mediaeval manuscripts
made by the Jewish sect of the Karaites. The editor of these
manuscripts, which were found at the end of the last century,
Solomon Schechter, significantly called them 'The Zadokite Fragments'.[19] In the sections now published by Wacholder, instructions
appear which are similarly contained in the letter 4QMMT and
in the Temple Scroll. This applies, for example, to the exclusion
of unclean people from the temple as provided in 4QMMT B 39.
There is a similar list in the fragment CD De 9.2.12-18. There this
group of people also includes the man who betrays the secret of
his people to the Gentiles or curses Israel. This very crime is also
mentioned in the Temple Scroll (11QTemple 62.7-12): according
to Deuteronomy 21.22f. it is to be punished with crucifixion, as
high treason. This regulation is also important for understanding
the charge against Jesus.[20]

By his comparison with the regulations and controversies in
the Mishnah, Schiffman has made many contributions to a better
understanding of the criticism presented in the letter 4QMMT
which illuminates the main concern of the 'Teacher of Righteousness' and also shows the abiding significance of these particular
controversial points. But caution is called for in such a comparison, extending over centuries. If we attach great importance to
the differences within Qumran we should also not overlook the
differences between the exegesis of the law in Qumran and
rabbinic doctrine in the Mishnah which was edited much later, at
the end of the second century CE. For example, it has become
customary to call the letter of the Teacher of Righteousness
4QMMT a collection of *halakoth* (from the Hebrew *halak*, 'go,
walk'), i.e. rules for a 'way of life' which accords with the Torah.
But significantly this rabbinic term *halakah* (plural *halakoth*) does
not occur in the Qumran writings, even in the letter of the Teacher
of Righteousness. This letter is new and unique in the corpus of
Qumran manuscripts, but it also differs from the Mishnah and
its *halakoth*. In the Mishnah the *halakoth* are put in thematic
order and presented as the doctrinal decisions of the wise.

Nevertheless they are also regarded as part of the old oral tradition given on Sinai.

As we have already said, no such tradition was known in Qumran, and therefore no *halakoth* were known either. And it seems that the latter were being mocked when the commentary on the prophet Nahum speaks of the *doreshe halaqoth*, the 'seekers after smooth things' (4QpNah 1.2,7; 2.2,4; 3.3,7), and by it meant the Pharisees: to the rigorously inclined Zadokites their *halakoth* seemed to be *halaqoth*, all too smooth and convenient exegesis. They did not want any doctrines handed down orally, especially if the relationship of these doctrines to the law of Moses was not always clear. The Zadokites were concerned with the right performance of the Torah given in writing and ordered by God through Moses, with the doing of the law and the 'works of the Torah'. This expression *ma'aseh ha-torah* used in 4QMMT also occurs in Greek form, *ta erga tou nomou*, in the apostle Paul (Romans 2.15; 3.20,26; Galatians 2.16; 3.2,10,23). The designation 4QMMT has rightly been chosen as the title for the letter of the 'Teacher of Righteousness', now published. It has been taken from the text of the letter, in which it appears as a kind of table of contents: 'We have written to you something (*miqṣat*) about the doing of the Torah (*ma'aseh ha-Torah*),[21] for the good (i.e. salvation) of you and your people' (C 28f.). By contrast the designation 'halakhic letter', which recalls the Mishnah and Pharisaic schooling, should be avoided, since the letter does not have a Pharisaic but a 'Zadokite', i.e. Qumranic, orientation.

So the 'Teacher of Righteousness' based himself on the principle 'scripture alone', and like Jesus judged that the command of God (given in writing) is to be observed and not the 'tradition of men' (Mark 7.8f.). In the view of the Zadokites and also of Jesus, Holy Scripture does not need any special doctrine as it were to accompany it on its course through history and protect it against misuse and false interpretation. It interprets itself, or is constantly revealed by God. Most of its commandments are manifest and clear (Hebrew *niglot*). What is still hidden (*nistarot*) is illuminated by men like the priest Zadok (CD 5.4f.), the prophets (1QS 8.16) or the 'Teacher of Righteousness' (1QpHab 8.2f.); God gives them his Holy Spirit (1QS 8.15f.). Therefore everything depends on the study of the Torah and the 'works of the law'. These are presented in the living sanctuary of the Qumran community as the right sacrifice (4QFlorilegium 1.6f.).

Along with 'insight', the theoretical understanding of the Torah, such works of the law are the criteria by which the behaviour of the Qumran members is measured (1QS 6.18). Human beings must base themselves only on them if they want to withstand the judgment of God at the 'end of time' (4QMMT C 32f). For there the doing of what is right and good will be reckoned to men and women as righteousness. The high-priestly addressee of the letter is directed to Holy Scripture for this: 'We have written to you so that you create insight into the book of Moses and the (words) of the prophets, into David (i.e. the Psalms) and the books of Chronicles' (4QMMT C 10f.). So here as early as the second century BCE we can see a division of the canon of the Old Testament into several parts.[22]

## A split within the Jewish priesthood

The letter of the 'Teacher of Righteousness' is not evidence, for example, of the disputes between Pharisees and Sadducees which are reported by Josephus (*Jewish Antiquities* XIII, 297) and the Mishnah (Yadayim 3-4), but attests a schism in the priesthood among the sons of Zadok themselves. This break led to the formation of the Qumran community, i.e. the Essenes. The Essenes in fact emerged from the Zadokites and called themselves 'sons of Zadok'. But under the 'Teacher of Righteousness' these priests, along with Levites and laity, formed an eschatologically orientated community, detached from the world. This brought them into sharp opposition to the secular attitude of the priesthood in Jerusalem, the party of the Sadducees, as we know it from the New Testament and Josephus.

The first 'editors' of 4QMMT pointed to a remarkable passage in the fragment 4Q171, which is a *pesher* (commentary) on Psalm 37. There Psalm 37.32f., 'The godless seeks to kill the just' is interpreted in terms of the 'Wicked Priest, who [watched the Teacher of Righteousness] that he might put him to death [because of the ordinance] and the law which he sent to him... And [God] will pay him his reward by delivering him (i.e. the wicked priest) into the hand of the violent of the nations, that they may execute upon him [judgment].' It could be that the letter 4QMMT is meant here; the 'law' attached to it would be the Temple Scroll (11QTemple), a form of the Mosaic law distinctive to Qumran. The reaction of the high priest was to attempt to do away with the 'Teacher of Righteousness', but evidently he did not succeed. The punishment of the 'Wicked Priest' by violent Gentiles best fits the end of the first Hasmonaean high priest Jonathan, who was lured into a trap by the Syrians and killed (I Macc.12.39-53).

In the Jewish-Christian writing the Pseudo-Clementines (*Recognitions* 1.53f.) we hear of a Sadducean schism: 'There was first a division among those who are called Sadducees (*Sadducaei*). Some began to separate themselves from the community of the people as being more righteous (*ut caeteris iustitiores*).' This report about the 'more righteous' who separated themselves from the people clearly recalls the letter of the 'Teacher of Righteousness' and its statement 'we have separated ourselves from the mass of the people' (4QMMT C 7). The separatist righteous were those 'sons of Zadok' (*b$^e$ne ṣadoq*) who regarded themselves as 'sons of righteousness' (*b$^e$ne ṣedek*, cf. 1QS 9.14). Figures like John the Baptist (Mark 1.1.11) and the hermit Bannus (Josephus, *Vita* 11), then small groups like the Boethusians, the Tobele Shaharin (who took a ritual bath in the morning) and the orthodox 'Sadducees' in the Mishnah (Yadayim 4.5) probably belonged to these circles. They developed the priestly principles of sacred service into the ideal of an ascetic, anchoritic or monastic community and an angelic life which was unique in Judaism but represented a preliminary stage to Christian monasticism.

We find this ideal in the rules of the Zadokite priests which have been discovered in the caves by the Dead Sea and also in the image of the Essenes as Philo, Pliny the Elder and Josephus have depicted it. Therefore it is still best to see these two groups as identical – a few small differences between the sources cannot change any of this. The Qumran community and the Essenes agree in many important points at which they differ in particular from all other Jewish groups. Above all the detailed descriptions which Josephus gives of the various religious parties in the first century CE brings out the Sadducees, Essenes, Pharisees and Zealots in sharp profile.

Against this background the theory of Robert Eisenman, which

Baigent and Leigh have merely copied, that Essenes, Pharisees, Zealots and Jewish Christians are one and the same anti-Roman rebel movement, is completely wrong. Baigent and Leigh's claim that the Essene consensus was launched by the Dominicans of the École Biblique to divert attention from points of contact with earliest Christianity is equally far-fetched. It was above all scholars like the Israeli Eliezer L.Sukenik and André Dupont-Sommer, an ex-Catholic priest, who laid the foundation of the Essene theory.

# 4

# Was Qumran a Fortress or an Essene Monastery?

A popular tourist destination – A Herodian fortress? – A training camp for the last battle? – An Essene settlement nevertheless? – A man called Messadié and Jesus as a novice at Qumran – The Essene resurrection of Jesus and the lawsuits of the world reformers – Pinchas Lapide and Paul's studies at Qumran

## A popular tourist destination

A tour of Israel without a visit to the excavations at Qumran is almost unthinkable. Hundreds of tourists are shown through the partially reconstructed ruins every day. Most of them will probably not remember a great deal of what the guides tell them here, at a place which is around a thousand feet below sea level and swelters under the heat that almost always prevails. Nevertheless the visitors will be aware that they are seeing the remains of an Essene settlement.

A number of ancient sources tell us about the Essenes. As has already been said, the Jewish philosopher Philo, who wrote in Alexandria in the Egyptian Diaspora around 40 CE, but also visited the Holy Land at least once, was a member of the group. We get even more extensive reports through the Jewish historian Flavius Josephus, who composed his historical works in the last third of the first century CE. He even wanted to be a novice among the Essene monks for a while (*Vita*, 10-11). Reports on the Essenes appear above all in two of Josephus' works, the so-called *Jewish War* (written between 75 and 81 CE) and the *Jewish Antiquities* (93 CE). Philo and Josephus describe the Essenes as members of a group which was particularly faithful to the law and which lived an ascetic life in monastic-type settlements throughout Palestine.

As has also already been said, the ruins of Khirbet Qumran, known from the middle of the last century, were excavated between 1952 and 1956 under the direction of Gerald L.Harding of the Jordan Department of Antiquities and Roland de Vaux of the Dominican École Biblique in Jerusalem. A provisional excavation report appeared in 1961, which was later further expanded and improved by de Vaux.[1] This publication already provides a wealth of material from which it is possible for other scholars to examine de Vaux's conclusions.[2] In their book *The Dead Sea Scrolls Deception*, Baigent and Leigh significantly do not refer to other archaeologists for their judgment that the survey was 'amateurish'.[3] The scholarly world would have occasion for thorough criticism here had it thought that necessary. De Vaux presented his result in, among other places, a series of lectures organized by the British Academy. Unfortunately it is by no means rare in archaeology that a final report on the excavations has yet to appear. It must also be remembered that Roland de Vaux died suddenly in 1971, not long after his production of an improved provisional excavation report. Robert Donceel is now working on a final excavation report on the basis of the documentary material available.[4]

One of de Vaux's main theses was that those who settled at Khirbet Qumran were also the owners of the scrolls found in the caves. On the basis of ancient sources and some archaeological observations he also draws the conclusion that this was an Essene settlement. It existed from the second half of the second century BCE up to 68 CE; there was evidently a gap in occupation during the reign of King Herod the Great (37-4 CE). With very few exceptions the scholarly world – whether Jews, Christians or atheists – followed de Vaux's two theories. Criticism was fundamentally only of details. Only since the middle of the 1980s has there been a new discussion on the character of Qumran. Here some divergent views have been put forward, and we turn to them next.

*A Herodian fortress?*

In a number of academic articles,[5] but also in a public campaign, the American Jewish orientalist Norman Golb has put forward a counter-theory to Roland de Vaux, for which he has found some support in Germany from the Protestant New Testament scholar Matthias Klinghardt[6] of the University of Augsburg. According to Golb, Qumran is a Herodian fortress. However, the arguments that he offers for this theory are so weak that hardly any other scholar has been convinced by them. The existence of a fortified tower within the settlement is no argument in itself. This tower offered a possibility of temporary protection in times of danger. To take an example from Western Europe: the fact that a church has a tower for defence does not make it a robber's castle.

Golb's argument that the neighbourhood of an important road would indicate that Qumran was a military settlement is a strange one. Not every village past which a Roman road went was necessarily a castle. In Qumran there are just no walls thick enough for defensive purposes. Nor have ramparts and ditches been found. Furthermore, there are none of the Roman baths typical of Herodian fortresses in which the non-Jewish mercenaries could have refreshed themselves. Finally, so far not a single weapon has been found in any of the twenty-six graves excavated in the cemetery of Qumran.

Golb combines his unquestionably unsuccessful archaeological theory with another view which in itself is quite worthy of discussion. He believes that the scrolls which have been found are parts of libraries which were evacuated from the Holy City before the siege of Jerusalem by the Romans in 70 CE. As early as the 1950s, the German New Testament scholar Karl Heinrich Rengstorf (1903-1992), then head of the Institutum Judaicum at the University of Münster, whom Golb does not name, had put forward the view that they were part of the temple library.[7] In general, however, a connection between the settlement of Qumran and the hiding of the scrolls must be maintained. Most caves (4Q-10Q) are right next to Qumran, as is clear from even a fleeting glance at any plan of the settlement (map 3). Cave 4, which at one time must have been the fullest, was evidently a library, since in it there are the remains of bookshelves in the rock. So Golb's

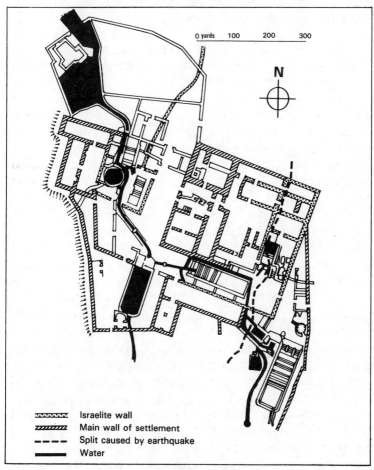

4 Plan of the Qumran settlement

statement that letters and documents of the kind that might be
expected in an archive of Qumran settlers is not true. According to
the list of publications which has now appeared, such documents
were also preserved in Cave 4 (4Q342-358).[8]

The argument that no discoveries of leather scrolls or papyri
were made in the settlement is also untenable. One need
only assume that the Qumran group were thorough in hiding
their writings. Moreover there are also positive indications of a
connection between the caves where the writings were found
and the settlement. Thus the jars in which the writings were

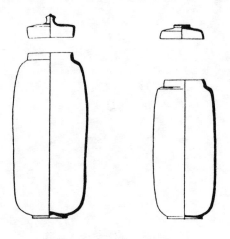

*5. Jars from Qumran and Cave 1*

stored are of the same typical pottery as that found in Qumran (diagram 5).

Furthermore, the spectacular discoveries in the settlement also include a number of inkwells. There are at least four, probably five – an unusually large number; so far only one inkwell from the period before 70 CE has been found in the whole of Jerusalem.[9] Furthermore, remnants of clay have been found which could have been made into tables. Two of the inkwells (diagram 6) were discovered with the remains of the tables, so the latter can be interpreted as writing tables (either for writing or for unrolling the scrolls), though this has always been disputed.[10] In one particular room in the Qumran settlement there was evidently regular literary production,[11] while military settlements elsewhere were not regarded as centres of writing. Furthermore, in Qumran itself at least brief inscriptions have been found on jars or potsherds (including a complete practice exercise of the alphabet).[12] The script used here is comparable to that which is to be found on many scrolls. Anyone who does not insist on a library stamp (*Ex libris conventus Essenorum Qumran*) has no good reason for doubting that most of the caves where discoveries were made were connected with the settlement.[13]

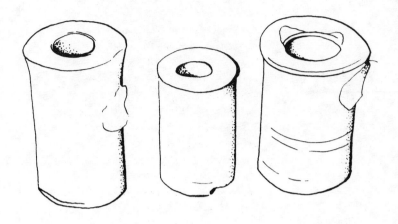

*6. Inkwells from the Qumran scriptorium*

There is one convincing argument against the assumption that the Qumran scrolls came for the most part from Jerusalem libraries or even from the Temple archive. According to all that we now know, among the very large number of discoveries there is not a single text which beyond doubt is Pharisaic or Sadducean. By contrast there are a great many texts which can be counted among the teachings of the group which we know from historical sources as Essenes (Ch.3). Now it is true – again to make a comparison – that the Vatican library has probably the greatest collection of heretical literature in the world. So it would also be possible for writings to have been collected in the temple archive which in the eyes of the Sadducean priesthood were unorthodox. However, it must be explained why only Essene writings survived in the Qumran caves, in addition to biblical and apocryphal writings widely in circulation. No one can really assume that in the face of the threat of a siege to Jerusalem people evacuated only the heretical writings from the temple and left the orthodox ones behind in the Holy City. So we would have to assume that for some reason only Essene writings have survived, although other documents were also hidden. But that would mean taking

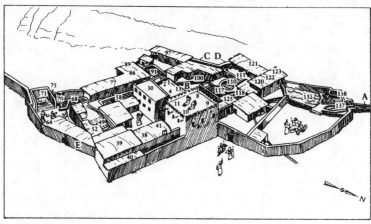

*7. Reconstruction of the Qumran settlement*

A. Entrance of aqueduct
B. Main water channel
C. Western wall of settlement
D. Western supporting wall
E. Eastern wall near the cemetery

1–2 Upper rooms
4 Room with low seats (council room)
8–11 Tower
13 Stairs leading to terrace
30 Scriptorium (where inkwells were found)
38–41 Kitchen
49 Large cistern
52 Laundry
58 Large cistern

64 Kiln
68 Ritual bath
70 + 75 Pottery workshop
77 Large assembly room
86 + 89 Room for pottery vessels
91 Large cistern
97 Stable?
100 Mill
110 Cistern (8th–6th century BCE)
111 Courtyard
117 Large cistern
118 Large cistern
120–123 Store rooms
132 + 137 Overflow basin
138 Ritual bath

chance as an explanation where there is a plausible reason: this is the treasured library of an Essene group which was hidden close to their settlement – namely Qumran.

## A training camp for the last battle?

Baigent and Leigh again show their talent for helping the theory of a military settlement to gain more publicity by crude exaggeration: 'What de Vaux, his colleagues and adherents of the consensus chose continually to overlook is the unmistakably military character of some ruins... There is another structure whose function may not be immediately apparent. In fact it is the remains of a well-built workship – with its own water supply for tempering the tools and weapons crafted within it.'[14] De Vaux was hesitant about defining the precise character of the workshop.[15] Frank M.Cross, a member of the international team and advocate of the scorned Essene theory, to whom Baigent and Leigh suddenly refer here in a positive way, thought that the place was possibly a forge.[16] So let us assume that it really was.

However, now Baigent and Leigh take the fatal leap in their argument. In view of the finds, the fact that de Vaux does not venture to define the place more closely 'is rather like not venturing to define the purpose of empty cartridge cases and spent projectiles of lead scattered around the OK corral in Tombstone, Arizona'.[17] One is amazed, reads the sentence once more and clarifies the logic: any tractor factory could equally well serve for the production of tanks. And the fact that no weapon was found in the Qumran forge is conclusive proof that it was a forge for weapons. Even if weapons of the Qumran settlers had been found (the origin of one arrowhead is uncertain), this would not be a proof that militant Zealots rather than pacifist Essenes lived here. We know from Flavius Josephus that although the Essenes were fundamentally peace-loving (*Jewish War* II, 135), they carried weapons with them on journeys as protection against attacks from robbers (ibid., II, 125).

In any case, Baigent and Leigh have not asked one decisive question in connection with the hypothesis of a Zealot military camp. The Qumran settlement existed from the second half of the second century BCE until 68 CE. Did the Hasmonaean ruler, King Herod Agrippa I, and the Roman procurators tolerate this nest of resistance so near by? Rome sent a whole legion to subdue the last Zealot bastion of Masada in the Jewish war after 70 CE. If Qumran had been a Zealot settlement, it would only have taken a few platoons to make short shrift of it and drive out its inhabitants.

But among the Qumran texts there is the so-called 'War Scroll'. This belongs among the first discoveries from Cave 1 and is cited with the abbreviation 1QM, after the Hebrew word for war (*milḥamah*). The scroll depicts the eschatological battle of the Jews who remained faithful ('sons of light') against the adversaries of God ('sons of darkness'). The battle is decided by the intervention of God. So is this a kind of military handbook for the last battle and thus a proof of the Zealot character of Qumran? However, such a work relating to the end-time is far from saying anything about the conduct of its authors and readers in the present. This can be clarified well by means of a modern example. No security police in the world would persecute Mennonites simply because their Bible includes the Revelation of John, which similarly speaks of eschatological wars. Despite their predilection for the Apocalypse of John the Mennonites were and are resolute pacifists.

### An Essene settlement nevertheless?

We have seen that virtually everything is in favour of the majority of the non-biblical Qumran texts being regarded as Essene writings (ch.3). Furthermore, strong archaeological evidence points to a connection between the writings in the caves and the Qumran settlement. In that case the texts which have been discovered are an almost indisputable indication that this is an Essene settlement. There is also a series of archaeological peculiarities in Qumran itself which best fit an Essene settlement. Here are just four examples:[18]

1. The ingenious and expensive system of water channels, cisterns and large baths with steps is extremely striking for an ordinary settlement, but is immediately explicable if a Jewish group lived here which had an extra need for cultic purity of the kind we know from the Essenes.[19]

2. The largest room in the settlement is marked out by its length and a special platform in the West orientated on the Holy City of Jerusalem.[20] Quite obviously religous meals took place in this room, as is shown by an adjacent room with dishes and ritually buried animal bones immediately next to it.[21] This is markedly reminiscent of the meals led by a priest in an Essene community house of which Josephus writes (*Jewish War* II, 129-31).

3. Josephus reports a further Essene peculiarity: they used a trenching-tool to bury their excrement (*Jewish War* II, 148). Such a trenching-tool was found at Qumran.[22]

4. The Temple Scroll describes at length niches in house walls which were to take priestly garments (11QTemple 32-33). A series of niches in Qumran can be connected with this regulation.[23]

Roland de Vaux never made a secret of the fact that the graves of some women were also found in the Qumran cemeteries.[24] But this is no decisive argument against the assumption of an Essene settlement. We know from Josephus (*Jewish War* II, 160f.) and the Damascus Document (CD 7.6f.) that there were also married Essenes. As we shall see, above all a contemporary historical account suggests that Qumran was a monastic settlement. It is striking that in the gigantic, carefully prepared main cemetery, so far only male skeletons have been found (in 26 out of about 1100 graves), all lying in a north-south direction. So far the female burials have been demonstrated only in separate small unorganized burial fields. In contrast to the male burials in the main cemetery, in some of the female graves remnants of wood coffins have been found, which indicates that these women were brought here from elsewhere.[25] There could have been married Essenes or women living celibate lives as presupposed by the Temple Scroll (11QTemple 53,14ff.),[26] in settlements associated with Qumran (like En et-Turabe, En el-Juwer and En Fesha).[27] Similarly, occasionally peasants' wives from neighbouring settlements would be buried in the cemeteries of isolated Christian monasteries.

One very interesting fact is that not a single ossuary has been found in Qumran, and the burials are exclusively earth burials. Ossuaries are small limestone coffins in which the bones of the dead were buried after corruption. This second burial was an originally Pharisaic custom,[28] and does not occur in Qumran. Since according to Josephus the Zealots were Pharisees in their theological views, apart from their need to carry on an armed freedom fight against the Romans (*Jewish Antiquities*, XVIII 23), the lack of ossuaries also tells against Qumran as a Zealot nest. The simplicity of the earth burials is a further strong argument against Qumran being a Sadduceean or Herodian villa. In that case one would have expected splendid rock tombs and stone coffins like the examples which are present in Jerusalem in abundance. But probably there were not the rock walls for making monumental tombs in Qumran.

We shall go on to mention other three ancient sources which more or less clearly indicate that Qumran was an Essene settlement. A letter from the time of the Bar Kokhba revolt (132-135

CE) which was found in the Wadi Murabba'at mentions a settlement *meṣad ḥasidin*, 'citadel of the pious' (Mur 45,6). This settlement is best identified with Qumran.[29] As for the mention of a fortress, it must be recalled that after their conquest of it in 68 CE the Romans made Qumran a lightly-fortified military post.[30] 'Citadel of the pious' was not, as we shall see, the original name for Qumran used by its inhabitants. Nevertheless the later name is interesting. It preserves the recollection that this was an Essene settlement. For the Greek term *Essaioi, Essenoi* is most probably connected with the Hebrew word *ḥasidim*.[31]

The most exciting but also most enigmatic texts from Qumran are the two-part copper scroll found in Cave 3, which originally formed a whole. It contains a list of a total of sixty-four hiding places for treasure. At present scholars are again becoming firmly convinced that this is an authentic Qumran document and not a popular legend from the period around 100 CE.[32] Norman Golb sees the Copper Scroll as particular support for his theories, but quite wrongly. The Scroll mentions the hiding places of the treasure in a very definite geographical order.[33] Some of the hiding places are in the area of the River Yarmuk (3Q15 8.1-10.4), which is a tributary of the Jordan south of Lake Gennesaret. It is not evident how parts of the temple treasure could have been hidden in an area which soon after the outbreak of the Jewish War fell into Roman hands. However, for a Qumran document hoards of treasure in this area would make good sense. Nowadays scholars are more than ever assuming, with full justification, that the 'land of Damascus' of which the Damascus Rule speaks (CD 7.15-19) is not a code name for Babylon or Qumran but in fact refers here to the city in southern Syria.[34] The Essene group had been in exile in the 'land of Damascus' for a while at the beginning of its foundation and after that some of the members evidently remained in this neighbourhood. Equally important is the concentration of hiding places south of Jericho (map 2, p.6); here a place called Secacah appears four times (3Q15 4.13f.; 5.1f., 5,12). Now this designation is none other than the Old Testament name for that Iron Age settlement (Joshua 15.61) which existed in the area of Khirbet Qumran in the eighth and seventh centuries BCE.[35]

Finally, mention should also be made of the famous description by the Roman author Pliny the Elder, written before 73 CE – he was thus an immediate contemporary: 'On the west side of the Dead Sea, but out of range of the noxious exhalations of the coast, is the solitary tribe of the Essenes, which is remarkable beyond all the other tribes in the whole world, as it has no women and has renounced all sexual desire, has no money, and has only palm trees for company. Day by day the throng of refugees is recruited to an equal number by numerous accessions of persons tired of life and driven thither by the waves of fortune to spend their days. Thus through thousands of ages (incredible to relate) a race in which no one is born lives on for ever, so prolific for their advantage is other men's weariness of life! Below them once lay the city of En-Gedi, second after Jerusalem [perhaps a miswriting of Jericho] in fertility and palm groves, but now also a heap of ruins. Furthermore, equally not far from the Dead Sea the citadel of Masada stands on a rock. Thus Judaea.'[36]

For all the rhetorical exaggeration, it is clear that Pliny is thinking of Essenes living a celibate life. In addition he gives us valuable geographical information: the main settlement of the Essenes which he is evidently describing here lay some way from the west shore of the Dead Sea, north of En-gedi. Greater accuracy is hardly to be expected from an ancient writer in describing the situation of Qumran.

The phases in the history of the Qumran community as they have already been worked out by Gert Jeremias on the basis of the Damascus Rule and the commentaries on Nahum, Micah, Habakkuk and Ps. 37[37] fit in well with the early periods of the settlement of Qumran.[38] Thus literary and archaeological evidence coincide. Frank M. Cross has commented somewhat sharply: 'The scholar who wants to "exercise caution" over identifying the Qumran group with the Essenes finds himself in an amazing position. He must in all seriousness propose that two major groups of religious communities founded settlements in the same region of the Dead Sea and in fact lived in the same two centuries, shared the same sometimes bizarre views, and performed similar or the same purification, ritual meals and ceremonies. Furthermore the scholar must assume that a community described so precisely in the ancient sources simply disappeared without leaving the remains of buildings or even potsherds behind. By contrast, the other community, which is so completely ignored by the classical sources, left behind extensive ruins and even a library.'[39] We must concede that James C.VanderKam[40] is right in saying that even to describe Qumran as Essene-like is an evasion; he bluntly calls Qumran an Essene monastery.[41]

## A man called Messadié and Jesus as a novice at Qumran

Like *The Dead Sea Scrolls Deception* later, the novel by the Frenchman Gerald Messadié, *L'homme qui devient Dieu* (The Man who Became God), found a firm place in the bestseller lists of *Meinung* magazine.[42] One could happily consign this book to oblivion did it not in an extensive postscript claim to be a historical novel on a factual basis.[43] Evidently Messadié did not properly understand the illuminating little book *Qumran and the Origin of Christianity*, by Jean Daniélou, who was later to become a cardinal.[44] Contrary to what Daniélou wrote, Messadié regarded it as proven that 'The Dead Sea manuscripts show that Jesus' teaching and indeed the structure of his teaching was essentially already in existence before him.'[45] However, Messadié betrays on the same page that his real informants are Edmund Wilson and John M.Allegro. Amazingly the German edition of *A Man Called Jesus* says that the scrolls were discovered in 1949,[46] i.e. one year before the publication of parts of them in academic journals (22).

Messadié obtains the time for a lengthy Qumran novitiate, during which John the Baptist is said to have initiated Jesus, by brushing aside as unhistorical Jesus' long stay in Nazareth. He does this with the hilarious argument: how could a carpenter have earned a living there when excavations have proved 'that the synagogue of Nazareth could not have contained more than around forty people'?[47] A look at a modern Bible lexicon could have shown the amateur historian that so far no synagogue from New Testament times has been found in Nazareth.[48] Already in his youth, Messadié says, he was indignant 'that the [Catholic] church could have been founded on a word-play which can only be understood in the Romance languages'.[49] We are to conclude from this that even up to the writing of his book Messadié can have read none of the many discussions of the Aramaic word-play[50] which underlies the Greek of Jesus' saying: 'You are Peter (*Petros*) and on this rock (*petra*) I will found my community' (Matthew 16.18).

As was to be feared after the success of his Jesus novel, Messadié has meanwhile also turned to the apostle Paul. In addition to the almost 500-page text, the novel *Un homme nommé Saul* (A Man Called Saul), which appeared in 1992, contains almost 150 pages of 'scientific' notes, which could also be a reason for the limited success of the work. For Messadié Paul's visions of Christ are the result of attacks of epilepsy on a personality which is already hysterical by disposition. Messadié's key thesis is that Saul was an offspring of the Herodian ruling house. His father was none other than Antipater, otherwise known only as one of the unfortunate sons of Herod the Great; his mother was Mariamne, daughter of the last Hasmonaean ruler, Antigonus. As a prince without hope of the Jewish throne, and torn to and fro between his partly Jewish and partly pagan descent, Saul resolved to found a religion. But because not a word of this is to be found in the work of the Jewish historian Flavius Josephus, Messadié must assume that 'the later copyists of both his works [*Jewish War* and *Jewish Antiquities*] carefully obliterated all references that they thought inappropriate. The day on which the Vatican opens its libraries will definitely produce some surprises.'[51]

With that the circle is closed. After some confused sentences on the term 'apostle to the peoples' (Romans 11.13), the new book *The Dead Sea Scrolls Uncovered* by Robert H.Eisenman and Michael Wise concludes: 'Where Paul is concerned, he very likely refers to his own Herodian origins and relationship to such "peoples" in Romans 16.11.'[52] It is striking that as early as 1987 Messadié was asserting that only twenty per cent (!) of the Qumran texts had been published and then spoke of an 'all too real conspiracy which casts a mantle of silence over the manuscripts from the Dead Sea'.[53] According to the context, this suspicion can only fall on the Vatican. It would certainly be interesting to investigate the closer connections between Eisenman and Messadié. At all events one could wish more truth and thoroughness from the authors, rather than shrill sensationalism and provocation.

*The Essene resurrection of Jesus and the lawsuits of the world reformers*

According to Messadié, the resurrection of Jesus from the dead was also a concocted deception. However, he embellishes the pseudo-death theory with a further, absurd variant: the ongoing life of a crucified Jesus who was not quite dead could have been in the political interest of both the Roman governor Pontius Pilate and the Galilean tetrarch Herod Antipas. The Roman hoped that Jesus would calm down the tense situation in Palestine. Herod wanted to play off Jesus (the son of David) against his step-nephew Agrippa (the later Jewish king of 41-44 CE) in order to secure rule for himself.[54] One is amazed that helpful Essenes do not also intervene in this situation, since elsewhere in Messadié they crop up on every occasion, possible and even more impossible. But this strong missing link in the chain of proof has recently been offered in another book.

This is *Das Jesus-Komplott* (The Jesus Plot), by Holger Kersten and Elmar R.Gruber, which also appeared in 1992. Both are well prepared for their disclosure story. Holger Kersten, a former teacher of religion, is the author of the bestseller *Jesus lebte in Indien* (Jesus Lived in India, 1983).[55] Elmar R.Gruber was academic assistant to Hans Bender, Professor of Parapsychology in Freiburg. *Das Jesus-Komplott* has the subtitle 'The Truth about the Turin Shroud'. Kersten and Gruber are convinced that the 1988 radio carbon test according to which the Turin Shroud comes from the fourteenth century is a skilfully arranged deception. In a series of interviews and investigations Kersten and Gruber can in fact point to a whole series of inconsistencies. Other authors have also voiced considerable suspicions about the way in which the tests were carried out,[56] so that we can only endorse the demands that the investigation should be repeated, this time in really controlled conditions, in order to make all speculations groundless.

What is new in Kersten and Gruber is that they make the Vatican responsible for the falsification of the radio carbon test. However, they explicitly rule out Pope John Paul II and thus suggest doubt about their own plot theory. Still, the two authors think that they have a convincing motive for the manipulations of the Vatican: the Turin Shroud shows that Jesus was only apparently dead! However, all serious experts who have so far occupied themselves thoroughly with the question are of the view that the crucified figure on the shroud, whoever he may have been, was in fact dead.[57] Kersten and Gruber regard their interpretation of the Turin Shroud merely as additional evidence. The Gospels, above all that of John, already betray to the unprejudiced historian that the resurrection of Jesus was the revival of someone who was apparently dead.[58]

For Kersten and Gruber it is certain that 'Jesus was close to the sect of the Essenes, and to all appearance even belonged to a branch of the sect'.[59] Since according to Josephus the Essenes were skilled in healing arts (*Jewish War* II, 136), it is presented as an irrefutable explanation that members of the sect began to cure Jesus in the cool rock tomb. Since the Essenes wore white garments at their liturgies (*Jewish War* II, 129), the young man in white garments whom the women meet at the tomb (Mark 16.5) could of course only have been an Essene. The aromatic stuff provided by Nicodemus (John 1.39) was just a dressing for the wounds. Jesus' knowledge of Yoga techniques and the abundant use of opium (the drink of John 19.29f.) had already seen to it that the crucifixion did not turn out too badly. So according to Kersten and Gruber the 'Risen Christ' is in fact only the 'revived Christ', who could soon leave the tomb (and set off for India).

Such Qumran stories are a lapse into the darkest times of the Enlightenment. The author of the Essene pseudo-death story was Carl Friedrich Bahrdt (1741-1792), who could look back on a life stamped by scandals and human inadequacies, which cost him both his Leipzig professorship and a chair at Erfurt. One almost feels sympathy with Albert Schweitzer, who had to work through Bahrdt's eleven volumes of almost three thousand pages for his critical account in *The Quest of the Historical Jesus*.[60] Anyone who has steeped himself in the relevant literature of the past soon sees how little new there is in modern speculations about the Essenes. One has only to read an account of the way the Essenes were depicted in the eighteenth and nineteenth centuries by the Leipzig Old Testament scholar Siegfried Wagner to be convinced about that.[61]

In a postscript to their book, Gruber and Kersten give a

summary of Paul's message which could hardly be briefer and clearer[62] – but only to brand Paul as the one who corrupted Jesus's simple ethic of love. Here we are given to understand that they want to re-emphasize the man Jesus's simple ethic of love so that humanity can survive the twentieth century. Kersten and Gruber agree with Karl Herbst ('No atoning death on the cross! no magic with bodies in the tomb!'[63]), and both express gratitude for his manifold help.[64] However, this friendship did not last long. When Herbst wanted to bring out his book *Kriminallfall Golgatha* (The Crime of Golgotha), Kersten and Gruber sought, and were granted, an injunction on grounds of plagiarism.[65] But presumably we must wait for the dawn of the kingdom of peace and love as long as experts only converse through their lawyers.

Karl Herbst is the religious inspiration behind Franz Alt, who claimed to be the first to have understood the Sermon on the Mount properly after two thousand years. Herbst's book has in fact now appeared,[66] with a bombastic introduction by Bernd März, who at the moment is making his name above all with an edition of sermons by Eugen Drewermann. But both Kersten and Gruber's 'Jesus Plot' and Herbst's 'Crime on Golgotha' are clearly to be counted as victims of the fall-out of *The Dead Sea Scrolls Deception*.

## Pinchas Lapide and Paul's studies at Qumran

In an interview with the Evangelischer Pressedienst in January 1993 the well-known Jewish free-lance writer Pinchas Lapide sharply atacked not only Baigent and Leigh's *Dead Sea Scrolls Deception* but also Robert H.Eisenman.[67] Grateful though we must be to him for some clarification here, the question arises whether this interview was not also connected with his book *Paulus zwischen Damaskus und Qumran* (Paul between Damascus and Qumran), announced for February 1993. The subtitle of this book once again mentions false interpretations and translation mistakes,[68] though these are those of Lapide himself, as was to be expected after his book *Ist die Bibel richtig übersetzt?* (Has the Bible been Translated Correctly?)[69] and other misguided contributions.[70]

Because some scholars identify the 'land of Damascus' of the

Damascus Document with Qumran, according to Lapide Paul was not converted near the Syrian city of Damascus,[71] but simply experienced a call at Qumran and also enjoyed theological studies there. That would explain points of contact between Paul's teaching and the Qumran writings. One historical blemish is that Paul not only mentions Damascus at his call (Galatians 1.17) but clearly means the metropolis of southern Syria when he refers to Damascus in another context (II Corinthians 11.32f.): there the ethnarch of the Nabataean king Aretas IV barred the city gates and wanted to arrest Paul.[72] Had the Nabataean ruler done that in Qumran, directly under the eyes of the Roman governor or the Jewish king, it would have been grounds for war. But the annals of Palestine are completely silent about such a war.

A personal experience of one of the authors (R.Riesner) may show how scepticism over some of Lapide's remarks is in place. In a television discussion Professor Lapide surprised the participants by saying that a prayer had been found in Qumran which is eighty per cent identical with the Lord's Prayer.[73] When asked after the discussion which text this was, he could not give a precise reference. In fact it can only be a prayer which is in one of the psalms attributed to the patriarch Joseph (4Q372) and has been edited by Eileen M.Schuller.[74] This is a further case to add to the few Jewish instances from the time of the Second Temple of God being addressed as Father.[75] But there the similarity ends. By comparison, Lapide was only exaggerating mildly when in the same broadcast he claimed that most of the Beatitudes of Jesus (Matthew 5.3-12) were already known from Qumran. The parallels here are indeed greater,[76] but that is not so surprising in the case of a literary genre already known from the Old Testament (Psalm 1.1) and the deutero-canonical books (Jesus Sirach 14.20-27).

Pinchas Lapide beyond question did great and abiding service in the first, difficult phase of the Jewish-Christian dialogue. Furthermore he defended the Vatican against unjustified accusations in connection with Hochhuth's controversial play *The Representative*.[77] But it cannot be ignored that in his numerous works, which appear in regular succession, there is much over-simplification and only approximate accuracy. To call him a Qumran expert would not do him justice. Still, his early commitment is to be treasured undiminished: as one of the Holocaust generation sorely tested by the severest suffering he argued for a new mutual understanding between Jews and Christians.

# 5

## Does James the Brother of the Lord lie behind the 'Teacher of Righteousness'?

Access to the unpublished Qumran fragments – Access to the history of earliest Christianity – Eisenman's confusion over method – Is the 'Teacher of Righteousness' at the same time 'James the Just'? – The slandering of the apostle Paul

### Access to the unpublished Qumran fragments

Not only has Barbara Thiering, whom we shall discuss in Chapter 7, put forward the theory that the Qumran texts offer new, revolutionary insights into Christianity which will shake the church's faith, but so too has Robert H.Eisenman, who has already been mentioned often. He is Professor of Middle East Religions at California State University, Long Beach, and is one of a new generation of Qumran scholars. In fact he can be described as a new star who has shone out particularly brightly on the stage of the Dead Sea Scrolls theatre, which has recently been illuminated with so lurid a glare. Of course there is some dispute as to whether Eisenman's 'currency and credibility have placed him among the most prominent and influential figures in his field'.[1] One looks in vain for his name in professional journals like the *Revue de Qumrân*, the *Revue Biblique* or the *Journal of Biblical Literature*; until recently his literary production even on Qumran questions was very small.[2]

Eisenman became known through the authors of the best-selling *The Dead Sea Scrolls Deception*, who needed a source on Qumran research obligated to scholarship and congenial to them, in order to give more credibility to their new and exciting discoveries about the rise of Christianity. Furthermore, Eisenman's attacks on the Qumran team established in Jerusalem also fitted in with their conspiracy thesis. He could also have seemed attractive to them above all because of his apparently adventurous, critical view that the 'Teacher of Righteousness' of the Qumran writings must be James surnamed 'the Just', the brother of Jesus, whose adversary was the apostle Paul, the 'Man of Lies'. The second, even weaker, part of *The Dead Sea Scrolls Deception*,[3] in which the secret of the Qumran community and earliest Christianity, allegedly so strictly kept, is to be revealed and the trusting eyes of believers are to be opened, is based on Eisenman's interpretation of the Qumran texts, above all the Habakkuk commentary.

Eisenman is beyond doubt an outsider with much self-confidence, energy and enterprise. Thus with a handful of enthusiastic students he has independently once again worked through the caves by the Dead Sea.[4] With his publication of the photographs of text fragments from Cave 4 Eisenman has done an indisputable service, but at the same time has earned sharp criticism for his illegal procedure. The facsimile edition in two stately volumes may offer only a photographic reproduction of pictures of the many fragments which had been taken some years before in the Palestine Archaeological Museum.[5] The pictures are also disordered and sometimes barely readable; often there are very small scraps with only a few letters on them (e.g. plates 311-14). Nevertheless the work as a whole is a treasure trove for the specialist who has patience and good eyes. One can also imagine the laborious work that such fragments present to a team of editors. On the other hand, it is hard to understand why such photocopies were not made accessible to the public long ago.

So it is a creative task to produce from the chaos of such mutilated fragments and scraps of texts the cosmos of meaningful statements and discussions which the teachers and writers in Qumran prepared on particular themes or the interpretations of biblical sayings. Eisenman worked on this task with Michael Wise, a young expert in Aramaic at the Oriental Institute in Chicago. They have edited and commented on fifty major fragments from Cave 4 (see above pp.28f.). *The Dead Sea Scrolls Uncovered* (1992) is the perhaps exaggerated title of their work. It enriches Qumran research to the degree that it offers easily readable Hebrew texts with translation and commentary. However, what is – to put it mildly – the wayward hypothesis of the fight between James and Paul cannot be sustained from it. Some statements in the Qumran fragments are compared with passages from the letter of James and the letters of Paul without really shedding much light. On the basis of the texts published by Eisenman and Wise, anyone can now test for themselves not only the viability of Eisenman's new revolutionary theory but also the views of Barbara Thiering (Ch.7) and Norman Golb and make up their own mind whether the old Qumran consensus, which has been attacked so harshly, has really been shaken.

In each of the introductions Eisenman is also concerned to praise the power, beauty and significance of the texts he has selected. Despite all the love of the subject-matter with which one must credit the editor, readers will often be disappointed. For the high expectations that they cherish as a result of Eisenman's praise are hardly matched by the translated text with its fragmentary sentences and even isolated words. One could calmly accept this apparently childlike zeal had not Eisenman drawn comparisons with the New Testament in the preliminary announcements of the German edition of this book: 'Anyone who wants to know what really happened in Palestine in the century before and after Christ should not read the Gospels but the Qumran scrolls,' Eisenman advises on the jacket text. Now there is indeed much that is edifying in the Qumran texts, but very little about the history of the Judaism of the time, far less about Jesus and the first Christians.

The few names from the history of early Judaism which occur in the new fragments of text all belong to the history of the Hasmonaean period: the high priest Yohanan, i.e. probably John Hyrcanus (143-104 BCE, cf. 4Q324 E 1.1f.);[6] then Shelamzion, i.e. Salome Alexandra (76-67 BCE) and her son Hyrcanus (4Q323 A 2,4,6; 4Q324 E.1,2,7);[7] also Aemilius (Scaurus), one of Pompey's generals (4Q324 D 2,4).[8] The fragments from Cave 4 may be exciting for those who, like Eisenman, compulsively look for references to James the Just and Paul in them. But the fact that they find the same concepts and phrases here and there does not mean much, seeing that both groups had the same Holy Scripture.

## Access to the history of earliest Christianity

Eisenman emphasizes that his interest in the Qumran texts and especially in the still-unpublished fragments from Cave 4 is historical and not, say, philological or even theological. He is tormented by the impatience of a historian who ultimately wants to know what really happened and therefore cannot spend long on the laborious task of editing and restoration and on pernickety translation problems. To proceed with any degree of certainty the historian needs an overall survey, a view of all available texts. So there should be no delay over their publication, nor should the eyewitnesses to the event be prevented from giving information about the origin of Christianity.[9] Unlike theologians – according to Eisenman – historians are not inhibited by any prejudices and other considerations; incorruptibly and freely they consider the phenomena they find and then offer the astounded world the truths which had previously remained hidden from it. At all events, Eisenman's propagandists Baigent and Leigh believe that his discoveries could 'shake' the Roman church. However, it seems that this church is at present more exercised by the criticism coming out of its own ranks from people like Eugen Drewermann than from the outsider Eisenman. But as Christianity cannot be overcome even by the gates of hell (Matthew 16.18), it will also survive the earthquakes of the new Qumran texts.[10]

How true is the interpretation of the Qumran text so passionately presented by Eisenman and the evaluation of Essenes and Christians associated with it? What is its basis, and what is so new or even threatening about it? Eisenman sees in James, as in Jesus and the Christians who emerged from Judaism, along with the Essenes and Qumran people, a species of Zealotism: for him, all these groups were supporters of the Palestinian protest movement against Roman rule, especially against the Roman administration of Judaea by the prefect of the emperor. After the deposition of Herod's son Archelaus, the king of Judaea, in 6 CE, Judaea and Jerusalem were put under a Roman prefect and attached to the province of Syria. This event and the Roman administrative measures connected with it led to the formation of the party of Zealots and Sicarii, with whom Eisenman wrongly also associates the Qumran people (Essenes) and the early Christians; the latter were more opposed to the Zealots and had a peaceful disposition.[11]

Martin Hengel[12] has portrayed the character of the Zealots particularly well in a monumental and basic work, while Eisenman blurs the major differences between the Jewish religious parties in the time of Jesus. The Zealots and Sicarii, defenders to the death of the honour of God and the purity of Israel, with their 'liberation theology' and their violent attacks on Roman occupation troops and Jewish collaborators, finally drove the people of Israel into a war against Israel which came to a catastrophic end in 70 CE with the destruction of Jerusalem and the abolition of the Jewish commnity. The Essene settlement by the Dead Sea was destroyed as early as 68 CE, and in a postlude in 74 CE the fortress of Masada with its heroic defenders was conquered.

The Zealot interpretation of the Qumran texts and the Jewish-Christian variant of the Zealot theory are not new. The Zealot hypothesis found significant advocates in Cecil Roth[13] and G.R.Driver.[14] Very soon after the discovery of the first scrolls, Jacob L.Teicher of Cambridge had conjectured that Ebionite Jewish-Christians rather than Essenes were their authors. For them Jesus had been the 'Teacher of Righteousness' and Paul a 'man of lies'. It is quite amazing that Eisenman still dares once again to bring out a theory about Qumran which has long been laid to rest. Furthermore, his historical assessment of the beginnings of Christianity is reminiscent of the scheme which Ferdinand Christian Baur (1792-1860), teaching in the middle of the last century in Tübingen, developed about the contrast between Jewish Christians and Gentile Christians and the transcending of it in the Catholic church.

According to Eisenman, the Qumran texts present a picture of the movement from which the Christian church came into being on Palestinian soil. However, this originally Jewish Christianity was completely different from the Christianity that we know from the New Testament and church history, namely 'Paulinized' Gentile, cosmopolitan, antinomian and pacifist Christianity. By comparison the Palestinian Christians led by James had been Zealots with a political commitment, nationalistic and xeno-phobic, faithful to the law and stamped by a messianic apocalypticism.[15] Here it must be said that this sharp distinction between Jewish Christians and Gentile Christians, which was also made by Ferdinand Christian Baur, but on another basis, can no longer be sustained in such a form in more recent scholarship. There was no gaping gulf between James and Paul. And Paul was to some extent much more 'messianic' than James and the supposedly messianic community of the Dead Sea. Nor can one simply describe Paul as an antinomian, as one who destroyed the law of Moses.[16] Conversely James too – like Paul – in his letter taught the 'royal law' of the commandment to love (James 2.8).

## Eisenman's confusion over method

How does Eisenman come to identify the 'Teacher of Righteousness', the great leader of the Qumran community, whose activity is usually dated to the second century BCE, with James the Just, for a while leader of the Jerusalem Christians, who lived more than two hundred years later? Is such a view worth discussing at all? First of all let us leave aside the 'un-Christian' content of the Qumran writings; yet other, external, circumstances tell against Eisenman. Second, there are the archaeological excavations in the ruins of Khirbet Qumran which indicate that there was already a settlement under the Hasmonaeans. Third, there is the palaeographical investigation of the texts, i.e. the determination of the age of the types of script contained in them. Of course Eisenman rejects this as too uncertain: 'These methods have in the past too often been employed illegitimately in Qumran research to confuse the non-specialist. The palaeographical sequences developed, while helpful [aha!], are too uncertain to have any real relevance to such a narrow chronological period [three centuries!].'[17] However, in this view he seems to stand very much alone (apart from Barbara Thiering). Nowadays palaeography is utterly taken for granted as a tool in archaeology. In favourable instances scripts can be dated precisely within two or three decades. At a very early stage it was clear that the Qumran scrolls belonged in the period between the second century BCE and the first century CE, and most of them even in the pre-Christian period.

Of course one can also measure the age of the writing material of the scrolls – leather, which contains carbon – and the linen wrappings (by the C 14 test). This was done relatively soon after the discovery of the scrolls, and at that time the year 'zero' was established for their manufacture (p.30) – with a margin of error of around ten per cent of the period between 200 BCE and 200 CE. In the meantime the process has been refined (AMS = accelerator mass spectrometry): the margin of error on normal presuppositions is now only around five per cent. In 1989 Eisenman himself had asked the Israeli Department of Antiquities for a more recent C 14 test; this was carried out in 1991 with international participation. The result was devastating for Eisenman's theory: most texts were written in the second and first centuries BCE, and only one is certainly to be assigned to the first century CE. The C 14 test meanwhile carried out in the Institute for Middle Energy Physics in Zurich in 1991 showed that of eight scroll texts coming from three different caves, six clearly and two probably are pre-Christian.[18]

Even this result did not bother Eisenman. His commentary on this investigation reads: 'The process is still in its infancy, subject to multiple variables, and too uncertain to be applied with precision to the kind of materials we have before us.'[19] But in that case why did Eisenman suggest the text at all? Indeed the radio carbon test is not infallible, above all if it is dealing with articles which are heavily polluted. But here the result corresponds perfectly with the other insights, the cumulative value of which Eisenman plays down because it does not fit his concept. Eisenman's remarks on the radio carbon test show his prejudice so clearly that Geza Vermes simply remarked: 'No further comment is required.'[20] Baigent and Leigh have treated the test even more lightly, since they simply keep quiet about it in *The Dead Sea Scrolls Deception*, though it was already known when the book appeared (in September 1991). Magen Broshi had published the result at a Qumran Congress in the Escorial in Madrid in the middle of March 1991.

Now to Eisenman's substantive, historical assessment of the Qumran texts. A new method of interpretation has allegedly led him to conjecture behind the title 'Teacher of Righteousness' the brother of Christ, James who was called 'the Just'. In describing this method and its controversial results we shall keep above all to the remarks which Eisenman made in the Festschrift for the long-serving editor of the *Revue de Qumrân*, Jean Carmignac, edited by Zdzislaw J.Kapera. Eisenman's contribution is entitled 'Playing on and Transmuting Words. Interpreting Abeit-Galuto in the Habakkuk Pesher'.[21] This title with its striking formulation is characteristic of the author's method of working. He assumes that word-play and the transmutation of terms is an interpretative and descriptive technique used by the authors of the Qumran texts which the modern interpreter must take into account, and therefore must rely on speculative thought. As an example of this, Eisenman chose the Hebrew expression Abeit-Galuto (*el beth-geluto*, i.e. 'to the place of his exile'), which is written with a remarkable abbreviation; this is said to be particularly full of meaning.

It is interesting to see how Eisenman puts his new method in place. He promises to proceed like the 'physical sciences', which seek to find the key to an explanation of the whole with the solution of a central problem. Accordingly Eisenman seeks to discover the secret of the phrase Abeit-Galuto, and from it to define the historical origin of the Qumran community. First of all he spreads a thick cloud of scepticism and confusion over Qumran research: the history of the Essenes, and also that of the Zealots and Christians, is still mysterious.[22] Internal pointers are cited in gay profusion: the 'star prophecy',[23] the 'making a way in the wilderness',[24] 'Holy Spirit Baptism';[25] in each instance these are supported by numerous references, but one dare not examine them more closely.[26] Finally there is 'a large swath of Qumran material which has an anti-Herodian thrust' – but no references are given for this, since the name 'Herod' never appears in the Qumran texts.

After that, palaeography and archaeology are sweepingly condemned: they are said to have explained very little of the history of Qumran but rather to have increased confusion. They are also said not to 'bend' to accommodate new data. Rather, in present Qumran research the reverse procedure is applied: 'The new data is [sic] bent to accommodate new theories'.[27] We shall see how Eisenman himself does precisely that and bends the statements of the Qumran texts, not least the expression Abeit-Galuto, to fit his theory.

*Is the 'Teacher of Righteousness' the same as 'James the Just'?*

The problematic passage investigated by Eisenman and used as the key to his theory about James occurs in the Qumran commentary (Hebrew *pesher*) on the prophet Habakkuk (1QpHab 11.4-8). The passage Habakkuk 2.15 is quoted in 1QPesher Habakkuk 11.2f.: 'Woe to him who gives his neighbour drink, who pours out his wrath! Yes, he makes them drunk to look on their festivals.' Then follows the *pesher*, the interpretation which brings the passage up-to-date and applies it to the community in the present: 'The interpretation of it refers to the godless priest who persecuted (*radap*) the Teacher of Righteousness, in order to swallow him up (*lebal'o*) in the wrath of his anger. In the place of his exile (*'abbeth galuto*) and at the time of the festival of rest on the Day of Atonement he appeared among them, to swallow them up and to bring them down on the day of fasting, the sabbath of their rest.'

This passage is usually understood as follows. The 'wicked priest' must have been the Hasmonaean high priest Jonathan (152-143 BCE), who was regarded as illegitimate. Surprisingly he had sought out the 'Teacher of Righteousness' in the land of Damascus or in Qumran to convince him that he was wrong, to make him change his mind, or even to kill him (cf. 4QpPs 37.4, 7-9). And that happened at the very time when the Teacher's community was celebrating the Day of Atonement with rest from work and fasting, but according to the sect's own solar-lunar calendar of 364 days in a year. For the High Priest and the other Jews who went by a lunar calendar of 354 days, the Day of Atonement fell on another date: so this difference in the festival calendar offered a good opportunity for such a punitive action.

Eisenman understands the phrase '*beth galuto*' as 'place of concealment' and thinks that this place of concealment must have been in Jerusalem.[28] But that is wrong. For first, the important Hebrew term *galut* means 'exile' and not 'concealment'; the second meaning of the verb *galah* is 'reveal', 'disclose', and thus the precise opposite of conceal.[29] Secondly, Jerusalem is anything but a *beth galut*, a 'foreign place of exile'. In the Qumran War Scroll *galut* is used for the exile of the children of light in the 'desert of the peoples', i.e. the Diaspora, and there is contrasted with the desert of Jerusalem (1QM 1.3). But Eisenman must translate differently, because he regards James the Brother of the Lord as the 'Teacher of Righteousness' and sees the high priest Ananus (Annas II) as the wicked priest. Annas had James and other Christians in Jerusalem condemned to death and stoned, as we know from Flavius Josephus (*Jewish Antiquities* XX, 200-3). We know nothing of an 'exile' of James, far less of his 'concealment' in Jerusalem. Here exegesis is 'bent' – to use Eisenman's term; not, however, on the basis of new data but in favour of a contrived and untenable theory. To quote Eisenman once more: the 'circumstances surrounding James' death could be considered a possible *Sitz in Leben* for this allusion, the expression *abeit-galuto*.'[30]

For the same reason the passage 1QpHabakkuk 9.1f. is also given a very arbitrary interpretation. It deals with the punishment of the 'wicked priest' (cf. 1QpHab 8.16) by his enemies: 'And they inflicted horrors of evil diseases and took vengeance on his body of flesh (*gewiyat besaro*).' This passage is rightly connected with the violent death of the high priest Jonathan (143 BCE), who according to I Maccabees 13.21-30 and Josephus (*Jewish Antiquities* XIII, 209-12) was lured into a trap by the Syrian Diodotus Trypho, ill-treated and finally killed. In Qumran this was seen as an act of retribution by God, who did not allow the commandments to be transgressed (1QpHab 8.8-13) and the actions against the 'Teacher of Righteousness' and his followers to go unavenged: God had therefore 'given the wicked priest into the hands of his enemies' (1QpHab 9.9-11). Eisenman connects this information in the Habakkuk *pesher* with the sorry end of the high priest Ananus, which the Jerusalem Christians must have seen as a divine punishment for the unjust death sentence on the pious James which Ananus had insisted on. Ananus had been killed, along with his Sadducean priestly colleagues, by the Idumaeans fighting for dominance in Jerusalem. Josephus reports how the Idumaeans seized the dead bodies and then threw them into the city (*Jewish War* IV, 316-18).[31]

Eisenman again adapts the Habakkuk passage to the 'Sitz im Leben' that he proposes for it: the redundant 'meaningless' expression 'body of his flesh' now gets its 'real meaning because of the outside events': what is really meant is the 'flesh of his corpse'.[32] But that is an inadmissible translation, simply changing the *nomen regens* of the construct chain to a *nomen rectum* in order to find a report and confirmation in the Habakkuk *pesher* of the profanation of the corpse of Ananus reported by Josephus. In the War Scroll the word *peger* is used for corpse (1QM 11.1). Eisenman feels satisfied that one could only arrive at such an interpretation if one were considering the biography of a particular person; that would relate here to the life or the death of James and Ananus. But the wording and the truth of texts must always have priority. The 'historian' Eisenman is guilty of begging the question, of slipping in the desired result by a wrong translation, which he cold-bloodedly declares to be a 'finer meaning' and a 'better construction': again the text is bent to fit the theory.

Eisenman obtains yet other phrases in the Habakkuk *pesher* for his James theory through speculative exegesis.[33] For the 'persecution' of the Teacher of Righteousness by the wicked priest he refers to Esau, who persecuted Jacob.[34] The verb 'swallow up (*bala'*, 1QpHab 11.3,7) is connected with the Edomite King Bela (Gen.36.32) and of course also with Balaam, who 'swallows up the people' (*bala' 'am*). The statement 1QpHabakkuk 12.6 is applied to King Agrippa II, the contemporary of James. It was he who with the high priest Ananus 'conspired to destroy the poor', i.e. to exterminate the Jewish Christians (Ebionites, from Hebrew *ebyon*, poor). The assertion, made repeatedly, that James was accused of blasphemy by the Jerusalem Sanhedrin and executed is plucked completely out of thin air and introduced mechanically from the trials of Jesus and Stephen.[35] By contrast, in the case of Josephus it is said that Ananus accused him and others of having transgressed the law (*Jewish Antiquities* XX, 200: *paranomein*, not *blasphemein*); nor does the Habakkuk *pesher* speak anywhere of blasphemy.

Finally, it is confusing that such a 'pregnant' expression as 'Abeit-Galuto' should also be used as a term of contempt for the Beth-din, i.e. for the 'court' that wrongly condemned James.[36] However, because Eisenman aptly points out that in all these operations he is treading new ground and has no certain proof,[37] in this expression 'Abeit-Galuto', which has still not been exhausted, he discovers another reference to the exile of the divine indwelling (Hebrew *shekinah*) reported in the Babylonian

Talmud. Before the destruction of the temple it left its place on
the ark of the covenant and returned to heaven (Rosh ha-Shanah
31a); at the same time the Supreme Court left the pillared hall of
the temple and went into its exile in the hall of merchants
(Sanhedrin 41a-b). For Eisenman, such late reports support
the theory that the Habakkuk *pesher* with the one pregnant
expression 'Abeit-Galuto' is referring in many ways to the events
of the 60s of the first century CE: the execution of James and the
destruction of the temple, which was regarded by the Christians
as divine punishment for the death of the righteous brother of the
Lord.

Eisenman is certainly right in asserting that no other theory
than his can conjure up such a wealth of meanings out of this
mysterious term, but not in celebrating his method of interpretation as the only one which does justice to Qumran,[38] and
regarding all other previous attempts at a solution as failures. The
exegete must always remember that the Qumran exegetes changed
words consistently in order to arrive at the desired interpretation:
otherwise the James hypothesis and the key it offers to the
interpretation of early Christianity and the history of the last
years of the Jewish state could not be found. This too we gladly
concede to Eisenman. But it is not true that in Qumran the biblical
statements were altered and pressed as 'consistently' as they are
by Eisenman in the case of the phrase 'Abeit-Galuto'. The rabbinic
method of speculative and synthetic interpretation which takes
into account the abundance and multiplicity of terms and
expressions cannot be replaced so freely by the historian who
wants to work precisely and, according to Eisenman, with scientific strictness: Eisenman is simply overcome with a delight in
making up stories.

## The slandering of the apostle Paul

The role which the apostle Paul is given in Eisenman's 'Christian'
interpretation of the Qumran texts is not only incredible, but
devastating to believers. Paul is demoted to being James's
opponent and has to take over the role of the 'man of lies' in the
Habakkuk commentary. His career now looks roughly like this.
Whereas the martyr Stephen (Acts 6-8) took the side of James

who was a strict observer of the law, Paul approved of the stoning of Stephen (Acts 8.1) and at the time was 'fanatic in his enmity towards the earliest church'.[39] After his conversion, which may have been prompted by his guilt-feelings as a persecutor, Paul is supposed to have spent a three-year novitiate in Damascus (which is of course at the same time Qumran!) (cf. Galatians 1.17f.). He was then sent into 'exile' in Tarsus by the leaders of the Jerusalem Christians, but later went to Antioch and there submitted himself to the Apostolic Council in Jerusalem headed by James.[40] According to Eisenman, the statements about the 'man of lies' in the Habakkuk *pesher* fit Paul's activity admirably: he rejected the law and led many astray to set up a community of lies.[41] He based his theology of faith on Habakkuk 2.4 and its interpretation in 1QpHabakkuk, but deliberately overlooked the doing of the law which is mentioned there alongside faith. That is the Jewish-Christian verdict on the apostle as Eisenman sees it.

This is supplemented by 'perceptive' conjectures by Eisenman the historian: Paul could have been an agent of the Romans.[42] That at any rate would be the best explanation for his rescue in Jerusalem and his favourable treatment by the legionaries, and finally also for his successful mission in the Roman empire. According to Eisenman, Paul, and not the Jesus who was faithful to the law, is the real creator of later Christianity. Here he has completely twisted the teaching of Jesus by making him a god who did miracles and a counterpart to dying and rising gods like Adonis, Tammuz and Attis in the Hellenistic East and wanting to know nothing of the historical Jesus.[43] Here Eisenman is following the interpretation of II Corinthians 5.16 which was put forward by Wilhelm Bousset (1865-1920) and Rudolf Bultmann (1884-1976): Paul's statement that from now on he no longer wants 'to know Christ after the flesh' refers to the fact that he wants to know nothing of the historical Jesus. But that is a false interpretation of this passage. Paul is only saying that he now has a different estimate of Jesus from that in his pre-Christian days.[44]

Eisenman attaches great importance to the accounts about Paul and James in the Jewish-Christian Pseudo-Clementines (third cenutry CE) and in Eusebius' *Church History* (fourth century CE), which he thinks should be preferred to the 'muddled and confused' conclusion of the Acts of the Apostles.[45] But Acts, which was written by Luke, a companion of Paul,[46] stands much closer to the events reported than, for example, the Pseudo-Clementines, in which the miraculous is exaggerated to a grotesque degree; moreover these works are dominated throughout by bitter anti-Pauline polemic.

# 6

# Does a Qumran Text speak of the Crucified Messiah?

The disputed fragment 285 from Cave 4 (4Q285) – God and the helping Messiah (4Q521) – The Son of God in a text from Cave 4 (4Q246) – Messianic expectation in Qumran and the Christ of the Gospels

## *The disputed fragment 285 from Cave 4 (4Q285)*

In November 1991 the sensational news was published in the daily papers that among the hitherto unpublished Qumran fragments a text had been discovered which attested the violent death of the Messiah.[1] Some press reports even spoke of a description of the crucifixion of Jesus.[2] According to its 'discoverer', Robert H.Eisenman, this new Qumran text does not in fact speak of Jesus, but that is precisely what makes it so important: 'The text is of the most far-reaching significance, because it shows that whatever group was responsible for these writings was operating in the same scriptural and Messianic framework of Early Christianity.' So an important connecting link between early Judaism and Christianity is said to have been discovered: the Jewish community or tendency from which Christianity emerged. Certainly we already knew that the Dead Sea Scrolls bear witness to a similar messianic expectation to that in the New Testament; but the notion of a dying Messiah in a Qumran text was claimed as new and 'explosive' (Michael Wise, Chicago). Elsewhere, too, people made very enthusiastic remarks about the new text.

It had previously been assumed that at the time of Jesus a triumphant Messiah was expected in Israel who would restore their lost political dignity to the people of God, but not a suffering and dying 'King of the Jews'. According to the apostle Paul, the

crucified Christ was a stumbling block for the Jews (I Corinthians
1.23), an unheard-of presumption, sharply condemned in the law
of Moses, indeed a blasphemy (cf. Deut.21.22f.). The discovery of
a 'slain Messiah' in the texts and theology of the Qumran
community seemed to put in question the uniqueness of Christian
faith. Precisely because the cross of Christ, God's anointed, stands
at the centre of the gospel, such a Qumran text could destroy the
character and divine power of the 'word of the cross'. Some other
articles of faith hitherto regarded as exclusively Christian were
already mentioned by the Jewish authors of the scrolls – at any
rate according to Eisenman and Baigent and Leigh in *The Dead
Sea Scrolls Deception*.

However, the euphoria over this discovery was damped down
by objections and important questions. First it should be noted
that the 'new' Qumran text, its interpretation and even the
significance attached to it, are not as new as all that. Thirty-seven
years ago it was already being hailed as a sensational document
which shook the faith of the church and put the uniqueness of
Christianity in question. In 1956, John M.Allegro, a member
of the first Qumran team at the Palestine Archaeological Museum
in Jerusalem, gave three lectures on British radio. In these he
claimed that central doctrines of Jesus and Christian rites had
their origin in Qumran, like parts of the Lord's Prayer, the
eucharist and even belief in the crucified and risen Christ. A letter
to John Strugnell indicates the spirit of Allegro's publications: 'I
shouldn't worry about that theological job if I were you. By the
time I'm finished there won't be any church left for you to join.'[3]

On 6 February 1956 an article appeared in *Time Magazine*
headed 'Crucifixion before Christ'.[4] The remarks made by Allegro
on this topic must have related to this text 'discovered' so much
later among the photographs of the Huntington library and
declared by the daily press to be a sensational find. One can infer
all that Allegro read out of it from the rebuttal which was
published on 16 March 1956 by the remaining members of the
Dead Sea Scrolls team:[5] 'We find no crucifixion of the "teacher",
no deposition from the cross, and no "broken body of their
Master to be stood guard over until Judgment Day". Therefore
there is no "well defined Essenic pattern into which Jesus of
Nazareth fits", as Mr Allegro is alleged in one report to have said.

It is our conviction that either he has misread the texts or he has built up a chain of conjectures which the materials do not support.'

But does not such an encounter reek of church apologetics, a desperate defence of the uniqueness of Christian faith? That is claimed by the authors of *The Dead Sea Scrolls Deception* when they describe this group of Christian scholars in the Palestine Archaeological Museum as a pack of hounds who are 'ganging up' on one of their number, Mr Allegro.[6]

But what is really in this text? In 1991 the author of this chapter (O.Betz) put it together on the basis of the few copies of the concordance compiled by the team of editors and then also discovered it among the Huntington Library copies.[7] In a paper to the Qumran symposium at the University of Eichstätt between 18 and 20 October 1991 he then translated and interpreted the text, which is preserved only in fragments.[8] Eisenman offers it in the first chapter of his *The Dead Sea Scrolls Uncovered*,[9] edited with Michael Wise and published in 1992, under the title 'The Messianic Leader' (*nasi*'); the fragment is now called 4Q285. This text begins with a reference to the prophet Isaiah and according to Eisenman and Wise reads: 'Isaiah the Prophet...'[10] (line 1). Then Isaiah 11.1 is quoted: 'A staff shall rise from the root[11] of Jesse...'(line 2); the branch of David... and they will enter into judgment with...' (line 3), 'and they will put to death (*wehemitu*) the leader of the Community'[12] or '...the leader of the Community will put him to death (*wehemito*)...' (line 4), 'and with wounds... and the priest will command...'(line 5) '...the slain of the Kittim...'(line 6).

One problem with this text is the verb-form *hmtw* in line 4. As the Qumran texts are not pointed, i.e. as a rule contain no vowels, this text can be translated in two ways: first, with the 'prince of the community' as the object of the killing ('they will kill him'), which is how Allegro, Eisenman and Wise interpret it, but also, equally possibly with the 'prince of the Community' as the subject: 'And he will put him to death'. The unnnamed object would be the evildoer of Isaiah 11.4.

Doubt about Eisenman's interpretation and his thesis of the 'slain Messiah' were already indicated by O.Betz in his paper to the Eichstätt symposium. What is important is the reference in the fragment to the prophet Isaiah and the obvious quotation from the famous chapter 11. This prophecy is included in the blessing for the 'prince of the Community' (1Q28b 5,20-26) and interpreted in terms of the Messiah who triumphs over the godless. That leads to the supposition that it is the victorious Messiah and not the suffering and dying Messiah who is probably also meant in the fragment BM 5,1-6 (now 4Q285), especially since the 'slain of the Kittim' is mentioned at the end. Geza Vermes and Marcus Bockmuehl arrived at the same result in a detailed investigation. Vermes, working at the University of Oxford's newly-founded Centre for Qumran Study, where there is a collection of 3300 photographic plates containing all the Qumran texts, translates: 'The prince of the congregation, the Branch of David, will kill him' and understands the leader of the hostile army to be the victim of this deadly blow.[13] Similarly, Markus Bockmuehl, working at Cambridge, interprets the passage: 'the prince of the congregation will kill him'.[14]

That puts in question the theory of the slain or even crucified Messiah in Qumran of which so much has been made: it is fundamentally untenable. Eisenman himself does not abandon it, but he is very uncertain. He still thinks that this text is 'potentially very explosive' and regards his interpretation of the slain *nasi'* (prince) as the most meaningful if the fragment is taken by itself.[15] But he adds in brackets to his translation 'And they will put to death the Leader of the Community, the Branch (of David)' the statement 'depending on the context this might also be read "and the Leader of the Community, the Branch of David, will put him to death" '.[16] Eisenman explains this text, which is unfortunately so mutilated, by means of the fragment 4QpIsa, a commentary on Isa.10.33-11.5.[17] However, that is not very helpful, especially as it does not contain the illuminating term 'prince of the community'.

Furthermore, it is inappropriate to put a question-mark against the messianic interpretation of this term 'prince of the community' or to speak of an allusion to the high priest (line 6). For in other Qumran writings, too, 'prince of the community' is a designation for the Messiah, and in line 5 there is only a simple *kohen* (priest).[18] Finally, something else which does not favour Eisenman's translation 'And they will put to death the Leader of the Community' is the conjecture which he himself mentions, made previously by Geza Vermes, that 'this messianic *Nasi*' text should be attached to the War Scroll': the latter is a document of 'violent militancy' and 'vengeful'.[19] A 'slain Messiah' does not fit particularly well into the context of a messianic nationalism and extreme hostility to Rome, characteristics attributed by Eisenman to the pious of Qumran and also the first Christians.

The only correct method is to use the blessing for the Davidic Messiah (1Q28b 5.20-26) as an aid towards interpreting the disputed fragment 4Q285. For this figure is similarly described there by the expression 'prince of the community', which is specific to Qumran and as in 4Q285 is interpreted in terms of Isaiah 11. In this blessing the Qumran Teacher (*maskil*) prays that God will 'renew the covenant of union for the prince of the community...', in order to establish the kingdom of his people for ever' and to 'judge the poor for ever with righteousness' (line 21). The wish 'The Lord raise you to eternal heights and like a strong tower on a high wall. And you shall smite the peoples with the power of your mouth and devastate the earth with your staff, and you will kill the godless with the breath of your lips' (*tamit resha'im*, lines 24f.), is particularly important.

In the last-mentioned promise the phrase Isa.11.4, 'he will kill the godless' (*yamit rasha'*), is taken up. In this particular phrase from Isaiah 11.4 we have the model for the statement about the 'death of the Messiah' in 4Q285 (line 4) of which Eisenman makes so much. So it must be translated differently, in the active: 'The prince of the community will kill him (i.e. the godless).' The fact that the Messiah himself is killed or even crucified is excluded on the basis of Isa.11.4 and above all because of the blessing 1Q28b 5.20-26. Moreover, in the latter his rule is given the predicate 'eternal'. God will raise him to an 'eternal' height, set up his kingly rule 'for ever' and judge the people 'for ever' with righteousness. These attributes of eternal duration are added to the prophecy of Isaiah 11 in 1Q28b 5.20-26. They come from II Samuel 7, the prophecy of the prophet Nathan about the Davidic dynasty, which is fundamental to Israel's messianic expectation: God's will is to establish the royal throne of the promised son of David 'for ever' (v.13); it is to stand 'in eternity' (v.16). Eternal duration is the characteristic of messianic rule.

Finally, Eisenman himself indicates a further problem for the translation with the death of the Messiah which he proposed. We do not know the context in which 4Q285 belongs, but the context is very important for the right translation. Eisenman put the questionable fragment in which the death (or better 'the killing') of the 'prince of the community' is mentioned in the seventh and last place among the other fragments which go with it. Immediately before it is fragment 6, in which the 'prince of the community' is mentioned three times. This fragment speaks of the shattering of godlessness, of resistance against enemies and a man who is 'brought before the prince'. Now it could be that fragments 6 and 7 should be put the other way round; in fact they were found separately and only later recognized as pieces which belong together. At all events, fragment 6 depicts a living and uncommonly active 'prince of the community' opposing his adversaries and also godlessness, whose death would be quite unexpected and is impossible if the fragments are put the other way round. His resolute battle against godlessness (*tennagep rish'a*, fragment 6, line 1) makes it very probable than in fragment 7 (line 4) he kills the godless one and does not fall victim to him.

Now this translation, which we regard as the only correct one, does not disclose, say, a striking similarity or even a disturbing identity between the Qumran texts and the New Testament over Essene and Christian messianic expectations, but a fundamental difference. To take Jesus' messianic activity, he too saw Isaiah 11.4 as a normative text: the ideal king of the end-time judges the poor and wretched in the land with justice. That is what Jesus does, for example, in the Sermon on the Mount, in which he promises God's saving righteousness to the spiritually poor, humble and oppressed, and declares that they are heirs of the kingdom of God (Matthew 5.3-12). And he wages his battle against godlessness in a desire not for the death of sinners but for their penitence and liberation from the enslaving, deadly power of evil. Therefore the driving out of demons is a characteristic of his activity as saviour; the sick and sinners are 'possessed', captives of the devil who are imprisoned in the strong man's fortress. Evil is a kingdom opposed to the kingdom of God (Mark 3.22-27), and it is Christ's purpose to destroy it.

The death of the Messiah is the central confession and characteristic of Christian faith, but is not confessed as such in the Qumran texts. The objection of the Scrolls team in Jerusalem led by the Dominican Fr Roland de Vaux to John M.Allegro, who wanted to find a crucifixion of Christ in the fragment 4Q285, was also completely justified from a scholarly point of view, and in no way dictated by the Vatican; Jewish scholars like Yigael Yadin or David Flusser have not agreed with Allegro either. But above all, the crucifixion of Jesus is not to be attributed to his nationalism and Zealot hatred of Rome, as Eisenman or Barbara Thiering (see Chapter 7) suppose. Rather, Jesus judged his messianic mission in the light of Isaiah 53: as Son of Man/Messiah he 'did not want to be served but to serve and give his life (by dying) as a ransom for many' (Mark 10.45). In the context of Isaiah 11 and the Qumranic messianic expectation the violent death of the 'prince of the community' would be a catastrophe; it would represent a triumph of godlessness, not an abolition of its power. From the perspective of Isaiah 53, the death of the Messiah Son of God is a saving event which can be proclaimed as gospel, and which gives believers the power of God.[20] For the death of the messianic servant atones for sins and does away with them (Isaiah 53.12); the righteous servant of God, who suffers innocently, justifies the many (Isaiah 53.11).

The messianic expectation of the pious of Qumran and the first Christians was largely built up on the same prophecies in the Hebrew Bible. But the messianic interpretation of Isaiah 53 and also Isaiah 43 by Jesus and the New Testament writers makes the difference.[21] The Qumran community hoped for a victorious Messiah because it was a 'congregation' of the pious which was under attack and indeed suffering; it also wanted to resist the power of sin and the devil through obedience to the Law of Moses; it wanted itself to have an atoning influence on the country and not to be atoned for by the death of a servant of God suffering in its stead. However, it is quite unjustified for Eisenman to regard the authors of the Qumran writings as 'warlike, xenophobic, apocalyptic and vengeful' and for this reason to think it impossible that they could have referred Isaiah 53 to the death of the Messiah;[22] evidently he does not find this text congenial. By contrast, Jesus himself took upon himself the sufferings of the pre-messianic time (*ḥeble mashiaḥ*) and did not seek, say, a Zealot or a political solution. Eisenman's pan-Zealot interpretation of early Judaism and the first Christians is right out of court.


## God and the helping Messiah (4Q521)

The anti-Zealot attitude of the Qumran pious can be seen from a further messianic text from the previously unknown 4Q fragments which Eisenman has selected, reconstructed well and translated. He has aptly assessed it as 'one of the most beautiful and significant in the Qumran corpus', but given it the not altogether happy title 'The Messiah of Heaven and Earth'.[23] In the commentary which he has supplied he emphasizes that this fragment stresses the righteous and the pious, the gentle and the faithful, and describes them as those commended to God's protection and friends of the Messiah. Eisenman therefore speaks of 'new themes', among which he also includes the gift of the spirit to the meek, the seeking out of the pious, the call of the righteous and their glorification on the throne of the eternal kingdom. He associates the content of these themes with the New Testament, and here of course the name of Jesus would have to be mentioned; instead Eisenman feels reminded of Jewish mysticism and the Kabbala. But that is too far-fetched, for the 'eternal kingdom' (*malkut*) of this text is in no way a reference to the tenth Sephirah (stage) of the kabbalistic system. In his commentary on this 4Q fragment Eisenman understandably says nothing of the Zealotism of the Qumran pious and the 'nationalist undertones' which he hears in the text of the 'slain Messiah';[24] 4Q521 in particular tells completely against the glorification of the strong, the militant and political.

This hymn of praise celebrates both the care and miraculous power of God and the saving action of the Messiah. The beginning sounds highly ceremonial: 'The heavens and the earth will obey His (i.e. God's) Messiah, [the sea] and all that is in them. He will not turn aside from the commandments of the Holy Ones.' Eisenman resorts to Daniel 7 in interpreting this task with its cosmic extension: the Messiah is 'to a certain extent a supernatural figure... (like) "the Son of Man coming on the clouds of Heaven" '.[25] Not only heaven and earth but also the 'Holy Ones' (*qedoshim*), i.e. the heavenly hosts, are subject to the command of the Messiah.[26]

But that is an exaggeration. For evidently this passage is not about the messianic rule over heaven and earth, far less about the rule of the angels. Eisenman translates the invitation to heaven and earth to 'hearken' (*yishme'u*) to the Messiah as 'obey', but that is not appropriate here. And in no way is an obedience of the angels meant – on the contrary; the Messiah 'will not turn aside from the commandments of the Holy Ones', i.e. from the instructions of God which even the angels, God's special heavenly servants, follow. So the Messiah is a human being and subject to the law.

Surprisingly, the middle of this hymn, lines 3-8, does not deal with the followers of the Messiah and his saving activity. Rather, it praises God's care for the pious and his redemptive power: he will name the righteous by name, and his spirit will hover over the meek; he will strengthen the faithful through his power, and glorify the pious on the throne of his eternal kingdom. Then – taking up Psalm 146.7 – the praise is uttered: 'He shall release the bound, make the blind see and raise up the downtrodden' (line 8). That almost gives the impression that a Messianic redeemer is not necessary at all. But further on, after the heavily damaged lines 9-12, a similarly miraculous saving action is promised – not, however, in the timeless participial style but in the future tense and with a reference to an eschatological change: 'Then he will heal the sick, resurrect the dead, and to the meek announce good tidings...'(line 13).

This is probably a description of the redemptive action of the Messiah, who will emerge at the point predestined by God, the great 'then'. However, elsewhere the resurrection of the dead is the eschatological action of God, as is shown for example by the second of the Eighteen Benedictions, which is still used today in synagogues. But the proclaiming of the good news to the poor, which is mentioned at the same time in the Qumran text, cannot be God's task. According to the prophet Isaiah it is part of the programme of the one anointed with God's Spirit and sent by him (Isaiah 61.1f.). And according to the Qumran text 11Q Melchizedek, too, it is the Messiah who brings the good news and proclaims the great year of the divine good pleasure (11

QMelchizedek 2,9,18). However, this year of jubilee is first proclaimed and ushered in in heaven. That happens with the enthronement of the archangel Michael, the angel of the people of Israel and intercessor for the pious (cf. Daniel 10.21; 12.1), among the heavenly ones, as *malki-ṣedek*, 'king of righteousness' (11QMelchizedek; 1QM 17/6).[27] Various texts of Holy Scripture, above all Psalm 82, are related to this change of rule in heaven, from which the change on earth then proceeds. For Michael will descend with the heavenly hosts and finally decide the long war of the 'children of light' against the 'children of darkness'. As he rules among the divine beings as prince, so the peoples of Israel will be lead on earth; this rule will prevail, according to the War Scroll, i.e. bring order, 'among all flesh' (1QM 17.7f.). This important function of the archangel Michael, who brings the turning-point in the eschatological struggle against the supremacy of evil and becomes the real helper of the people of God, tells against Eisenman's interpretation of the supernatural Messiah like a son of man in 4Q521. Rather, this is a human being who is obligated to human beings, the 'prince of the whole community' (1QM 5.1); as such he is clearly distinguished in the War Scroll from the angelic prince Michael and similarly in 4Q521 from a supernatural son of man. According to the War Scroll the names of the twelve tribes of Israel stand on the shield carried by the 'prince of the community' (1QM 5.1); they describe his sphere of rule, which is therefore on earth and represents the counterpart to the heavenly kingdom of the angelic prince Michael.

According to the Gospels Jesus was also active as Messiah as a human being among human beings. He proclaimed the redemptive action promised in 4Q521 (line 12) as a programme and a proof of his messianic mission. In the synagogue in his home town of Nazareth he preached on the text Isaiah 61.1f. and declared that this prophetic text was fulfilled with his coming:[28] as the one anointed with God's spirit he proclaimed the good news to the poor, liberation to the captives and sight to the blind (Luke 4.18-21). And to John the Baptist who doubted him he gave the following message: 'Go and report to John: the blind see, the lame walk, lepers are cleansed and the deaf hear, the dead are raised up and the good news is proclaimed to the poor' (Luke 7.22). As in

4Q521, the resurrection of the dead as a messianic action has been inserted into the statements based on Isaiah 61.1f. and 35.5f.

In 4Q521 the miraculous healing action of God which the pious already experience in the present and which is consummated with their glorification in the kingdom of God is closely connected with the redemptive work of the Messiah in the eschatological future; it is difficult to keep the two apart. In Isaiah 61.1 this unity of action is grounded in the mission of the anointed one and his endowment with the spirit, which are not really mentioned in 4Q521. According to the Semitic law of the messenger the one who is sent represents the sender and is to be accepted as the sender himself (cf. Mishnah, Berakhoth 5.5): he acts with his authority. According to Isaiah 61.1f. which is formulated as the introduction in which the divine emissary presents his credentials, God himself has anointed him with the power of his spirit. The fragment 4Q521 allows the conclusion that the Qumran exegetes did not relate the anointed divine emissary's introduction of himself to the prophets but to the Messiah. Jesus virtually declared it to be his messianic programme, and it can also be heard in the Beatitudes of the Sermon on the Mount (cf. Matt. 5.3f. with Isa. 61.1f.).[29]

But on the other hand there is an important difference. In 4Q521, in good Old Testament fashion, the praise of redemption is indebted to a legalistic piety. God is a God of the just; his care and glorifying power go out to the pious (*ḥasidim*), and the good news is proclaimed to the humble. Anyone who seeks the Lord is visited by him. However, for the pious of Qumran such a quest for God is engaged in by searching in his commandments (Community Rule 1QS 1,2; 5.11). That is confirmed by our text: the commandment is to be observed and is to be 'pursued' (4Q521, 1,3,1). Nor will the Messiah turn aside from the commandments which even the angels observe (1.2.1). Jesus had come to fulfil the Law and the Prophets (Matthew 5.17). But as Messiah he also knew that he had been sent to the lost sheep of Israel (Matthew 15.24); he called the sinners and not the righteous (Mark 2.17).

## The Son of God in a text from Cave 4 (4Q246)

Hitherto it has usually been assumed that the Messiah was not designated 'Son of God' in early Judaism, whereas this often happens in the New Testament (cf.Romans 1.3f.). In fact the Messiah was regarded as Son of David (*ben dawid*). The rabbis usually spoke of the Son of David when they meant the Messiah, and Jesus was addressed in this way by people seeking his help (Mark 10.47; Matthew 9.27; 15.22). Indeed he himself described the Messiah as Son of David, but saw divine Sonship as his real dignity (Mark 12.35-37). That is what is intended by Jesus' question about the son of David. In this conversation in Mark 12 he does not want, say, to challenge the Davidic descent of the Messiah; he himself was from the house of David. But according to II Samuel 7.14 the Messiah is the Son of God, so the king can address him as his 'Lord' in the Davidic Psalm 110.1. The Christ, says a Jewish-Christian confession cited by Paul at the beginning of Romans, is 'David's son according to the flesh' and 'Son of God according to the Holy Spirit' (Romans 1.3f.).

Now in 4Q246, a text composed in Aramaic, which Robert H.Eisenman defines more closely as a 'Messianic Pseudo-Daniel Fragment',[30] there is mention of a king with the title 'Son of God', 'Son of the Most High' (4Q246 2,1). Although the most interesting part of this Qumran text was known almost twenty years ago,[31] there has now also been a great turmoil about it in the press. Thus a leading English newspaper came out with the headline 'Scrolls Fragment Challenges Basic Tenet of Christianity'.[32] So we have to look more closely at this scroll fragment.

Who is meant by the Son of God in 4Q246? The context of this statement is highly problematical. The beginning, which is unfortunately very mutilated (4Q246 1.1), is reconstructed on the basis of the dream visions of king Nebuchadnezar which the prophet Daniel interprets (cf. Dan.2-5). There also seems to be such an interpretation here, but it remains very obscure in the first part of this document, which is only half preserved and even now needs a wise man to interpret it. First of all, everything that is to happen ever is announced in dark apocalyptic language, namely tribulation on earth and many wars (lines 2-5). Then the phrase 'king of Assyria' appears in a large gap (line 6); he will be great on earth and all will serve him (lines 7-8).

But at the same time we must ask: can the king of Assyria (i.e. Syria), by whom Qumran means a Seleucid ruler, have been expected as eschatological cosmocrator and even called Son of

God? Eisenman is probably right in asking this, and like Émile Puech[33] fills in the great gap in 4Q246 1.6 like this: '...[until the King of the people of God arises. He will become] the King of Syria and [E]gypt.' The important statement 'He will be called the son of God (*bereh di 'el*); they will call him son of the Most High (*bar 'elyon*)' (4Q 246, 2.1), the text of which has been well preserved, would then relate to this king by God's grace.

The continuation, the much more legible second column of 4Q246, presents some problems, this time above all in terms of content. First of all – so to speak as a contrast – there is once again mention of the chaos of pagan rule, with an eschatological intensification: human beings and peoples will trample on one another and annihilate one another. But even this self-destructive chaos can only be a brief intermezzo. It is compared with shooting stars, evidently because these fall rapidly and die out (4Q246 2.2f.).

Then follows the emergence of the people of God and with it the great turning point (lines 4-9):

4. Until the people of God arises and causes everyone to rest from the sword.

5. His Kingdom will be an Eternal Kingdom, and he will be Righteous in all his Ways.

6. He [will jud]ge the earth in Righteousness, and everyone will make peace. The sword shall cease from the earth.

7. And every nation will bow down to him. As for the Great God, with his help

8. He will make war, and He will give the peoples into his power; all of them

9. He will throw down before him. His rule will be an Eternal rule.

Accordingly, several factors define the time of salvation: God himself, the people of God, and possibly the Son of God.

But is not this latter a worldly ruler, say the king of Syria, who belongs to the provisional time of tribulation and stands in contrast to the true God and his people? In that case 2.1 would be polemic against the ruler cult of the Diadochi and would prepare the end for him through the emergence of the people of God.[34]

But the Son of God is probably thought to be the representative of the new age,[35] the Messiah/Son of Man of Daniel 7.13f. From 2.4 on the people of God then appear alongside him, just as in Dan.7.21,27 the people of the saints of the Most High take over the rule of the Son of Man. The eschatological trinity of kingdom of God (2.44), enthronement of the Messiah/Son of Man (7.13f.) and rule of the people of God (7.27) appear specifically in the book of Daniel. And as the whole apocalyptic fragment 4Q246 is inspired by the book of Daniel, this may be the best solution to our problem.

But the title 'Son of God' is absent from the book of Daniel; it must have been prepared for in our Qumran text 4Q246 by other Old Testament passages, and that is in fact the case. It is no surprise when one thinks of the messianic expectation of Israel and the confession of Christ in the New Testament. II Samuel 7.12-14, which represents the foundation of the messianic expectation of the old covenant, is also the basis of the two messianic titles 'Son of David' and 'Son of God'. For according to this prophecy, which the prophet Nathan proclaimed to king David and which the Qumran community referred to the Messiah (4QFlorilegium 1), the promised king who rules for ever will first of all be a physical descendant of David (II Samuel 7.12): hence the designation 'Son of David'. But God also promised that he would be like a father to this son of David and would bring him up like a son (II Samuel 7.14; cf. Psalm 2.7): the messianic title 'Son of God' was inferred from this promise.

Earliest Christianity explained the messianic dignity of Jesus as a twofold sonship (Romans 1.3f.). This twofold dignity of son already appears in the announcement of the birth of Jesus (Luke 1.32); it provides the best parallel to fragment 4Q246 (line 2.1). For the angel Gabriel says of Mary's child almost precisely what the Qumran text says: 'He will be great (cf. 4Q246 1.7) and will be called Son of the Most High (cf. 4Q246 2.1). And God the Lord will give him the throne of his father David (cf. II Samuel 7.12f.).' But the Qumran fragment 4Q246, which is also so strongly governed by Daniel, may also have derived the naming of the Messiah as 'Son of God' from II Samuel 7.14; so the statement in 4Q246.1 must similarly have related to the Davidic Messiah and not to a pagan king.[36] The Qumran fragment 4Q246 shows how at an important point in the Lukan birth narrative the language is not, say, pagan Greek, but Palestinian Jewish.

## Messianic expectation in Qumran and the Christ of the Gospels

When one reads the Gospels, one gets the impression that in the days of Jesus there was a burning expectation of the Messiah in large areas of the Jewish population. This impression has been challenged in various ways by exegetes. In the Qumran writings we now have original documents from the New Testament period which attest how pious Jews looked intently for a change of the times and also researched into the writings of the Old Testament with the deepest seriousness and the utmost effort. Here we see how attention was directed above all to passages which also play a major part in the New Testament, like Isaiah 11 or 61 or Daniel 7. At the same time we can see how much the interpretations diverged. Even the Essene movement does not seem to have found its way to a completely uniform messianic expectation. Some texts like, for example, the Community Rule (1QS 9.10f.) speak clearly of the appearance of two messianic figures, the king from the house of David and also a high priest set over him. In the Damascus Document, which probably refers back to a wider circle of Essene pious, the presupposition seems to be more the expectation of a single Messiah figure.[37]

But the Qumran texts also show how firmly rooted the expectation of a warlike liberator from the house of David was in the light of the Old Testament. Here we probably have a conviction common to most, if not all, of the Jewish groups. Against this background we can understand better how at Caesarea Philippi Peter could venture to question Jesus, whom he had just confessed as the Messiah (Mark 8.27ff.). Peter believed that he had the right exegesis of Holy Scripture on his side. The Qumran texts also confirm, despite assertions to the contrary, that there was no question at that time of the expectation of a suffering or even dying Messiah. In the combination of the suffering servant of Isaiah 53 who nevertheless, indeed precisely because of his obedient passion, is exalted by God to be Son of Man and ruler of the world with the Messiah king we encounter the new exegesis of Jesus and his unique consciousness of mission.

The 'Teacher of Righteousness' remains one of the most impressive figures of Jewish piety. His followers believed that God had given him an epoch-making gift, that of interpreting holy scripture. But this teacher never claimed to be a prophet or even the Messiah, just as Jesus first claimed that for himself indirectly and then with increasing clarity and resolution after Peter's confession. That is the insuperable difference between Qumran and earliest Christianity: the Qumran texts show us pious Jews who are waiting with great intensity for the messianic time; the New Testament proclaims unanimously through all its witnesses that the Messiah has already come and the turn of the ages has dawned through his death and resurrection.

# 7

# Do the Qumran Writings Criticize Jesus as the 'Wicked Priest'?

A professor from distant Australia – The late dating of the Qumran texts – John the Baptist as the 'Teacher of Righteousness'? – Jesus as the 'Wicked Priest' and 'Man of Lies'? – The eventful life of Jesus – A new way to decipher the Gospels? – Destructive and pseudo-scientific

## A professor from distant Australia

Barbara Thiering, who teaches at the University of Sydney, Australia, also counts herself among a new generation of Qumran scholars. She rejects the prevailing consensus of experts who assume a pre-Christian origin for the Qumran texts and the Essene movement. Like Robert H.Eisenman (Chapter 5), Barbara Thiering thinks that the 'Teacher of Righteousness' certainly did not emerge under a Hasmonaean high priest like Jonathan I (152-143 BCE) or his brother Simon (143-134 BCE) or perhaps even under the priest-king Alexander Jannaeus (Jonathan II, 103-76 BCE). She regards such a dating as 'one of the great errors of modern scholarship'.[1] Rather, this teacher is to be dated much later; he belongs in the New Testament period, specifically in the time of Herod. However, Barbara Thiering does not identify him with James the Just, the brother of Jesus, like Eisenman or Baigent and Leigh, but with John the Baptist. And his counterpart, the 'wicked priest', was not a high priest in office, but none other than Jesus Christ. This adventurous theory,[2] not previously put forward by anyone else, comes from a woman who has written professionally on the Dead Sea Texts. She is the author of two valuable articles which discuss the difficult problem of ritual purity and washing in Qumran.[3]

However, in recent years Barbara Thiering has left the sphere of academic journals; instead, her name appears in the headlines of the tabloid press. Thus in July 1992 *Bild-Zeitung* tried (in vain) to track down one of the authors of this book (R.Riesner) on holiday in order to get an opinion.[4] Incredible things are brought to light in her book *Jesus the Man* (US title *Jesus and the Riddle of the Dead Sea Scrolls. Unlocking the Secrets of His Life Story*). One learns some all too human things about the life of Jesus of Nazareth, who, according to Thiering, was an Essene and spent most of his time in the wilderness of Judaea: for example in September of 30 he married Mary Magdalene and in 33 was crucified with Simon Magus and the Zealot Judas, but at the last moment was taken down in a helpless state. He survived, arrived in Rome in the 60s and there attained the biblical age of seventy.

But what have these alleged disclosures about Jesus to do with the 'Riddle of the Dead Sea Scrolls'?

## The late dating of the Qumran texts

Let us return first to the thesis that the Qumran texts are to be dated late – i.e. to be moved from the Hasmonaean to the Herodian period – and that in them John the Baptist is referred to as the Teacher of Righteousness. As a consequence of this theory Jesus is degraded to being the 'Wicked Priest' and 'Man of Lies'. It already requires considerable thrust to transfer the statements about the great teacher of the Qumran community to the New Testament period. Barbara Thiering can certainly profit from the fact that the Qumran texts are written for insiders and therefore do not mention some things, and above all persons, by name. But in preparing the way for John the Baptist countless obstacles have to be removed. First of all, doubt has to be used as an instrument: things are difficult if the methods of scholarship so far applied are true and reliable. So Thiering looks compulsively for weaknesses, uncertainties or even contradictions which she can use to carry through her construction.[5]

She sees some discrepancies and problems in the palaeo-graphical dating of the texts, above all as carried out by Frank M.Cross,[6] but these are tendentiously exaggerated. First she points out that 'semi-cursive script' fluctuates and varies from case to case and is therefore difficult to classify. Furthermore, there is a custom of writing in an archaizing way which can lead to texts being wrongly given an early date. In addition, one should be flexible in dating and - as with the radio carbon test – allow a margin of plus or minus fifty years. A further shift could arise from the time span during which a younger scribe was being trained by an older one. Thiering has one-sidedly added such possibilities together to support her late dating. The Temple Scroll and the *pesharim*, commentaries, are decisive for her. In her view 'There is no sound palaeographical barrier to a Herodian dating of the Temple Scroll (11 QTemple), the script of which, while classified as "Hasmonaean semi-formal", displays Herodian features'.[7] And she thinks that the *pesharim*, the typical Qumran commentaries on biblical books and passages, all come from the Herodian-Roman period; this is the time in which the prophecies of the ancient prophets were fulfilled.

The question of the alleged 'Herodian' content of the specific Qumran writings is decisive. Like Robert H.Eisenman, Barbara Thiering takes up the passage in the Habakkuk *pesher* which speaks of the attack of the 'wicked priest' on the Day of Atonement (1QpHab 11,8). However, this supports the Hasmonaean dating and hardly gives Thiering's theories a chance. But she does not argue like Eisenman with his speculative rabbinic exegesis. And she does not fall upon the note about the exile of the 'Teacher of Righteousness' (Abeit-Galuto), from which Eisenman wrested so many references to a late date. Rather, she seeks to disarm those passages in the Qumran text which can be set against her late dating.

It is said of the 'wicked priest' and his time in office that he 'was called by the name of truth at the beginning of his standing' but then erred from the way (1QpHab 8.9). That fits very well with the Hasmonaean high priest Jonathan I or with Alexander Jannaeus, i.e. in the second or perhaps first century BCE. But Thiering understands the expression 'truth' (*'emet*) as it were in a technical way, in a sense specific to Qumran; it is the embodiment of the special teaching of the Essenes. They have covenanted with the truth because they interpret scripture truly and also do the truth. If the wicked priest was called in the name of truth, he became a member of the 'community of truth'. The same applies to him as applies to the 'Man of Lies'; the latter is expressly said to have belonged to the community and later to have turned his back on it (1QpHab 2.2: 10.8; CD 20.15). 'Wicked Priest' and 'Man of Lies' are merely different names for one and the same person (Eisenman differs!), namely for the rival of the 'Teacher of Righteousness': but a Hasmonaean high priest could never have been a member of the Qumran community.

Barbara Thiering wants to demolish bit by bit the thesis of the 'wicked high priest' and opponent of the Teacher as it is put forward in the Qumran consensus. But that necessitates extremely unusual exegetical steps. For Thiering the information that the 'Wicked Priest' 'ruled' (*mashal*, 1QpHab 8.9f.) over Israel is quite devastating. The unprejudiced reader has to think here of a king or high priest in Israel; and that would be the Hasmonaeans, who ruled as priests and kings. So like the term 'truth', the term 'Israel' is now understood in a sense allegedly specific to Qumran. It does not mean, say, the nation, but in particular the laity in the community as distinct from the clergy, for in the Damascus document 'Israel' is mentioned alongside the priests and Levites as a third state (CD 14.4-6). Accordingly, the 'wicked priest' will have 'ruled' the laity of the community.

However, these pedantic interpretations go against the Qumran terminology. For both terms, 'truth' and 'Israel', are predominantly used in a more general Old Testament sense. Granted, on particular occasions the 'truth' can specifically be the teaching characteristic of Qumran, but – like righteousness – in the vast majority of cases it is God's quality and mode of revelation. Similarly, 'Israel' is primarily the people elected by God but now in need of repentance, in whose midst the Qumran community maintains God's covenant. Moreover the sharp distinction between clergy and laity in Qumran tells against a mixing, which would have been the case were the laity led by a priest. Finally, such a task of leadership would never be described with the word 'rule'.

The attack on the Qumran consensus which is pressed so energetically, 'There is no Hasmonaean high priest in the scrolls', gets nowhere. For in the fragments from Cave 4 now published by Eisenman and Wise, several Hasmonaean rulers or high priests are even mentioned directly by name, including Salome Alexandra

(76-67 BCE), her son Hyrcanus II (from 67 BCE) and presumably also John Hyrcanus (134-104 BCE).[8] By contrast there is no name from the Herodian, New Testament period, though that is the period in which according to Thiering the prophetic writings are to be fulfilled.

In the *pesher* on the prophet Nahum the names of the Syrian kings Antiochus and Demetrius are mentioned; when asked for help by the Pharisees the latter threatened Jerusalem and Alexander Jannaeus, the priest king ruling there, with his army (cf. 4QpNah 11.2f.). However, he withdrew. Thereupon Alexander had 800 Pharisees crucified for high treason. This cruel punishment is reported both in the Nahum *pesher* (4QpNah 1.6-8) and by the Jewish historian Josephus (*Jewish War* I,92f.; *Jewish Antiquities* XIII, 377f.). Thiering now puts these events around 100 and thinks that Pilate carried out a mass crucifixion after the Jewish protest against the Roman standards; it is this act that is referred to in the Nahum *pesher*. However, there can be no question of that. There was no bloodshed then, since Pilate, taken by surprise, gave way to the Jews (cf. *Jewish War* II, 169-74; *Jewish Antiquities* XVIII, 55-9). Quite apart from that, one cannot relate a conflict within Judaism under Alexander Jannaeus to a later Jewish-Roman incident.

Barbara Thiering relies above all on the Temple Scroll from Cave 11 which – as is also often judged to be the case by others – she claims have been made even before the emergence of the Teacher. Thiering sees the extension of the Jerusalem temple undertaken by Herod the Great in 26 BCE as the main reason for the preparation of this scroll: with its precise description of the buildings, courtyards, sacrificial cult and festivals, and also the commandments relating to cleanness, it was to serve as a model in the form of a programme proclaimed by God to Herod at the building of the temple. However, Herod is said then to have rejected it because the strict royal law which it contains did not correspond to his own relaxed way of life.[9] Moreover the Temple Scroll is said to have been composed by a mixed group of pious which included Essenes along with Pharisees and Zealots. After the severe earthquake which severely damaged the Qumran site in 31 BCE and made it cultically impure, the Essenes had settled in Jerusalem. That there was a settlement of Essenes under Herod in Jerusalem and that the Temple Scroll had some influence on the rebuilding of the temple under this Jewish king are viable theories which have also been put forward by other scholars independently of Thiering.[10] But these theories are still far from supporting a dating of the 'Teacher of Righteousness' to the Herodian period.

Now Thiering does not think that Essenism (the Qumran community) belongs exclusively in the first century CE. Its history began in the second century BCE, when Qumran was inhabited by exiles who had separated from official Judaism. In the early phase of a radical and also nationalistic Essenism, biblical books were copied, and pseudepigraphical writings like Enoch, Daniel, Jubilees and the Testaments of the Twelve Patriarchs were composed.[11] After the earthquake of 31 BCE the Essenes had lived in Herodian Jerusalem. But from 6 CE, when Judaea was occupied and administered by the Romans, a group with Zealot tendencies returned to Qumran and other places on the Dead Sea, including Masada; it was then that the War Scroll was written. According to Thiering, Zealot disturbances under Vitellius necessitated a time of exile in the land of Damascus for part of the Essenes. In Palestine these disturbances finally led to the first Jewish rebellion (66-70 CE), the fall of Jerusalem with the destruction of the Temple (70 CE), and the end of the Zealots in Masada (73/74 CE). Here Thiering comes near to Eisenman's defective pan-Zealot hypothesis.

## John the Baptist as the 'Teacher of Righteousness'?

By the term alone, Barbara Thiering wants to prove that she has solved the riddle posed by the title 'Teacher of Righteousness' correctly. The Hebrew expression *moreh sedeq*, usually rendered 'Teacher of Righteousness', can also be translated 'the one who baptizes in righteousness', 'who pours out righteousness (like water)' (cf. Joel 2.23). For her, in the allegorical interpretation of the Gospels, John, who was officially born on 16 September of the year 8 BCE to Elizabeth the wife of the Zadokite priest Zechariah, originally bound to celibacy for a lengthy period, is also the 'man who went from Jerusalem to Jericho' (98).[12] That took place in the year 26 CE, when Pilate came to Judaea as a Roman governor, twenty years after the beginning of the 'time of wrath' in the Damascus Document (CD 1.9-11), which began with the Roman administration of Judaea. John left his parents and led the life of an ascetic in the wilderness as a pious and zealous observer of the law, before taking over the leadership of the Qumran community. His strong personality and authority are expressed in the Qumran hymn 1QHodayot 2.8-13 (Thiering, 91f.).

John, she goes on, was firmly convinced of the imminent dawn of the end of the age and dated it to 29, 30 or 31 CE. In contrast to the enlightened Jewish friends of the Gentiles, like James, Caiaphas, Gamaliel or the young Saul he was a 'Hebrew of the Hebrews', i.e. full of pride in the Old Testament Jewish tradition. For five years he ruled a Qumran coalition consisting of radical nationalist Essenes and Essenes friendly to the Gentiles. Then Herod Antipas had him arrested, first because he was angry about the Baptist's criticism of his marriage to Herodias, and secondly, because the xenophobia in the Baptist's preaching seemed to him to be politically dangerous. Moreover the prophecy of a turning point that would bring salvation had not been fulfilled even in 31. Finally the Baptist was executed as a false prophet (Thiering, 556).

John also made enemies among the Essenes by his rigorous, unforgiving attitude. While he was working as 'Teacher of Righteousness' there was a schism in his community: 'the split (*schizomenoi*) heavens' in the story of the baptism of Jesus (Mark 1.10) indirectly indicates this and the Damascus document describes it clearly: a majority opposed to John's rigorous attitude declared themselves in favour of the conciliating 'man of lies' (CD 20.13-15). On the Day of Atonement there was a conflict: the rival was accused of working for the death of the 'Teacher of Righteousness' (cf.1QpHab 11.8), a charge which was not unfounded. After the execution of the Baptist, retribution also overtook the 'wicked priest' and 'man of lies'. Because of his guilt over the 'Teacher of Righteousness', God gave him into 'the hands of his enemies... that he might be humbled by means of a destroying scourge, in bitterness of soul, because he had done wickedly to his elect' (1QpHab 9.9-12). Thus begins the story of Jesus. In the Habakkuk pesher he is referred to under the names 'wicked priest' and 'man of lies'.

This picture of John is a complete caricature and developed in free fantasy:

1. John the Baptist was anything but a nationalistic Zealot who had the political prosperity and mission of the people of Israel in view. Thiering diligently overlooks the fact that John's preaching of penitence – like that of the 'Teacher of Righteousness' – decisively changes the notion of the unity and uniqueness of the people of God and puts belief in election and salvation on a new basis. That is shown by the threat, 'Do not think that you can say "We have Abraham as our father." For I say to you, God can raise up children to Abraham from these stones' (Matt.3.9 and parallels). That means that salvation is in no way guaranteed for Israel as a nation. The true people of God is made up of individual 'children of light' predestined by God, the true sons of Abraham. It is a hidden entity, created by God.

We know nothing of any leadership of the Qumran community by John the Baptist. Had that been the case, Flavius Josephus would have reported it. John may indeed have grown up as a child in Qumran (cf. Luke 1.80), but he then separated from the community and prepared the way in the wilderness for the coming Lord as a preacher of penitence (Mark 1.2ff.).[13]

3. There was no breach between him and Jesus, who took on the Baptist's ministry after his arrest (Mark 1.14) and praised him as the greatest of all prophets (Matthew 11.11); however, after his arrest by Herod Antipas John did doubt Jesus' messianic status (Matthew 11.2-6).


## Jesus as the 'Wicked Priest' and 'Man of Lies'?

Barbara Thiering wants to look for the real, historical Jesus and not the Christ and Son of God whom the church confesses and venerates. She alleges that the man of flesh and blood is presented by the '*pesher*' of the four Gospels, i.e. not their clear text but their second, deeper sense, towards which they are directed. This sense has to be searched out, since it lies under the surface. Thiering attempts to depict Jesus in her way as a sympathetic person: he was probably short in stature, since Mary Magdalene thought that she could take him away (John 20.15); he also had long hair and the beard of a Nazirite, i.e. someone dedicated to God (100). Although destined for royal office, Jesus went around among the lowly and supported the oppressed and exploited, the poor, the handicapped, the socially excluded (100). He was generous, open to strangers and those of other opinions; he personally observed the ascetic discipline of the Essenes in which he had been brought up.

But why was this peaceable man, of all people, described in a discriminatory way in the Habakkuk *pesher* as a 'wicked priest' and 'man of lies'? According to Thiering, primarily his open nature, the way in which he was above nationalistic Jewish zeal and strove for universal peace, were crucial here. To the orthodox wing of the Essenes, aware of tradition and loyal to the law, and an ascetic like John the Baptist, this attitude seemed to be a godless evasion of the true obedience demanded by the law. It was thought particularly irresponsible because, on the basis of his descent from the family of David, Jesus was destined to be heir to the royal throne in Israel. But he also had to bear the stigma of his birth, the circumstances of which – strongly condemned as they were by the law – made him seem an illegitimate heir of royal dignity and therefore a man of lies. Recognition or repudiation depended on the high priest of the time. But such insecurity and the threat of humiliation made Jesus sensitive to those who were discriminated against in society and ready for peace with anyone, including the Gentiles from Rome.

Thiering has established with amazing exactitude the most important dates in the life of Jesus, which for the most part was lived in the wilderness by the Dead Sea and not, say, in friendly Galilee: he was born not far from Qumran in March of the year 7 BCE. At the age of twelve he underwent a first dedication in a life filled with all kinds of ceremonies and rites; he was accepted as a novice among the Essenes and in 17 CE fully received into the order. His father Joseph died in 23 CE. The baptism of Jesus by John, the then leader ('Pope') of the Essenes, took place in 29 CE. However, this also sparked off the schism in which Jesus, along with the apostolic council of twelve,[14] separated from John. In September 30 CE he married Mary Magdalene, first for a three-year trial marriage of an Essene kind; as a Davidide he had an obligation to provide a physical son as successor to the throne.[15] On the Day of Atonement, 32 CE, which had been expected to be the turn of the ages, Jesus appeared to his followers in the robes of the high priest. Thiering infers this from the Transfiguration story (Mark 9.22ff.). But his claim as a son of David at the same time to be a 'son of Zadok' was an unprecedented, intolerable break with tradition for everyone.

At the end of this year Jesus then took the side of the Zealots and entered Qumran (!) in March 33 CE, riding on a mule. Because Judas Iscariot had again vainly hoped for a miraculous divine intervention here, in disappointmnet he betrayed Jesus to Pilate. Pilate appeared in Qumran to arrest Jesus, along with Simon Magus and the Zealot Judas from Galilee, condemned them to death and had them crucified outside the settlement. (Thiering even offers a photograph of the place of execution.) It proved possible to take Jesus down from the cross, anaesthetized by a poisoned drink and deeply unconscious (154-60), put him in one of the neighbouring caves – 7Q – and restore him to life with healing herbs.[16] After that he appeared to many and then ascended to 'heaven', the place of 'gods and angels', though this only means the Essene place of prayer. So Thiering adds yet a new variant to the unending story of the pseudo-death of Jesus.

Jesus would thus largely have remained associated with the Essenes. In 36 CE a daughter was born to him by Mary Magdalene and in 37 CE a son, Justus. But in 44 CE his wife separated from him, after which in 50, in a second marriage, he married the purple dyer Lydia of Philippi whose 'heart he had opened' (Acts 16.14, Thiering, 195-8).[17] He visited Jerusalem in 58 CE and in 61 CE went with Paul to Rome, where Paul – along with Peter – suffered martyrdom in the Neronian persecution. At that time Jesus reached the biblical age of seventy. We know nothing of his end; perhaps he died at a ripe old age in Rome or sought refuge with his family on Herod's estate in the south of France.

## The eventful life of Jesus

Those are just the most striking events of Jesus' life. There is further information in a second detailed chronology (Thiering, 281-390), though this has to be inferred from a bewildering number of dates. They bear witness to a highly eventful political and spiritual struggle between parties and persons who are known to us by name from the New Testament, the writings of Josephus and the sources of early church history. The portrait of Jesus fluctuates in this newly disclosed history, distorted by the hatred or favour of the parties; sometimes it is also completely concealed again. But now at last, Thiering claims, the possibility of a biography of Jesus, which scholars have previously claimed quite categorically to be impossible, becomes a reality. She recovers, reconstructs and gives a precise date (sometimes to the nearest five minutes) to the 'lost years' between Jesus' birth and first public appearance. After his public ministry, there is a further phase in the life of Jesus, even if its pages are almost completely blank; in it he is overshadowed by Paul, whom he accompanies on his missionary journeys.

Thiering, as it were, deciphers the Gospels and Acts and offers their real, hidden, meaning: they are 'allegorical', i.e. tell a different story from what appears at first sight. Thiering calls this a *'pesher* procedure'. It enables her, she claims, to infer from the Lucan infancy story (chs. 1-2) further events of Jesus' youth; in this way it proves possible to fill years which were previously empty. She then sees Jesus' miracles in terms of natural reality and interprets the parables historically by giving names to their anonymous figures. For example, Luke is said to present no fewer than twelve 'historical' parables: the first four deal with the history of the Essenes, a further six with the house of Herod, and the last two with the first generation in the thousand-year kingdom of David (Thiering, 575). As we have seen, the man who went 'from Jerusalem to Jericho' (Luke 10.30) was none other than John the Baptist, who joined the Essenes by the Dead Sea; his fate is related in the parable of the Good Samaritan (Thiering, 98).

The father in the parable of the Prodigal Son is the Essene Simon, who was able to interpret the dream of King Aristobulus (Josephus, *Jewish Antiquities* XVII, 346-7) and is identical with the aged Simeon in the story of Jesus (Luke 2.25). His younger son was Theudas, the revolutionary from Acts 5.36; he was not killed, as everyone had previously believed; after his failure he adopted the life of a hermit! As leader of the Egyptian Therapeutae (a species of Essene) he introduced communal life with women in distant Qumran and squandered his father's possessions by buying weapons for the fight against the Romans (Thiering, 81f.). So for the peace-loving Jesus he became the prodigal son and the 'seeker after smooth things'. The older son in the parable can only be the Zealot Judas, the Galilean of Pharisaic origin, and the fatted calf Archelaus son of Herod, who was killed in 6 CE, i.e. deposed by the Romans (84-5). After such samples one is really inclined to stop reading these Gospel *pesharim* and also spare the reader such offerings.

### A new way to decipher the Gospels?

There is method behind what seems to be grotesque fantasy. Everything that Barbara Thiering presents in her book with its wealth of material is well ordered and worked out with 'scientific' accuracy. The reader is offered many guidelines: the bulk of the book is not made up of the narrative of thirty-five chapters, brief and exciting in its way, but of the appendixes. There is a 'Who's Who in the History', i.e. a guide to persons and events (Thiering, 530-61). Furthermore a vivid topography is offered, containing sketches and pictures of where Jesus went and worked; unfortunately they do not take us into the attractive landscape by the Sea of Galilee but into the bleak wilderness of Judaea by the Dead Sea (Thiering, 391ff.). The chronology which is offered in many forms is mind-boggling, first in a compressed survey of the most important events from 7 BCE to 64 CE (530-602) and then in the detailed chronological table already mentioned; this is prefaced with a methodological indication of how one can arrive at minutious (in the literal sense) datings of the life of Jesus with the aid of *pesher* exegesis. The various calendar systems are explained and then the indications of time used in the Gospels. Very general adverbs ('immediately', 'then', etc.) are said to have a precise sense which can be expressed in figures.

But is the word *pesher* understood rightly here? Does it mean a method of scriptural exegesis comparable to the moralizing allegory of Philo, or, even better, the twofold scriptural sense of the kabbalists? Thiering claims to have taken over this kind of scriptural exegesis from Qumran and thinks that it is also presupposed by the evangelists. In Chapter IV of her book, which is supposed to explain and justify the *pesher* technique, she cites some instances from the commentary on the prophet Habakkuk.

Thus for example she connects Habakkuk 1.7, which speaks of enemies provoking terror, by which is meant the Babylonians, with the Romans, who fill all peoples with fear. She then explains that the biblical term *pesher* can be the 'interpretation' of a dream, say in the Joseph story or the book of Daniel (29). So she compares the *pesher* with the solving of a riddle or the interpretation of a cryptogram; one has to find the key to it, apply a special technique. In her view *pesher* exegesis implies two levels of meaning, the first conveying general religious truths, as it were for babes in the faith, and the second, special level with mysterious, historical depths which only the dedicated exegete can discover.

But that is clearly a false assessment of the *pesher* as we find it in Qumran. The exegete who wrote the Habakkuk commentary does not regard his basic text as a riddle. He does not interpret it allegorically, but as a quite meaningful analogy. The righteous person remains righteous and the godless person is understood as an evildoer. However, both are more closely defined in the *pesher* and related to people of the present: what the Chaldaeans did then is predicated of the Romans, the present enemies. That is a quite legitimate and illuminating procedure which takes to heart the abiding significance of the Word of God. Certainly the mysteries of God are addressed in the Habakkuk *pesher* (1QpHab 7.8), but there is no exegetical secretiveness. The form of the *pesher* in Qumran is clearly defined. First of all a passage is cited from the Old Testament, then follows an updated application of the passage, usually introduced by the formula *pishro* (the interpretation of it).

Now we also find comparable passages in the Gospels, where an Old Testament saying is cited as being fulfilled in the activity of Jesus (Matthew 1.22f.; 2.15 etc.). But that is something quite different from Thiering's *pesher* procedure, for which she abuses the Qumran expression to give her fantasies a touch of seriousness. Nowhere in the New Testament is a word or an action of Jesus cited with the claim that it is a cryptic reference to a completely different historical event. To interpret the Gospels and the Acts of the Apostles throughout by the *pesher* method is sheer whimsy. They do not ask to be understood as cryptograms nor even as *pesharim* in the Qumranic sense. What they report about Jesus' activity is irrevocably past. Nor do the miracles and parables of

Jesus ask to be interpreted allegorically in such a way that they tell of the struggles of heads of rival parties; they are about people like us who are called on by God and invited to believe in Jesus Christ.

## Destructive and pseudo-scientific

Was Jesus the 'wicked priest' of the Damascus Rule and the Habakkuk *pesher*? Not at all. Thiering's late dating of the Qumran writings and identification of their main figures with John the Baptist and Jesus are as false as Eisenman's attempt to identify the anonymous 'Teacher of Righteousness' with James the brother of the Lord. James and Jesus were Davidides, not Zadokides. They were condemned to death by the Sadducees, and Jesus was resolutely against the attempt of the Pharisees and Essenes to proscribe priestly rules of cleanliness even for the laity and thus to raise all Israel to a higher level of holiness (Mark 7). He also did away with the sacrifice offered in the Temple by his messianic self-sacrifice. In the Transfiguration story (Mark 9.2ff.) Jesus did not reveal himself as high priest but as the servant of God of Isaiah 53, prepared for vicarious suffering and glorified in anticipation.

It is no consolation that Thiering dates the Gospels very early, the Gospel of John being the first, no later than 37 CE. For believing Christians, many of Thiering's fantasies about Jesus are blasphemous. We have gone into the content of the book in some detail here so as to spare as many people as possible an unnecessary reading of it. The damage that has been done is already great enough. Thiering's theses were popularized in Australia by a nationwide television broadcast on Palm Sunday (!) 1990, which attracted more attention than any religious programme for a long time. A journalist's book on the broadcast heightened its influence.[18] Even the German tabloids took it up immediately. 'Woman Theologian: Jesus was Quite Different', announced the *Hamburger Abendblatt* on its front page.[19] *Quick* magazine then took it upon itself to enlighten its readers in the last issue of 1992. Here the Qumran plot à la Baigent and Leigh and Thiering's scandal story were mixed into an unpalatable brew,[20] all in the regular column 'Know More', adorned with a portrait of Albert

Einstein. It is significant that over two large pages all the Hebrew words are printed upside down.

Thiering's book is an insult not only to Christian faith but to serious scholarship. She and Eisenman show the by-ways one gets into with the allegedly transmuted meaning of the Qumran texts. Both complain to have cracked the Qumran code, but each solution excludes each other. Their methods do not open up the texts, but only make way for whimsy. By Thiering and Eisenman's methodological aberrations one can claim whatever one likes about Qumran, Jesus and the early Christians, from whatever motives. In the *Biblical Archaeology Review* the review of Thiering's book is headed 'Review of a Silly Book'. Its author is the Jewish journalist Hershel Shanks. He writes: 'The real mystery (of the book) is how Harper San Francisco, a sub-division of HarperCollins, generally known for solid academic books, could have decided to publish this weighty tome. Doubtless the answer has something to do with what was on the tables that Jesus overturned.'[21]

# 8

# Were Manuscripts of the New Testament found in Qumran Cave 7?

Irresponsible sensationalizing – The debatable hypothesis of a Spaniard with an Irish name – The academic dispute: from Rome via Münster to Eichstätt – Fragment 7Q5 = Mark 6.52-53? – The present state of discussion: possibility or probability?

## Irresponsible sensationalizing

Brilliant sales successes have been achieved because of the burning interest of Christians in Israel. Sensationally inflated reports from the sphere of biblical archaeology are particuarly lucrative. Thus on its front page the *Jerusalem Christian Review* proudly indicates a circulation of more than 200,000 copies. Its topic at the end of 1992 was the discoveries at Qumran.[1] Right at the beginning it claimed that the discovery of the Dead Sea Scrolls had irrefutably proved that the Old Testament used by the Jews of the first century, including Jesus, was *word for word* the same as the one we use today. Statements of this kind are even used as promotion by serious Christian publishing houses. Nevertheless, such claims are false.

The Old Testament scrolls from Qumran show that there is a very good tradition behind the Hebrew text which underlies the Jewish and Christian Bible, at least for an age to which printing was still unknown and in which books had to be copied laboriously by hand. In antiquity, with longer manuscripts there are hardly two copies of one and the same work which are identical in every character. That is also the case in Qumran. The incomplete Isaiah manuscript from Cave 1 (1QIsaᵇ) corresponds in an amazing way with the so-called Massoretic text produced by the rabbis of the first centuries, but is not completely identical with it. The better-known complete Isaiah manuscript from the same cave (1QIsaᵃ) clearly shows more deviations from this form of the text.

It is not enough that the statements about the copying of Old Testament books in this newspaper are crude, not to say irresponsible. 'Undeciphered Scroll from the Dead Sea may prove to be Gospel of Luke' runs another headline. Granted, the article itself does not say quite that, but the reader is left with the impression that after further deciphering, part of the Third Gospel could emerge. The text concerned is 4Q246, which we have already examined earlier (pp.93–7 above). This fragment is highly significant because here beyond question the term 'Son of God' is used for an eschatological figure in a pre-Christian document. But to see this text as part of the Gospel of Luke is so absurd that even Eisenman and Wise were restrained here.[2] Furthermore the decisive part of the text has long since been deciphered and published, something of which the author of this article was evidently unaware.[3] In 4Q246 there are some words and phrases which recall Luke 1.32–35 – no less, but also no more. If 4Q246 were to be part of the Gospel of Luke, one could equally claim that the War Scroll was the Gospel of Matthew, since the expression 'poor in spirit' appears in both (1QM 14.7; Matthew 5.3).

## The debatable hypothesis of a Spaniard with an Irish name

The proposals introduced into the academic debate by José O'Callaghan in 1972 are to be distinguished from such cheap showmanship. O'Callaghan was Professor of Papyrology at the Biblical Institute in Rome, and since his retirement has been head of the Papyrological Seminar at San Cugat del Vallès (Barcelona). As a specialist on the Septuagint, the most important Greek translation of the Old Testament, he has also been concerned with Qumran. The great surprises among the finds are fragments of Greek manuscripts of the Bible. Fragments of two manuscripts of Leviticus, one of Numbers and two of Deuteronomy come from Cave 4.[4] If there were already Greek texts of the Bible in a conservative Jewish community like the Essenes of Qumran, we can imagine how widespread knowledge of this language was at the time of Jesus.[5] It must be mentioned that the Jesuit Fr

O'Callaghan was by no means concerned to find New Testament texts at Qumran at any price; he would have been quite content with Old Testament fragments.

O'Callaghan paid special attention to the sparse Greek fragments from Cave 7. The editors[6] had identified one of these (7Q1) as a fragment of Exodus 28.4-7 and another (7Q2) as a fragment of the so-called Letter of Jeremiah, which as an appendix to the book of Baruch is part of the deutero-canonical works of the Catholic Bible. The other seventeen fragments had remained unidentified. O'Callaghan now hoped to make sense of them. But all attempts at identification with the help of extensive concordance work failed.

So O'Callagan made the attempt with New Testament texts. To his surprise New Testament attributions proved possible for several of the unidentified fragments. In order of probability, which O'Callaghan himself judged to differ in each case, these were 7Q4 (I Timothy 3.16-4.3), 7Q5 (Mark 6.52-53), 7Q6 (Mark 3.28), 7Q7 (Acts 27.38), 7Q8 (James 1.23-24), 7Q9 (Romans 5.11-2), 7Q10 (II Peter 1.15) and 7Q15 (Mark 6.48). O'Callaghan himself regards only 7Q4 and 7Q5 as certain. The Spanish scholar published these proposals in the famous journal of the Biblical Institute.[7] Soon afterwards, not only did a discussion begin among the professionals, but many articles appeared in the church and world press.

## The academic dispute: from Rome via Münster to Eichstätt

How explosive O'Callaghan's theories were becomes clear when one thinks of the majority views on the dating of New Testament writings. According to the hitherto undisputed view, Cave 7 too was sealed in 68 CE on the approach of the Romans. If O'Callaghan were right in his proposals for identification, Acts and II Peter would have been written before this year. However, most scholars date Luke's work to the 80s of the first century and some regard II Peter as an inauthentic letter and put it only at the beginning of the second century CE.[8] In the case of the Gospel of Mark, a dating shortly before or after the destruction of Jerusalem in 70 CE predominates.[9] But the papyrus fragment 7Q5 (Mark 6.52-53?) is written in the so-called Herodian decorated style, which is usually assumed to come to an end around 50 CE.[10] So do we have to put the composition of the Gospel of Mark in the 40s, which John A.T. Robinson for other reasons thought to be at least possible in his provocative book *Redating the New Testament*?[11]

O'Callaghan's theories were taken up in Protestant fundamentalist groups in the USA even more strongly than in conservative Catholic circles. The popular evangelical magazine *Eternity* chose for an issue devoted to the topic the title 'Could One Small Fragment Shake the World?'[12] For many people two centuries of critical biblical scholarship seemed outdated and valueless.

In the scholarly world O'Callaghan's proposals met with widespread criticism. For many New Testament scholars the question was settled when the much-respected textual scholar Kurt Aland rejected the identifications in two articles.[13] The great confidence in him as an expert is understandable since his great achievement has been to have developed the Institute for New Testament Textual Research in Münster with its unique documentation centre. Aland was a leading figure in the preparation of the twenty-sixth edition of Nestle-Aland, the most widely used edition of the Greek text of the New Testament.[14] When well-known evangelical exegetes also came out against the proposals for identification, things increasingly settled down.[15] From the end of the 1970s the discussion seemed to have been decided in the negative, though ultra-fundamentalist authors who in other respects could hardly be regarded as friends of the Catholics continued to take Fr O'Callaghan's side.[16]

However, one should never say 'never' too quickly, in politics or in scholarship. In 1984 the German literary critic Carsten Peter Thiede opened up a new round of disussion[17] by defending O'Callaghan's identification of 7Q5 with Mark 6.52-53 (the end of the feeding of the five thousand and the beginning of the healings of the sick in Gennesaret). The German edition of Thiede's book, now in English as *The Earliest Gospel Manuscript? The Mark Fragment from Qumran and the Beginnings of the Written Tradition of the New Testament*, went through three editions in a short time[18] and was translated into several languages. In the scholarly world, Thiede in part gained cautious to clear assent[19] and in part harsh criticism.[20] A Catholic philosopher

engaged in interdisciplinary work wrote most on the topic after
Thiede: Ferdinand Rohrhirsch of the Catholic University of
Eichstätt pointed out that Kurt Aland had not noted in his
computer researches that the papyri from 7Q were not fragments
of a codex written on both sides (as in the case of other New
Testament manuscripts) but fragments of a scroll written on one
side.[21] Trained in the scientific criticism of the British philosopher
Karl Popper, Rohrhirsch put forward the view that the identification of 7Q5 with Mark 6.52-53 was the only possible proposal
out of all those made so far.[22] As long as this identification was
not falsified (by an identification which fitted better), one could
work with it.

In October 1991 scholars with different ideolological back-
grounds, from several countries, met in Eichstätt for a symposium
on 'Christians and Christian Elements in Qumran?'. Alongside
the question whether there was an Essene quarter in Jerusalem
(see Chapter 10 below), the problems of Cave 7 and especially
the identity of 7Q5 were a focal point of discussion. The
conversations were held with a fairness which cannot always
be taken for granted in controversial academic debates. The
arguments for and against were openly advanced, and inadequate
ones were openly conceded. New Testament scholars arguing
with Thiede and Rohrhirsch for the identification of 7Q5 with
Mark 6.52-53 included Harald Risenfeld of Uppsala and Eugen
Ruckstuhl of Lucerne, and the distinguished papyrologist Herbert
Hunger of Vienna. Objections were made above all by the exegete
Camille Focant of Louvain and the philologist Stuart R.Pickering
of Macquarie University, Australia. The discussion has been
documented in a collection edited by the Eichstätt New Testament
scholar Bernhard Mayer.[23]

There has been a further important development since then.
On 12 April 1992 Carsten Peter Thiede was able to clarify further
the reading of disputed consonants by an investigation of the
fragment 7Q5 in an Israeli police laboratory, using techniques
employed in criminal detection.[24] The glass plate with the 7Q
fragments was allowed to leave the Rockefeller Museum for a
few hours under a special permit. It proved possible to make
further fragmentary consonants visible. This new analysis supports the assumption by O'Callaghan and Thiede that the Greek

```
                    ]ε[
                 ]υτωνη[
          ]η     καιτι[
                 ]γνησ[
     5           ]θησα[
```

Transcription of the letters deciphered from 7Q5

Mark 6.52–53
```
          [συνηκαν]ε[πιτοισαρτοισ]
          [αλληνα]υτωνη[καρδιαπεπωρω]
          [μεν]η  καιτι[απερασαντεσ]
          [ηλθονεισΓε]γνησ[αρετκαι]
     5    [προσωρμισ]θησα[νκαιεξελ]
```

Reconstructed complete text of the five lines of
the fragment 7Q5

```
[συνῆκαν] ἐ[πὶ τοῖς ἄρτοις,]
[ἀλλ'ἦν α]ὐτῶν ἡ [καρδία πεπωρω-]
[μέν]η ·  ⁵³Καὶ τι[απεράσαντες]
[ἦλθον εἰς Γε]γνησ[αρὲτ καὶ]
[προσωρμίσ]θησα[ν. ⁵⁴καὶ ἐξελ-]
```

Complete, text-critical version

Mark 6.52–53 in the reconstructed text according to the RSV.

'. . . understand about the loaves,
but their hearts were hard-
ened. And when they had crossed over (to land),
they came to Gennesaret and
moored. And when they . . .'

consonant *nu* appears in line 2. Parts of the investigation were also filmed by German television's second channel.

## Fragment 7Q5 = Mark 6.52-53?

The fragment 7Q5 is at most 3.9 centimetres high and 2.7 centimetres wide, i.e. just larger than the average special issue postage stamp. It contains twenty consonants or fragments of consonants in all, on five lines. There is no controversy over the reading of ten of the consonants, and of the others, ten are disputed to some degree. It is easy to understand why there is a dispute over the identification of Papyrus 7Q5 if one compares it with the famous Papyrus 52. Charles H.Roberts undertook the identification of the latter with part of the Gospel of John, 18.31-33 on the recto and 18.37-38 on the verso, in 1935.[25] Since then no one has disputed it. $P^{52}$ is dated around 125 CE and thus is barely three decades later than the most probable date for the composition of the Gospel of John.

Three factors above all make the identification of $P^{52}$ certain as compared with 7Q5.

1. There are 105 certain consonants as opposed to 10 uncertain consonants.

2. Some words or roots are recognizable on $P^{52}$ which are particularly typical of the Gospel of John, like *hoi Ioudaioi* (the Jews), *semaino[n]* (showing), *apothneskein* (die), *mart[yreo]* (attest), *aletheia* (truth). In 7Q5 only the common word *kai* (and) can be read with certainty, in the third line; because of a preceding space at the beginning it seems to stand at the beginning of a new section. Sentences beginning with *kai* are very frequent in Mark.

3. In contrast to the Qumran fragment, the John Rylands Papyrus is written on both sides; this facilitates an identification and usually makes it more certain.

The question of the identification of the fragments from Cave 7 cannot be discussed in detail in this chapter. Here we must limit ourselves to considering briefly the pros and cons of three subject areas:

1. *Deviations from the text*. An identification of 7Q5 with Mark 6.52-53 presupposes two textual variants which are not to be found in any New Testament manuscript of this Gospel. That is

Transcription of the letters visible on the papyrus

*recto*

         οι ιουδαι  ημε
         ουδενα ϊνα ο λ
         πεν σημαινω
         θνησκειν ισ
5      ριον ο π
         και ειπ
           ιω

*verso*

         το γ γ νν  μαι
         σμον ϊναμαρτ
           κτης αληθε
         εγει αυτω
5         ιτουτ
           ουςι
           εμι

9. *Papyrus 52 – what remains of the text (according to C. P. Thiede)*

quite a lot for such a short fragment. What we have is the miswriting of *d* as *t* in line 3. Moreover because of the stichometry (the average length of the reconstructed lines), at the end of the third line we must assume the omission of the words *epi ten gen* (to the land). Those supporting the identification can point out that the miswriting assumed can also be demonstrated in other biblical and non-biblical manuscripts.[26] One must also assume an omission of the two words *eis touto* (for this), not otherwise attested, in line 2 of the verso of Papyrus 52, and one cannot get by in fragment 7Q2, which has been identified beyond dispute as the 'Letter of Jeremiah', without assuming omissions.[27]

2. *Questions of date.* It is objected against the identifications of 7Q fragments with the New Testament that Acts, James and II Peter certainly came into being only after 70 CE. It would therefore

be impossible to find them in a cave which had already been sealed up in 68. However, a significant minority of New Testament scholars argue that Acts and James were written before 70 CE. Some exegetes even regard James as the earliest writing in the New Testament.[28] In the case of II Peter one can count the scholarly supporters of a dating before 70 on the fingers of at most two hands, and O'Callaghan himself says that the identification of 7Q with II Peter 1.15 is only very hypothetical. But in principle at any rate the dating of writings which cannot be dated by external evidence or indisputable internal references must always be subject to revision on the basis of new evidence. Whether it is plausible to identify 7Q fragments with New Testament writings must be decided internally, i.e. on the basis of the consonants.

3. *The location.* Had the 7Q papyri been discovered in the more remote caves 11Q or even 3Q, it would be relatively easy to dispute a connection with the Essene settlement. One could then e.g. assume that Jewish Christians hid New Testament writings in a cave on their flight from the Holy City. But 7Q is right next to Qumran and not far from Cave 4, in which indubitably Essene writings were discovered and which must even have been a library for the monastic settlement. It is not very easy to explain how Essenes would have come by early Christian writings.

However, supporters of identifying the fragments with the New Testament can point to two striking peculiarities of 7Q: only in this cave have exclusively papyri been found, and without exception only Greek fragments. Any German university library has its 'poison cupboard', including among other things some works from the Nazi period. Was 7Q a *geniza* (Jewish store place for unused writings) for heretical documents, as the Qumran scholar Hans Burgmann assumed?[29] Other scenarios, too, were proposed to the Eichstätt symposium.[30] It is desirable that Cave 7Q, considerable parts of which have collapsed into the Wadi Qumran, should once again be investigated by modern archaeological methods. Fortunately the archaeologist responsible, Yitzhak Magen, has this in mind.[31]

*The present state of discussion: possibility or probability?*

As a provisional conclusion to the discussion we might say that while the identification of 7Q5 with Mark 6.52-53 is not certain, it does remain very possible. The dispute is over whether one can talk in terms of probability. It would be resolved if one could justify clearer identifications than those proposed by O'Callaghan. However, the reading of 7Q5 proposed by O'Callaghan is supported by the Ibycus computer programme, which covers the whole of extant ancient Greek literature. This demonstrates that of this material, the fragment corresponds only with Mark 6.52-53.

However, Professor Hartmut Stegemann of the Qumran Research Department of Göttingen University is optimistic that it will be possible to demonstrate that 7Q5 is a genealogy.[32] It had already been proposed earlier that the sequence of consonants *nnes* in line 4 could be expanded to form the Greek word *[ege]nnes[en]* (he begot). So the debate goes on. Hopefully the fact that extreme Catholic traditionalist groups are nailing the fragment 7Q5 to their standards in a triumphalistic way will not have a negative effect.[33] Although Baigent and Leigh and Eisenman and Wise could use it as grist for their mills, neither of them discusses the question of the 7Q papyri. Nor does Barbara Thiering make any connection between what she assumes to be the tomb of Jesus in 7Q and the fragments which have in fact been found there. We must regard this as good fortune in many ways, since this remarkable silence certainly contributes to a more objective discussion.

Three attitudes from most recent times show how far we still are from a scholarly consensus. Émile Puech of the École Biblique, to whom we owe splendid reconstructions of Qumran fragments from the portion assigned to Jean Starcky, speaks brusquely of 'fanciful identifications'.[34] By contrast, Shemaryahu Talmon, who is a member of the new control body for editing the Qumran writings, judges that: 'Some attempts at interpretation must be regarded as scientific and therefore also have a justified claim to be discussed by scholars. Here I am thinking above all of the publication by Carsten Peter Thiede, who has taken up the work of the Spanish expert José O'Callaghan.'[35]

Let us leave the last word to Ferdinand Rohrhirsch, a supporter of the identification of 7Q5 with the New Testament, who nevertheless states: 'In my view, at present no clear judgment in favour of a particular direction is possible. Anyone who claims that the identification of 7Q5 with Mark 6.52-53 is *certain*, and consequently thinks that all doubt over the identification has finally been removed, can announce that as a private opinion. But there is no scholarly justification for such a statement. However, the contrary must also be said: there is no certain proof against the possible identification of 7Q5 with Mark 6.52-53. In my view the theory that they are identical may be taken up in scholarly discussion as a useful working hypothesis.'[36]

# 9

# What is the Significance of the Qumran Texts for Understanding Jesus of Nazareth?

The joint work by Jews and Christians on the Qumran writings - Multiplicity and unity in the Qumran texts – The 'Teacher of Righteousness' and Jesus – The Sinai tradition, Qumran and the Sermon on the Mount – The great difference: Jesus' concern for sinners – Qumran and the life-style of Jesus' disciples – Qumran and the so-called 'historical Jesus'

## The joint work by Jews and Christians on the Qumran writings

Putting all the Qumran texts into the New Testament period and making them speak cryptically of John the Baptist and Jesus, James and Paul does not make them specially relevant for Christians. The Dead Sea Scrolls were written by Jews: they should not be Christianized, so to speak dragged away to be baptized. They are important and of value to Christians specifically as testimonies to a piety which was both pre-Christian and contemporary with Christianity. We may regard them as an unexpected, great gift of God, learn much from them and understand our Christian belief better through them. Nor do we need to regard Jesus as an Essene, as Frederick the Great already did, and as has happened time and again since the discovery of the Qumran writings. However, there is some support for the view that John the Baptist was brought up in the Qumran community: the nature of his baptism and his preaching, and above all the note in Luke 1.80 that he grew up as a child in the wilderness.[1]

Dating the Qumran writings to the pre-Christian period in no way happens as a piece of desperate apologetic or out of a fear that Christianity has such contacts with Judaism; nor is it dictated by the Vatican. It is accepted as a scientifically assured fact by Protestant and Jewish Qumran scholars and those with no religious commitment. No dogmatic consensus has done violence to the interpretation of these texts and hindered free research into them. The obstacles come far more from some of the new 'solutions' to the Qumran problem which are born out of protest against the consensus and also against Christianity. Sometimes these 'solutions' seem to be prompted by a desire to be different or adventurous, even at the risk of academic suicide. Total solutions are offered without the necessary texts for them. It should at least have made people suspicious that the inter-confessional academic team of editors who knew all the texts never thought of abandoning the Essene theory in favour of the hypothesis that the Qumran caves served as a deposit for various writings from Jerusalem libraries, or of replacing it with the assumption that political or religious battles fought by the Zealots or the early Christians were perpetuated in the Dead Sea Scrolls.

The Qumran writings have led Jews and Christians to a fruitful collaboration which has already lasted for decades and brings them together at a number of congresses. And if there have been differences, they were rarely connected with the dating or the content of these documents; rather, they concerned problems of a technical or a legal kind. Even the fact that the Dead Sea Scrolls went separate ways in politically divided Palestine, on the one hand being bought by Israel and coming into the hands of Jewish scholars, and on the other being purchased by a Metropolitan of the Syrian church and being entrusted to American scholars, did not stop the rapid publication and the beginning of study of them. From a purely academic perspective it did not matter who had the scrolls. Qumran research has overcome not only the barbed wire in Jerusalem but also the Iron Curtain: research was being done in the Qumran texts in Russia, Poland, Roumania and Czechoslovakia even before 1989, privately or in the institutes for oriental languages. The Jewish Russian scholar Joseph Amussin, among others, did valuable work and was also persecuted for it by the Communist regime.[2]

Joint international scholarly research on the Qumran writings continues to remain important. These texts are of great significance for Jews and Christians and therefore need a joint effort. Apart from the necessary specialists in archaeology and palaeography, Hebrew and Aramaic, history and geography, polymaths are also needed. For despite its basically orthodox Jewish attitude and connections with holy scripture and the Hebrew language, the Qumran community also belongs in the world of Hellenism, that synthesis of Oriental and Greek culture.[3] Accordingly Qumran scholars should not just have a one-sided education in Judaistics, but also a good understanding of the languages of classical antiquity, above all Greek. Philo and Flavius Josephus wrote in Greek, and the Greek translation known as the Septuagint existed alongside the Hebrew Bible; the Apocrypha and Pseudepigrapha, many of which are close to the Qumran writings, are sometimes extant only in translations into Greek, Latin or other languages.[4]

## Multiplicity and unity in the Qumran texts

Since the publication of the 4Q fragments it has increasingly been said that the Qumran texts are multifarious and indeed differ among themselves, and a unitary Essene origin has been put in question. A final decision is not possible until all the fragments have been published in legible form and have been exhaustively discussed. Moreover, some differences would be quite possible even if all these documents came from the same religious party, in other words were Essene. At all events, a period of 200-250 years is to be assumed as the time during which they came into being. Even a 'congregation' of the kind that the Qumran community claims to represent can undergo a development over so many years, and experience changes. We should recall the multiplicity of the New Testament writings; it has increasingly led exegetes to the erroneous assertion that already in the first beginnings of Christianity the juxtaposition of various groups led to mutually exclusive 'theologies'.

Above all, however, it must be noted that according to Philo there were Essenes throughout Palestine (*Apology* 1), and that Josephus knows two different groups, some living a celibate life and others married (*Jewish War* II, 160f.). In contrast to the Community Rule which fits the order of monastic celibate Essenes,

the Damascus Document could have been written for members
of the Essenes living scattered about the land; thus in it wife and
husband are mentioned almost as a matter of course (CD 16.10).
Such 'outside Essenes' evidently did not practise communism of
possessions as strictly as this was enjoined in the Community
Rule and as it is praised in the descriptions by Philo, Josephus and
Pliny; there is mention of private property (CD 12.7), and the
selling of animals and agricultural products to Gentiles is forbidden (CD 12.8-11). Nevertheless, for these groups, too, communal
life is envisaged under the leadership of an overseer and a priestly
adviser (CD 13.11).

The newly appearing fragments from Cave 4 also contain clear
references to people who exist in worldly conditions and have
possessions. Wisdom-type admonitions are meant to teach one
how to deal with people who are not trustworthy, do not do their
work carefully and are regarded as hypocrites; so these can hardly
be members of the Essene community. It is these people in the
world, in particular, who according to the text 4Q424 (formerly
4QS1 61) see to the administration of the community possessions,
obtain goods, and serve the needs of those being taught here. One
should not put a 'man with a covetous eye' (cf. Luke 11.34-36) in
charge of one's possessions (*hon*). The content and terminology
of these wisdom rules recall the parables of Jesus, above all
that of the unjust steward (e.g. Luke 16.1-13).

## The 'Teacher of Righteousness' and Jesus

The new generation of Qumran scholars rightly stresses the great
importance of the historical question: the origin and historical
development of the Qumran community, its relationship to the
Jewish religious parties and other political factors, and its influence
on early Christianity. However, it was not the purpose of the
writers of the Qumran scrolls to inform outsiders about their own
history and to provide them with historical information. Rather,
they wanted to guide and console members of the community,
instruct them about the will of God and his eschatological way;
the 'wise man' (*maskil*) can be heard in them. Without Philo and
above all Flavius Josephus we would not know much about the
history of the Essene Qumran community. But the discovery of

their writings has also enlivened historical research into the New Testament and above all had opened a door to the 'historical Jesus' which had been long closed.

The great significance of a teacher personality who also influenced the schooling of the rabbinic masters equally emerges from the Qumran writings: according to the Damascus Document even a movement of penitence and reform which seeks God with a whole heart remains blind and for long years only feels its way laboriously as long as it is not given a 'Teacher of Righteousness' to guide it on the way according to God's heart and make it aware of the *kairos* of the eschatological decision (CD 1.8-12). Granted, the Qumran writings do not themselves mention whether they were written by the 'Teacher of Righteousness', but in some of the hymns the speaker expresses his great authority and influence so clearly (e.g. 1QH 2-4; 7-8) that one must attribute some of the hymns to this teacher.[5] The same is probably also true of the Community Rule (1QS) and above all of the sections attributed to the wise man (*maskil*); presumably he is also the author of the Temple Scroll.[6] By contrast, the New Testament Gospels report explicitly what Jesus taught and did. That makes any doubt that we can no longer know what the authentic proclamation of Jesus was all the more unjustified.[7]

But above all, we can clearly recognize against the background of the Qumran texts where Jesus agrees with the convictions of the 'Teacher of Righteousness' and what separates the two. Both stand under the impact of the imminence of the end of history, the feeling that God's righteousness will soon be revealed in the world. However, Jesus did not proclaim the great turning point as punitive judgment, as did the Teacher of Righteousness in the Habakkuk pesher (1QpHab 2.6f.; 7.1-8), but as the coming of the rule of God and the revelation of salvation for all who need God and repent (Mark 1.14). Indeed the new time begins with his activity. If he drives out the unclean spirits with the spirit of God and thus successfully breaks into the kingdom of the evil one, the rule of God is already there (Matthew 12.28). His proclamation is accompanied by healing miracles and is thus described as the good news of redemption, as the gospel (Matthew 4.23-25). That is a sign that Jesus was aware of being sent as God's Messiah, and this is not only attested in the Gospels but also presupposed by Paul.

## The Sinai tradition, Qumran and the Sermon on the Mount

The ancient world – Philo and Pliny, and also Josephus – was particularly impressed by the Essene communal life: an ascetic monastic life-style with its renunciation of possessions, celibacy and obedience to God's commandment. This life-style, which was neither Old Testament nor Jewish, had influences which lasted down to Christian monasticism, and Jesus and his disciples also seem to be stamped by it. Both the 'Teacher of Righteousness' and Jesus preached repentance and called for a new self-understanding in the face of the kingdom of God; they wanted everyone, as it were, to practise the final judgment every day and test themselves in the light of the absolute will of God. But that was to happen in the community of the people of God. For that Israel had to become once again what it had been called to be, namely God's holy people, consisting of the twelve tribes of the time of Moses. A council of twelve men (lay?) and three priests was formed in Qumran (1QS 8.1). Jesus called twelve disciples who were to rule over Israel (Matthew 19.28).

The great model for the striking life-style of the Essene Qumran community had been given by the Sinai tradition.[8] After their exodus from Egypt the Israelites went into the wilderness of Sinai and camped at the foot of the mountain; thus they waited for the appearance of God and the manifestation of his holy will. The penitents under the 'Teacher of Righteousness' acted in a similar way: they left the cultivated land as if it were unclean Egypt, went into the wilderness, dwelt in camps, and sought to prepare the way for the coming God. How did that happen?

Probably the translation of the old Sinai tradition into the life of a second-century BCE Jewish community was exclusively the work of the 'Teacher of Righteousness': the much-admired monastic life of the Qumran community goes back to him. The people of Israel had been defined ideally at Sinai as 'God's holy possession and a kingdom of priests' (Exodus 19.5f.). The response to this designation was the unanimous declaration, 'Everything that the Lord commands, we will do!' (Exodus 19.8).

God's first instruction related to the ritual purification of the people as preparation for the appearance of God: 'Go to the people and order them to be clean today and tomorrow and to wash their clothes and be ready for the day after' (Exodus 19.10f.). Sexual continence was also part of this readiness: 'Let no man approach a woman' (Exodus 19.15). The 'Teacher of Righteousness' used this commandment of sanctification together with the ordinance for priestly service (Ezekiel 44) to shape the holy, ascetic monastic community life in Qumran. Here the temporal limits to the instruction about for purity and continence were removed and it was extended from three days to an indeterminate period: one could not know when God would appear for judgment, and people wanted to be ready at any time. Moreover, what according to Ezekiel 44 was to apply to priestly service in the temple was, as it were, democratized and extended to the laity, because priests and laity at Sinai formed a 'congregation', in unanimous obedience to God.

This people of God, the 'congregation' (Hebrew *yaḥad*), with priestly purity, performed a holy service with cultic significance. In the wilderness of Judah, away from Jerusalem, in accordance with the Community Rule they formed a living sanctuary as a 'kingdom of priests', 'to expiate for the land' (1QS 8.8f.,6). The royal priesthood of the Qumran community was to achieve what the sacrificial cult in the Jerusalem temple was meant to achieve but could not because of its impure priesthood; it was to expiate for the polluted land and in this way protect it from the divine judgment. The sacrificial praise of lips, liturgy in harmony with the angels in heaven and the works of the law were better than the incense and animal sacrifices in the Jerusalem sanctuary (1QS 9.4f.). The surrender to God's community of one's own life, of the whole person with its spiritual and physical power, and of one's private possessions (1QS 1.11f.) was the presupposition for participation in the service of the royal priesthood. For in this community the personal properties and possessions of the worldly person were purified by God's truth; only then did they have expiating power (1QS 1.12f.).

Jesus, too, took up this Sinai tradition and transformed it for eschatological service. But as Messiah he did not so much follow the example of Israel as that of Moses, the 'first Redeemer'. So

Matthew rightly modelled Jesus' Sermon on the Mount on what
happened on Sinai: Jesus goes up the mountain and speaks to
the people camped before him, the Israel of the new covenant
(Matthew 5.1). He himself proclaims the God who rescues from
slavery (Matthew 5.3-12; cf. Exodus 19.4) and the destiny of the
true people of God, extending this beyond Israel and transforming
it: the kingdom of priests will be realized by Israel becoming the
salt of the earth and the light of the world and doing its good
works before men (Matthew 5.13-16; cf. Exodus 19.5f.). And he
alone says the great 'yes' to the unlimited doing of the will of God:
'I have not come to abolish the law or the prophets. I have not
come to abolish but to fulfil' (Matthew 5.17; cf. Exodus 19.8).
This fulfilment comes about through the doing of the better
righteousness (Matthew 5.20) and through performing the commandment to love (Matthew 5.43-48).

## The great difference: Jesus' concern for sinners

Jesus differed from the ethic of the Qumran community in his
radical interpretation of the love commandment in the Sermon
on the Mount. The Qumran community thought, as its Rule says,
that they must 'love all that God has chosen and hate all that he
has rejected; that they must abstain from all evil and hold fast to
all good; that they must practise truth, righteousness and justice
upon earth' (1QS 1,3-6). It is striking that this ethical maxim has
a theological foundation and is orientated on the action of God;
because he has foreseen and predestined good and evil, the
children of light and the children of darkness; because in their
actions and way of life they are fulfilling God's glorious plan until
the judgment and final separation (1QS 3.13-4.8), people should
also follow this decision in dealings with their fellow human
beings and love those whom God has chosen, but not those who
are rejected by him.

When Jesus interpreted the commandment to love one's neighbour for the people of the new covenant, he could similarly
point to God's exemplary action. Here he probably had the
interpretation given in Qumran in view when in the last of his
antitheses he said: 'You have heard it said that you shall love your
neighbour and hate your enemy' (Matthew 5.43). Hatred of the

enemy is nowhere commanded in the Old Testmaent. But it is in the Community Rule of Qumran, where there is a direct reference to God. Jesus contradicted this interpretation with his messianic authority: 'But I say to you: love your enemies and pray for those who persecute you, that you may be sons of your Father in heaven. For he makes his sun rise on the good and evil and the rain fall on the just and unjust' (Mathew 5.44f.). Thus it is no longer the action of God in election, before time, hidden and far transcending human wisdom, that is to be normative for our actions towards one another, but the goodness of God, experienced daily and made evident through sunshine and rain, which he gives to all creatures without distinction. Jesus' theology and his interpretation of the commandment to love is not governed by belief in God's predestination but by trust in the providence and concern of the heavenly Father (Matthew 6.19-34).

The different pictures of God have consequences for the nature of this service to the world, which is particularly urgent in view of the imminent coming of the kingdom of God and the threat of judgment. As the community of the 'Teacher of Righteousness' reckoned on the predestining action of God, its commitment to human salvation was limited. In its holy settlement it could await the coming of the elect, who as 'volunteers' begged for admission to the community of salvation (1QS 5.1-4). On the basis of their notion of priestly purity, which was governed by Ezekiel 44, the pious of Qumran wanted to keep themselves free from the world and unsullied. For only the worship of a holy people and a royal priesthood could have an expiating effect and preserve the land of Israel from judgment. The bond to the priestly Torah and the extension of it to the whole community thus called for detachment from the world, if holy service was to be successful and well-pleasing to God.

By contrast, Jesus went into the unclean world and addressed his preaching of repentance to it as an invitation to the kingdom of God (Matthew 4.17-25). He understood his messianic task as being in accord with the limitless commandment to love: he was particularly aware of being sent to the lost sheep of Israel (Matthew 15.24) and wanted to gather the whole people together and win them for the rule of God, the doing of the better righteousness, and the new covenant. It was not Ezekiel 44, the

Magna Carta for perfect priestly service, but Ezekiel 34, the chapter about the good shepherd, that defined Jesus' attitude to Israel. And because the quality of a royal shepherd is revealed by concern for the sick and the strays among the flock (Ezekiel 34.4, 12, 16), Jesus turned especially to the outsiders in Israel (Mark 2.17); he sought the lost (Luke 15). The ritual commandments about cleanness and the democratization of the priestly Torah were an obstacle to such proceedings which Jesus resolutely broke through (Mark 7); this removal of the barriers of cultic purity prepared the way for the gospel to the Gentiles and thus made possible the world mission of the apostles after Easter.

The gathering of Israel and service to publicans and sinners would also have stood in the way of a Zealot zeal for the political liberation and theocratic purification of Israel, although it is precisely this that is now once again attributed to the Jesus movement by authors like Baigent and Leigh and Eisenman. But Jesus's teaching and activity was anti-Zealot. He warned against condemning one's brothers in court and against fanatical actions: one is not allowed to exterminate the impure and the godless from the people of God by violence and to remove the tares from the wheat before God's harvest (Matthew 13.24-30). That was the goal of the Zealot Sicarii who believed that they had to purify Israel and for God's greater glory rid it by murder of collaborators with Rome. Rather, the people of God had to be saved and purified by the Son of man/Messiah understanding himself as servant of God and giving his own life for the many (Mark 10.45). He expiates by such a ransom, not for the land, but for the people of God, whom he saves from their sins (Matthew 1.21). The vicarious expiating death of the Christ and Son of God had an effect which extended beyond the boundaries of Israel, precisely because he revealed eschatologically the love of God for both just and unjust. The forgiveness of sins and the righteousness which stands before God are now no longer earned by fulfilling the law but through faith alone.

This universal saving significance of the cross of Christ was the real basis for the world mission and expansion of Christianity to the ends of the then known world. Missionary recruitment to the faith was unknown at that time among both Jews and Gentiles. It clearly goes back to Jesus. The sending out and authentication of the twelve disciples to whom Jesus delegated his own task deviates from the attitude of the Qumran pious, nor is it prepared for in the Old Testament in this form: they were to drive out demons, heal the sick and lepers, and proclaim that the kingdom of God had come very near (Matt.10.17f.). In this way his messianic activity was continued further by way of mission. The disciples whom the master had called to discipleship and to his community were now sent out as apostles. This centrifugal, expanding power of the service of Jesus stands in opposition to the centripetal tendency of the activity of the 'Teacher of Righteousness' and his building up of a community in Qumran. For there the whole concern was for the demarcation, security and defence of the small group of the faithful: the community is described not only as a sanctuary but also, in the hymns of praise, as a fortified city which has to assert itself against the onslaught of godlessness, the eschatological unleashing of the powers of chaos (1QH 6.26ff.). By contrast, Jesus went on the offensive in his battle against evil;[9] he broke into the fortified house of the 'strong man' – the devil – to rob him of his booty, captive human beings (Matthew 12.29).

## Qumran and the life-style of Jesus' disciples

We also find in the Gospels the twofold life-style which is stamped by the expectation of the rule of God: in some respects it is related to the common life of the Essenes.[10] Jesus and his disciples formed a community which had detached itself from the normal Jewish way of life, but constantly remained in agricultural territory. They had given up their ties to jobs, family and village community: Peter could say to Jesus, 'Behold, we have left all and followed you!' (Mark 10.28). Jesus' answer stresses the need to leave the family group for his sake (Mark 10.29f.). 'Anyone who loves father or mother more than me is not worthy of me' (Matthew 10.37). The 'Teacher of Righteousness' and his disciples formed a kind of spiritual family which took the place of physical parents, brothers and sisters, as the hymns show (1QH 7.20-22; 9.33f.).

Jesus could describe those who do the will of God as his true relations (Mark 3.35), and his disciples were to be like brothers to each other (Matthew 23.8). Like John the Baptist, he himself was unmarried. This was quite exceptional among the Jews of the time, apart from the Qumran Essenes. Among these, celibacy was based on the imminent expectation of the holy God and on priestly principles: Jesus was celibate for the sake of the kingdom of God. He may have been thinking of the Essenes when he made the obscure remark about 'eunuchs of the kingdom of heaven' (Matthew 19.10-12). By that he meant people who in the face of the coming great change and the demand for the whole person renounced marriage and family for the kingdom of God. The apostle Paul took the same line: because of the imminent eschatological tribulation it is good not to be married (I Corinthians 7.26); the unmarried are concerned for the Lord's affairs (I Corinthians 7.32).

The twelve disciples, too, shared their possessions. They had a common purse from which their meals were paid for and the poor were looked after. Judas Iscariot, who carried it (John 13.29), was their steward. And as among the Essenes, such communal meals were held in anticipation of the messianic age, of complete 'community' at the supper in the kingdom of God. However, whereas in Qumran the meal was confined to full members, as those who were completely clean, the meals where Jesus was head of the table were open to all possible guests: that is shown, for example, by the Feeding of the Five Thousand in the wilderness (Mark 6.35ff.). And just as Jesus could sit at table with some Pharisees (Luke 7.36-50), so too he could eat with publicans like Levi (Mark 2.13-17) and Zacchaeus (Luke 19.7). It is also worth noting that the earliest Jerusalem community broke bread in each other's houses, so that the common meals of the disciples with Jesus and the sharing of possessions continued (Acts 2.42-27). In addition there were also pious people who supported Jesus' cause, just as the second order of Essenes (those who were married) may have provided support for the nucleus living in the wilderness. These supporters included the married women who according to Luke 8.1-3 provided for the disciples out of their resources. The verb 'serve' is a specifically Christian term orientated on the model of Jesus (Mark 10.45; John 13), but the substance of such service could also be found in the Qumran community. This service is also characteristic of Jesus' three friends living together in Bethany. Mary, Martha and Lazarus were not married; perhaps they originally belonged to the 'second order' of Essenes living outside the monastery.[11] They welcomed Jesus and his disciples and gave them hospitality (Luke 10.38-42). According to Josephus, such hospitality was characteristic of the Essenes: 'When adherents arrive from elsewhere, all local resources are put at their disposal as if they were their own, and men they have never seen before entertain them like old friends' (*Jewish War* II, 124). Jesus, too, approached this family in the same matter-of-course way. The figures depicted by Luke in his infancy story, Zechariah and Elizabeth, Joseph and Mary, Simeon and Anna, have the piety of the humble or the poor (*'anawim*) which characterized the Essenes.[12] They are people who set their hope wholly on God, from whom they expect the eschatological consolation, the redemption of Israel.

### Qumran and the so-called 'historical Jesus'

On 10 December 1991, Norddeutscher Rundfunk broadcast a television programme on the Dead Sea Scrolls taken from the USA, in which Robert H. Eisenman had a central role as the expert. The ending differed from the American original by stating: 'Perhaps the history of Christianity has to be rewritten. The historical Jesus will have to be separated from the Christ of faith. For the church this is a blasphemous undertaking. For the church, historical and archaeological research has always been an instrument of the devil. Rightly, as we now see.'[13] This verdict is as stupid as it is offensive. The churches have never seen historical and archaeological research as such as an instrument of the devil, but have encouraged it and carried it on successfully, particularly in the Holy Land. For more than a century organizations like the Palestine Exploration Fund, the American Schools of Oriental Research and the German Association for Research into Palestine have been working alongside many other foreign schools and institutes in geographical and archaeological research into the land and its biblical sites. The results of this work help the exegesis of the Bible; they have led both to the confirmation and to the correction of previous assumptions.

The same applies to the Qumran texts. Their discovery was sensational; their content has surpassed the first expectations and of course has also given us more precise knowledge about Judaism, the environment of Jesus and the New Testament writings. But that has not essentially changed the historical picture of Jesus or shaken belief in Christ – on the contrary! All divergent hypotheses have swiftly disappeared from the scene, and we can forecast that the same thing will happen even to what now seem to be bestsellers. Their Jesus figures are like snowmen which quickly melt in the sunshine of serious scholarship.

One need only recall two events from the past history of research. The reports of the Mari texts (from the beginning of the second millennium BCE) about court prophets in this Syrian city on the Euphrates can be compared with accounts of the emergence of the classical prophets of the Bible. But the uniqueness of the revelation given to the prophets for the people of Israel becomes clear precisely because there are similar themes and even details in the surrounding world.

The Gnostic documents which were found in 1945 in Nag Hammadi in Egypt have also had the positive effect of disillusioning those exegetes who thought that Paul's or John's picture of Christ was stamped by Gnosticism or produced the dualism of the Fourth Gospel. The discoveries show that Gnosticism belongs in church history and not in the prehistory of the New Testament.[14] Gnosticism is a Christian heresy; we know no real Gnostic text from the period before the New Testament. By contrast, the Essene Qumran community is earlier than the Christian church. In its writings we find the best parallels to the dualism that encounters us in the Johannine writings, namely the ethically relevant opposition of light to darkness, truth to lie, children of light to children of darkness, spirit of truth to spirit of lies. The forms of thought and language in the Fourth Gospel are therefore not Hellenistic and Gnostic but Jewish, and have their roots in Palestine.

The Qumran writings are also a great help over many difficult questions relating to the trial of Jesus.[15] Against the background of the exegesis of the important passage Deut.21.22-23 which is offered in the Temple Scroll (11QTemple 64,6-13), the whole proceedings against Jesus become clearer. In the Temple Scroll the hanging of the delinquent 'on the tree' (Deut.21.22f.) is interpreted as crucifixion, to punish the crime of high treason against the people of God. The proceedings before the Sanhedrin with the hearing of witnesses, the question about messiahship and the condemnation of Jesus which Mark depicts in a highly concentrated way (Mark 14.53-65) also makes complete sense in the light of other Qumran writings.[16] So the course of the trial of Jesus as reported in the Gospels seems historically well founded.[17] This is no legend born of the community's belief in Christ and the anti-Judaism of the evangelists, as has often been assumed.

To those who claim that the history of Christianity must be rewritten, the answer must be: while the history of Christianity happened only once, new accounts of it need constantly to be written. This task is not an unfortunate 'must', now forced on us by the Qumran texts. Since Luke's Acts of the Apostles and Eusebius' *Church History* attempts have been made again and again, with joy and not with the resolve of despair. That will also continue to be the case in the future. The terms and notions offered by the Qumran scrolls are finding a place in the biblical lexicons, the commentaries on the New Testament, the books on Jesus and the accounts of the theologies of Paul or John: everything is gratefully received. The editing of the Qumran texts is, of course, still incomplete, but no sensational discoveries or shakings of Christianity are to be expected.[18] Nor is the 'consensus' over the identification of the Qumran community with the Essenes seriously endangered. Nevertheless, there is much detailed work to be done, by Jewish and Christian biblical scholars. Topics like 'Qumran and early Judaism' or 'the Qumran writings and the New Testament' will be important subjects for a long time yet.

As for the call to separate the historical Jesus from the Christ of faith, that is no shattering new enterprise for Christian theology. Such a distinction was made precisely a century ago by the conservative theologian Martin Kähler (1835-1912). His work, which was very influential, bore the title *The So-Called Historical Jesus and the Historic, Biblical Christ*.[19] In it Kähler stressed that the Christ attested by the Bible, proclaimed by the church and at work in its history is to be distinguished from the constantly changing, subjective and therefore very short-lived pictures which are given the label 'historical Jesus'. This is true of Jesus novels like that of Ernest Renan and of *The Dead Sea Scrolls Deception* or Barbara Thiering's Jesus *pesher*. But the Qumran writings in particular can also help us to see that the 'historic Christ' of the Bible is not simply different from the Jesus of Nazareth who can be discovered by historians: he knew himself to be called by God as Messiah and connected this task in a unique manner with the way of the suffering servant of God.[20]

# Did the Essenes turn to Jesus as Messiah?

The similarities between Qumran and earliest Christianity –
From the pious of the Persian period to the penitential movement of John the Baptist – The Essene quarter in Jerusalem and
the earliest community – Positive and negative influences of
converted Essenes – The significance of the Qumran texts for
the New Testament

## *The similarities between Qumran and earliest Christianity*

The sensationalized Qumran books, beginning with Johannes
Lehmann's *Jesus-Report*,[1] are based on the fact that there are
indeed phrases, interpretative techniques and forms of life and
thought which were common to the Qumran Essenes and the first
Christians. This was in no way concealed by Christian Qumran
scholars from the beginning, as Michael Baigent and Richard
Leigh claim.[2] Certainly there were occasionally attempts largely
to dispute the present similarities, but such unnecessary apologetic
concerns remain a minority activity.[3] There are many articles
by Christian scholars, and among them in particular Catholic
scholars, on the topic of Qumran, Jesus and early Christianity
which investigate the parallels between the Qumran writings and
the New Testament without prejudice. The results of this work
were made accessible to wide circles in a whole series of books
and collections of articles in English.[4] (There were valuable
German accounts in the 1950s and 1960s, but they are now out
of print.)[5] We have already pointed out that scholars in Germany
over the last thirty years have really neglected to inform an
interested public to any degree.

The similarities between Qumran and the New Testament were,
moreover, uncongenial not only to some conservative Christians
but, interestingly, also to some Jewish scholars. Thus the famous

Qumran patron Manfred R.Lehman, who himself has contributed some articles to Qumran research as an amateur scholar, writes: 'The members of the covenant community [of Qumran] were Sadducees and not Essenes, and as Sadducees they had a much stricter attitude to the halakah (the oral tradition of the law) than the authentic Pharisaic rabbis in Jerusalem. One consequence of this is that the widespread popular idea that the scrolls represent a kind of genealogical link between Christianity and Judaism is totally false... We must reject the often repeated assertion of *The New York Times* and others that [Jewish] Christianity and "rabbinic Judaism" were born at the same time. That is a misleading claim. Authentic Judaism goes back 3500 years. Christianity came into being around 1800 (!) years ago from a mixture of pagan rites and Pauline doctrines.'[6]

We have seen that a Sadducean origin of the Dead Sea Scrolls is untenable (Ch.3). In other respects, too, many Jewish scholars today would contradict such claims, perhaps if not publicly in a journal article, certainly in the protected area of scholarly publications. The completely unbroken line of tradition between Moses and present-day orthodox Judaism is a historical fiction. Pharisees, Sadducees and Essenes were Jewish religious parties which came into being at approximately the same time, in the Hasmonean period. Before 70 CE it had still by no means been decided which of these religious parties represented Judaism at its most authentic. Even rabbinic Judaism after 70 was not an uninterrupted continuation of the Pharisaism of the previous period.

Christianity came into being before 70 CE, and in the form of Jewish Christianity; externally it first seemed to be a new Jewish religious party. A comparison with the Qumran texts shows time and again how Jewish the New Testament is. Nor does that seem surprising, since with perhaps one exception the authors of the New Testament writings were Jews. The controversies over the Jewish character of ancient Jewish Christianity are not just a thing of the past. How one answers the historical questions will also have an effect on whether Jewish Christians today can be full citizens of the state of Israel.

We must be cautious about any straight-line explanation of the contacts between the Qumran writings and the New Testament.

One reason for some parallels is simply that both Essenes and Christians lived by the Old Testament. But that is far from being a complete explanation. At least two other explanations must be added, to which brief reference will be made here. Many of the first followers of Jesus came from that great religious movement of the *ḥasidim* which begins to surface from the Persian period on. Essenes, Pharisees, baptist groups and Jewish Christians drew on this broad apocalyptic stream of tradition. But even that is not in itself the whole answer to our question. The assumption that has already often been made, that some Essenes were also Christians, has now been corroborated by modern archaeological findings. So we shall pursue briefly the source of some renewal movements in Judaism after the Babylonian exile, down to the New Testament period.

## From the pious of the Persian period to the penitential movement of John the Baptist

The roots of the Judaism of the time of Jesus lie above all also in the fourth and third centuries BCE, when after the return of Jews from the Babylonian exile Palestine was under the rule of the great Persian kings. Unfortunately we have relatively few historical sources for this period, so many details remain obscure to us.[7] Already before the period of the Maccabaean fight for freedom, around 175 BCE the 'assembly of the pious' (*synagoge Asidaion*) represented a fixed group in Judaism (I Maccabees 2.42). Otto Plöger has demonstrated the probability that their prehistory extends far back into the Persian period.[8] The pre-Maccabean 'pious' nurtured prophetic traditions – though in a form which was on the way to apocalyptic – and were perhaps really the spiritual heirs of earlier 'prophetic conventicles' (cf. Ezekiel 8.1; 14.1ff.; 33.31). We cannot exclude the possibility that the voice of the 'community of the pious' (*qᵉhal ḥasidim*) can already be heard in some late post-exilic psalms (like 149.1) and some apocryphal Qumran psalms (11QPsᵃ 18.4). Many scholars also assume that this Jewish pietistic movement stands behind the Maccabaean parts of the book of Daniel (e.g. chs. 11-12). The 'pious' were characterized above all by faithfulness to the Torah, intensive research into scripture, regular prayer and a tendency to asceticism (fasting), and they came from a not particularly well-to-do sector of the population. In this connection the term 'poor' (Hebrew *'ebyon* or *'anaw*) had already taken on a religious colouring in the pre-New Testament period.[9]

During the rule of the Hasmonaean king and high priest Jonathan (152-143 BCE) the Essene community was founded under the leadership of the 'Teacher of Righteousness', and soon afterwards it split off from the Pharisaic movement. As well as the development within Palestine, there were perhaps also links between early Essenism and the Babylonian Diaspora.[10] In addition to the lay piety of the Hasidim, which was shaped by prophecy and apocalyptic, there was a markedly priestly element among the Essenes (probably above all via the 'Teacher of Righteousness'). We can go on to ask whether traditions of the Rechabites (Jeremiah 35.1-19; Nehemiah 3.14) did not also have an influence here.[11]

Now life tends to be varied. So it is most improbable that all the pre-Maccabean Hasidim went the way of exclusive Essenism or strict Pharisaism.[12] There could have been 'pious' who, like the Essenes, regarded the old priestly solar calendar as divinely willed, but did not make the observance of it a precondition for continuing to take part in the temple cult. The Pharisaic communities (*ḥaburot*) in the making also probably took over the Hasidic legacy with varying degrees of strictness. There were possibly Pharisees who to a large degree shared in the theological convictions and attitudes which were otherwise customary for the Essenes. That is far from saying that Robert Eisenman's theories about the mix of Jewish nationalist groups in the New Testament period is right. There really were Essenes, Pharisees and Zealots to whom one could attribute clearly defined basic convictions. However, there is no need to dispute certain contacts and overlaps between the groups.

It is very important always to remember that Essenism did not just undergo a two hundred-year history, but represented quite a broad movement which was in no way limited to the desert monastery of Qumran and its branch settlements. Both Philo (*Apology* 1) and Josephus (*Jewish War* II, 124) agree in attesting that there were Essenes throughout Palestine. Furthermore it is becoming increasingly clear that the 'land of Damascus' which is mentioned many times in the Damascus Rule (CD 6.5ff.; 7.15ff.; 8.21; 19.34; 20.12) is not a code name for Babylon or Qumran but in fact denotes the neighbourhood of the Syrian metropolis. Here and elsewhere in northern Transjordan there were Essene settlements[13] about which we are also given important evidence above all by the Copper Scroll of Qumran (3Q15). The regulations of the Damascus Rule, which do not seem to have been quite as exclusive as other Qumran writings, seem above all to relate to these settlements. The married branch of the Essenes may in any case have had closer contact with the rest of the Jewish population than the elite in the monastic settlement of Qumran. It is striking that the Damascus Rule seems to expect only one Messiah figure. So some Essene groups could have been closer than others to the mainstream of pious Judaism in some of their theological convictions.

John the Baptist's great movement of baptism and penitence was prepared for by the Hasidim and Essenes. There is much to be said for the claim that John originally came from an Essene background.[14] His diet (Mark 1.6) resembled that of an Essene living outside the community settlements.[15] Perhaps John wanted to make it clear by observing the strict rules of purity that he had not separated from the Essene movement lightly, but had been set on a new way by God's prophetic call (Luke 1.80). John baptized above all in places near to Essene settlements.[16] The tradition behind the Johannine writings, with its priestly stamp, could be related to the Essenes through John the Baptist.[17]

The family of Jesus might also have belonged to the wider circle of the hasidic movement.[18] The language in the birth stories in Luke 1-2 and in the Lucan special tradition generally has a kind of Hebrew stamp and comes close to linguistic forms and notions which have their closest parallels in the Qumran writings.[19] The expression 'men in whom (God) is well pleased' (Luke 2.14) is only the most famous example of that (cf. 1QH 4.32f.; 11.9).[20] An old problem of textual criticism here could be resolved by the Qumran text.[21]

A quite conservative Protestant biblical lexicon edited by Fritz Rienecker in 1960 put forward the suggestion, in the light of the Qumran writings, that 'a connection with the Jewish circles which were waiting for God's saviour (Luke 1; 2.27-38) does not seem

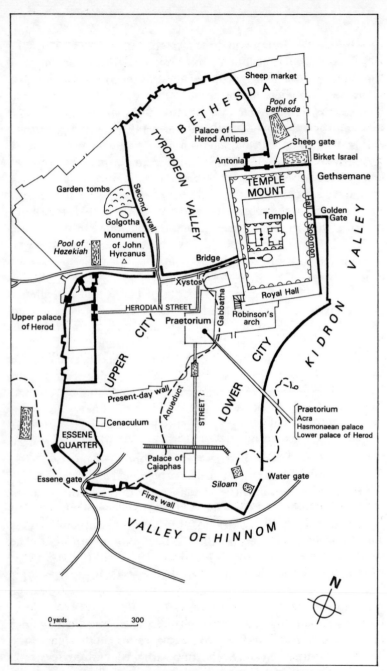

10 Jerusalem in the New Testament period (B. Pixner)

to be ruled out.'[22] The Catholic scholars Rudolf Mayer and Joseph Reuss made similar comments. They were looking for an answer to the puzzle that while the New Testament mentions Sadducees, Pharisees, Sicarii and probably also Zealots, it does not mention the Essenes: 'Perhaps the members of the Qumran community, like the Essenes, are included in that group which is described as "those who were waiting for the kingdom of God" (cf. Mark 15.43; Luke 23.51; 2.25; 2.38).'[23] If Jesus could draw followers even from the wider circle of the pious Hasidim, the question how the Essenes reacted to the earliest Christians' post-Easter proclamation of the cross and resurrection of Jesus becomes even more urgent.

## The Essene quarter in Jerusalem and the earliest community

We know for certain that some former Pharisees became Christians. The apostle Paul is only the most famous example (Philippians 3.5). There is some *a priori* probability that individual Essenes also attached themselves to the new messianic faith. Indeed many scholars see the remark in Acts 'and a great many of the priests became obedient to the faith' (6.7) as a reference to the conversion of Essenes.[24] The high-priestly party of the Sadducees was generally hostile to the earliest community, but in contrast to the Essenes with their marked priestly stamp they were a lay movement. But presumably Essenes became members of the first church at a still earlier period.

One of the most beautiful parts of the present-day Old City of Jerusalem is the south-west hill which is now called Mount Zion. The local Christian tradition has transferred the earliest Christian community's first meeting-place there.[25] As this local tradition can be traced back in the sources to the end of the first and beginning of the second century CE, it may be regarded as reliable.[26] In the immediate vicinity of the place to which the local Christian tradition leads (diagram 11), the Benedictine archaeologist Bargil Pixner has excavated a gate from New Testament times.[27] It can only be that gate which Flavius Josephus calls the 'Essene Gate' (*Jewish War* V, 145). Since the great English

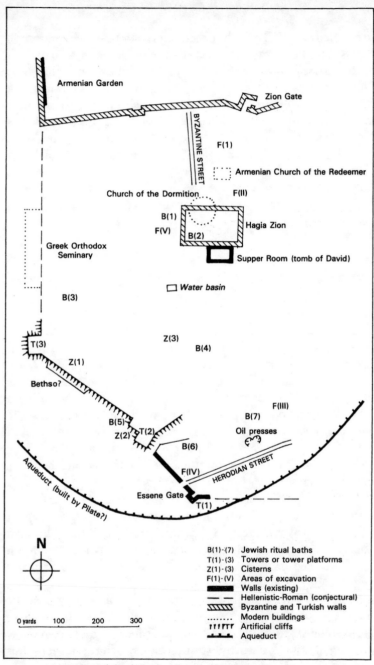

Armenian Garden

Zion Gate

BYZANTINE STREET

F(1)

Armenian Church of the Redeemer

Church of the Dormition

F(II)

B(1)

F(V)

B(2)

Hagia Zion

Supper Room (tomb of David)

Greek Orthodox Seminary

Water basin

B(3)

Z(3)

B(4)

T(3)

Z(1)

Bethso?

F(III)

B(7)

Oil presses

B(5)

Z(2)

T(2)

B(6)

F(IV)

HERODIAN STREET

Aqueduct (built by Pilate?)

Essene Gate

T(1)

N

0 yards    100    200    300

B(1)-(7)    Jewish ritual baths
T(1)-(3)    Towers or tower platforms
Z(1)-(3)    Cisterns
F(1)-(V)    Areas of excavation
▬▬▬    Walls (existing)
– – –    Hellenistic-Roman (conjectural)
\\\\\\    Byzantine and Turkish walls
......    Modern buildings
ⲧⲧⲧⲧⲧⲧ    Artificial cliffs
▬▬▬    Aqueduct

11 Plan of the Jerusalem Essene Quarter (R. Riesner)

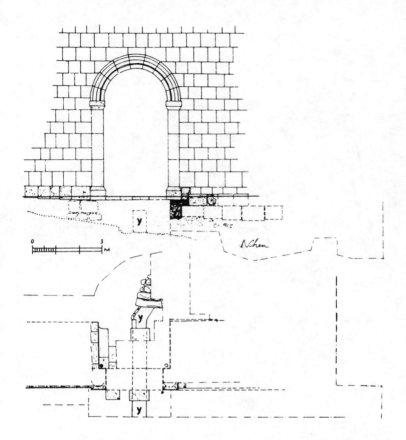

*12. The Essene gate – excavation and reconstruction by D. Chen, 1989. View
from outside the gate.*

*y = drain*

*The unfinished work connected with the insertion of the Herodian gate into The
Hasmonaean wall can be seen clearly under the right flank-stone.*

scholar J.B.Lightfoot,[28] scholars have continually argued that the
name of the gate derives from an Essene settlement in Jerusalem.[29]
Very large ritual baths comparable to those in the monastic
settlement of Qumran fit the assumption of such an Essene settlement well. The Essene quarter in Jerusalem is most likely to have
been formed at the beginning of the reign of Herod the Great (37-

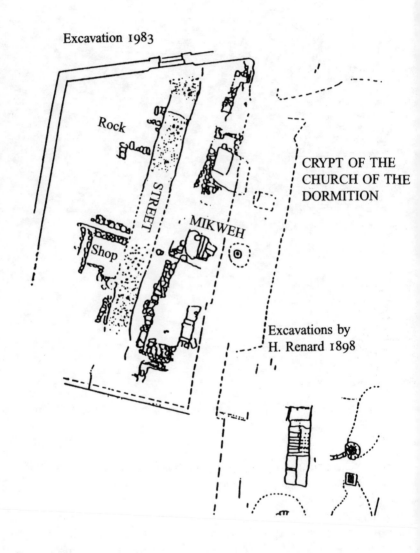

Excavation 1983

Rock

STREET

MIKWEH

Shop

CRYPT OF THE
CHURCH OF THE
DORMITION

Excavations by
H. Renard 1898

13. *Buildings from New Testament times on Mount Zion: plan of excavation and reconstruction following D. Chen and B. Pixner, 1991*

Isometric reconstruction

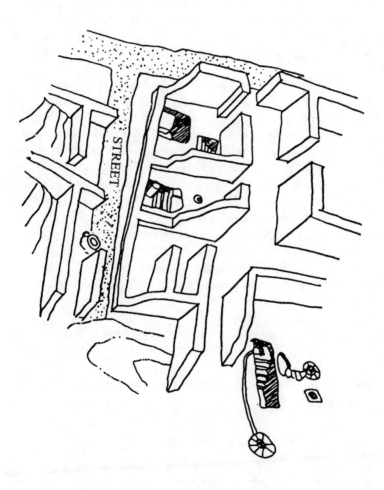

4 BCE).[30] At the beginning of his reign Herod was very well disposed towards the Essenes (*Jewish Antiquities* XV, 373-9). The assumption that Qumran was abandoned during the reign of this Jewish king, which still has good archaeological support, fits in with this.[31] Resettlement clearly took place on a smaller scale. That could indicate that only some of the Jerusalem Essenes returned to Qumran, perhaps the stricter and more exclusive ones.

According to the archaeological and literary evidence, then, Essenes and the earliest Christians lived as it were next door to each other in Jerusalem. There are possible recollections in the Pentecost account of the conversion of a significant number of Essenes.[32] There is mention of 'pious men dwelling in Jerusalem' (Acts 2.5). If we translate the Greek word for pious (*eulabes*) into Aramaic we get *hase'*. This term probably underlies the Graecized designation *Essenos*. Two observations in particular support Essene connections with Pentecost (Acts 2.1f.).

1. The way in which the Sinai event underlies Pentecost has clear parallels in Qumran texts.[33]

2. The striking life-style involving a strict sharing of possessions which initially characterized the greater part of the earliest Jerusalem community (Acts 2.44-45; 4.32-35) can best be explained as assimilation to an Essene environment.[34]

If the first Jerusalem community developed in the lee of the Essene quarter, which had a kind of religious autonomy, it would also be easier to explain how the first Christians could remain in the Holy City, though it was dominated by the enemies who had executed their master.

## Positive and negative influences of converted Essenes

As among the newly converted Pharisees, so too among the Essenes who came to believe, there were some whose prior background made them a gain and some who became a danger for early Christianity. While Ebionitism was not the original form of Palestinian Jewish Christianity, as Hans-Joachim Schoeps thought,[35] it had evidently been a danger from earliest times. Traces of this Jewish Christian heresy with its striking points of contact with Essene ideas can be traced down to the Pseudo-

Clementine literature of the second and third centuries CE.[36] Jewish scholars in particular also believe that Hebrews is a critical discussion of ideas which could have formed among Jewish Christians under Essene influence.[37] Above all Jean Daniélou, the great expert on Jewish Christianity, investigated the influence of an Essene trend in Jewish Christianity.[38]

But let us keep to those converted Essenes who with their prior background represented an enrichment for the early church. An influential trend in research into the Gospels was founded by Rudolf Bultmann[39] and Martin Dibelius.[40] This so-called 'classical form criticism' expressed its widespread scepticism about the tradition in the first three Gospels. Two main points were made in the argument. 1. The Christians of the first two centuries belonged to the uneducated classes and therefore were neither willing nor able to hand down a reliable tradition about Jesus. 2. They had written virtually nothing because they had an ardent expectation of the end of the times. A comparison with Qumran is very helpful in connection with these assertions, above all if one thinks in terms of converted Essenes.

Like the first Christians, the Qumran Essenes lived in the expectation of an imminent end of the world. But that does not mean that they were mere messengers before the end. Rather, precisely for this reason the intensive study of Holy Scripture was of prime importance to them; according to the Community Rule a quarter of the daily routine was devoted to it (1QS 6.6-8).[41] It is quite striking how often the Essenes and the earliest Christians refer to a quite specific group of Old Testament texts.[42] We may have the same exegetical tradition here. Of course it must have begun with Essenes and not Christians. Despite their tense expectation of the end the inhabitants of Qumran were not dissuaded from writing. Rather, their book production was immense, and not just in the late period of the group, as radio carbon testing has recently shown. Neither among them nor – to judge by the analogy of present-day Christian charismatic movements in which 'of the making of many books there is no end' (Ecclesiastes 12.12) – in earliest Christianity can the intensive activity of the Holy Spirit have been an obstacle to writing things down.

The text *miqsat ma'ase ha-torah* from Cave 4, which has not been published so far, is particularly interesting for the question

1. Essene Gate (Josephus, archaeology)
2. South-west tower of the city wall
3. Way through Gehinnom to Bethlehem and path along the southern wall
4. Street from the Essene gate to the city centre (archaeology)
5. Oil press and steps (archaeology), which led to the east gate (Copper Scroll) of the monastic part of the Essene quarter
6. Drainage channel which ran along street 4 and emptied out into Gehinnom here (archaeology)
7. Entry into Essene monastic area (Copper Scroll)
8. Guest house (KATALYMA, Mark 14.14) with room for supper
9. Ritual baths (archaeology) outside the city wall (cf. Deut. 23.10) with a gate for escape (MANOS, Copper Scroll)
10. Water supply for nos. 7 and 9 (archaeology)
11. Water cistern under the city wall (Copper Scroll, archaeology)
12. Tel Kochlit (Copper Scroll)
13. Two ritual baths within the monastery complex (Copper Scroll, archaeology)
14. Peristyle with large cistern (?Copper Scroll)
15. Bethso (Essene latrines: Josephus, Temple Scroll)
16. War tower (*Milham*, Copper Scroll)
17. Wall around the monastery area; behind it the garden of the Herodian palace
18. Aqueduct (of Pontius Pilate?) to the Temple Court (archaeology)
19. Valley of Hinnom (Gehenna)

# The Essene Quarter
## Reconstruction

of the formation of the earliest Christian tradition. As we have seen, this is probably a letter by the 'Teacher of Righteousness', i.e. the founder of the group (ch.3). Fragments of at least six copies of the letter are extant, which shows how important it was for the community to preserve the teaching of its founder. Given such a contemporary example, it is difficult to understand why the first Christians should not have written about Jesus until twenty years at the earliest after the cross and resurrection. Using other arguments, Rudolf Pesch[43] and Gerd Theissen[44] now put the composition of essential elements of the Synoptic tradition before 40 CE. If converted Essenes had come upon the earliest community, it would have included a group with a developed scribal training who knew how to deal with tradition.[45] We must also be careful not to assign well-considered theological statements automatically to a later period. Rather, such doctrinal convictions can be very early and Palestinian.

## The significance of the Qumran texts for the New Testament

To sum up, the significance of the Qumran discoveries, which is hardly to be underestimated, lies in the fact that here beyond question we have documents which show us the faith of pious Jews before the emergence of Jesus. What is particularly illuminating for us is the eager expectation of the coming of the messianic age, and the interpretation of Holy Scripture which arises from this. So we may reckon that a whole group of Essenes were converted to Jesus as the Messiah. These converted Essenes formed a body of theologians who were highly qualified for their time. They were capable of working out at a deep intellectual level who Jesus was and how he had brought salvation. A comparison with the Qumran texts shows that New Testament expressions and notions which many people regarded as Greek and late are, rather, Palestinian and early. That applies to such disputed parts of the New Testament as the Gospel of John and the first chapter of Acts. The early church reflected a great deal on the way in which God had already prepared for the revelation of the gospel in the course of world history. They thought, for example, of the bringing together of the then world into the one political unit of the Roman empire or of the dissemination of

Greek. Perhaps despite all the clear differences, we may reckon that the Essene movement, too, is part of this preparation for the gospel.

# Postscript

The great renewal of interest in the Qumran scrolls over the past five years is a remarkable phenomenon. There are both welcome and suspicious reasons for the strong public interest. It can only be welcome that recently people have increasingly come to realize that we can judge the present properly only if we know history. That explains why we should pay particular attention to the beginnings of Christianity. Finally, no other movement has shaped the Western world so markedly, both inwardly and outwardly, down to the present day. The awareness that a spiritual or religious movement which right from the start has been bound up with lies, hatred and violence must be greeted with the utmost scepticism is also correct. Furthermore the amazement, indeed the displeasure, of large groups at the extremely long delay over the last twenty years in the editing of the remaining unpublished Dead Sea Scrolls is also understandable.

The mixture of interest in unique ancient original documents and dissatisfaction at some of the events which have accompanied research into them has been exploited by some authors in a skilful but irresponsible campaign. Above all in Germany, these authors can use the neglect of serious scholarship to their advantage: the many non-specialists who are interested in the Qumran discoveries and the beginnings of Christianity have not been sufficiently informed. In particular, there have been no general books on Qumran, Jesus and the earliest church in Germany since the 1960s.

This vacuum made possible the great success of less valuable literature, indeed literature which falsifies the situation. It will not be easy to limit or indeed repair the damage that has been done. Those who come upon sensational claims often do not go on to read the later refutations, even if these have the truth on their side. That was the main reason why the authors of this book decided on speedy publication, something which always poses problems for scholars. Nevertheless it is better to give the interested public a rapid response which may perhaps be further enlarged on in the future than to leave the field to largely dubious claims and interpretations.

The great success of Barbara Thiering's book in Australia and of *The Dead Sea Scrolls Deception* in Germany is of course also connected with the spiritual mood in large parts of the Western world. Any book or programme which claims to be making disclosures or breaking tabus can reckon on high sales and viewing figures. Like many other phenomena, the rumpus over the alleged Vatican plot to suppress the Qumran texts indicates a deep crisis in our media society. Criteria seem to be completely lacking, not just in explosive ideological questions, but also in the purely academic sphere. If large publishing houses and influential media figures in future allow just about anything to be claimed as scholarship, the credibility crisis of the academic word will in due course become even greater than it is now. It was a necessary development that a critical eye should come to be cast on the scholarship of the first half of our century. But it would be equally wrong to replace credulity over scholarship with mere randomness. The controversy over the Qumran texts is a positive indication that scholars with very different world-views (Jews, atheists and Christians) can come to an agreement over many things, because there is a limit to the manipulation of facts.

The controversy over the Qumran scrolls is only one sign among many of the deep crisis in which the major churches at present find themselves. Certainly in the past, too, those who really believe were also only a minority in society. But at an earlier stage the churches to a remarkable degree succeeded in convincing large groups of the population – not through pressure but through solid information – that the New Testament account of Jesus and earliest Christianity corresponds to historical reality. Doubt about this arose at the periphery of the churches or outside them, but in the meantime it has penetrated deeply into their ranks. It is an ominous development that an influential trend in exegesis should have been uninterested in the historical charcter of the New Testament sources or even largely denied it. Here we have a repetition of an experience which occurs throughout missionary history: without a vivid and credible picture of the person and activity of Jesus, belief in him cannot be disseminated. The apostle Paul already knew this (Galatians 3.1). To the degree that the public are interested in Christian faith, they want a picture of Jesus. If they are not given it by serious scholars, then sensationally exaggerated fantasies have a hey-day.

It is certainly regrettable how many false and indeed slanderous theories are put forward about Jesus and earliest Christianity. But one could also put forward the view that dispute over the figure of Jesus is better than the deathly silence of complete lack of interest. Post-Christian Western society clearly cannot get rid of Jesus so easily. If people already do not believe in him, they at least want to prove that he either belongs completely in the sphere of religious legend or was one of the main freedom-fighters against the power of Rome. Where he may no longer be Son of God and Redeemer, people want at least to keep a sympathetic human being as a model. Whereas earlier they wanted unattainable ideal figures, Jesus is now to be a leading figure who was human, all too human. In a situation in Germany when towards the year 2000 every other marriage will end in divorce, it is of course reassuring to be able to refer to an allegedly divorced Jesus. Behind many so-called disclosures we can see the relief that there is now finally a reason for dismissing Christian faith. But underneath this there is often a remnant of bad conscience, indeed even a hidden desire that Jesus might be what the New Testament claims him to be.

So the sharp controversy over Jesus and the Qumran scrolls is in no way just a painful problem, but also a great opportunity. In the light of the Qumran texts it is becoming increasingly clear both how firmly rooted Jesus was in the Judaism of his time and what an unprecedented claim he made about his person. Like the pious people of Qumran, he lived by the Old Testament. But he interpreted the Old Testament with a direct divine authority and related it to himself in a way which far transcends the Essene awareness of being at the end of time. Jesus was a Jew and not the first Christian; however he was not just any Jew, but the Christ, the Messiah of Israel and the Redeemer of the whole world.

Essenism did not survive the catastrophe of 70. Its way of

believing may have been in some ways a preparation for Christianity, but in the end it was doomed to perish. Christianity not only survived the persecutions of the first centuries but has also survived the two anti-Christian ideologies of our century, and indeed has conquered both of them. That indicates that Christians do not live in heroic imitation of a past model, but in the power of the risen Lord. The Qumran community expected the resurrection of the dead, but this already began in history with the resurrection of Jesus. That is a decisive difference. The Qumran texts make the historical picture of Jesus more vivid, but they do not just reduce it to the level of ongoing history. In the light of the Dead Sea Scrolls, too, we can continue to say what a pious Jew (who was perhaps close to the Essenes) said about Jesus (Luke 2.34): 'Behold he is set for the falling and rising of many [not just] in Israel, and a sign that will be spoken against.'

# Books on Qumran

The controversial books discussed here are:

Barbara Thiering, *Jesus the Man*, Doubleday 1992, paperback Corgi Books 1993
Michael Baigent and Richard Leigh, *The Dead Sea Scrolls Deception*, Corgi Books 1993
Richard Eisenman and Michael Wise, *The Dead Sea Scrolls Uncovered*, Element Books 1992

For the Qumran texts and their background see especially:

Geza Vermes, *The Dead Sea Scrolls in English*, third edition, Penguin Books 1987 (a fourth edition is in preparation)
Geza Vermes, *The Dead Sea Scrolls. Qumran in Perspective*, SCM Press and Fortress Press 1982 (a new edition is in preparation)
Josephus, *The Jewish War*, revised edition, Penguin Books 1981

Other useful books

M.Black (ed.), *The Scrolls and Christian Origins*, Nelson 1961
Millar Burrows, *The Dead Sea Scrolls*, Viking Books and Secker and Warburg 1955
– , *More Light on the Dead Sea Scrolls*, Viking Books and Secker and Warburg 1958
P.R.Callaway, *The History of the Qumran Community*, Sheffield Academic Press 1988
F.M.Cross, *The Ancient Library of Qumran and Modern Biblical Studies*, Eerdmans $^2$1980
Roland de Vaux, *Archaeology and the Dead Sea Scrolls*, Oxford University Press for the British Academy 1973
A.Dupont-Sommer, *The Essene Writings from Qumran*, Blackwell 1961
M.A.Knibb, *The Qumran Community*, Cambridge University Press 1987

J.T.Milik, *Ten Years of Discovery in the Wilderness of Judaea*, SCM Press 1959

L.H.Schiffman (ed.), *Archaeology and History in the Dead Sea Scrolls*, Sheffield Academic Press 1990

Hershel J.Shanks (ed.), *Understanding the Dead Sea Scrolls. A Reader from the Biblical Archaeology Review*, Washington 1992 and SPCK 1993

K.Stendhal (ed.), *The Scrolls and the New Testament*, SCM Press 1958

# Abbreviations

| | |
|---|---|
| *ANRW* | *Aufstieg und Niedergang der Römischen Welt* |
| *BA* | *Biblical Archaeologist* |
| *BARev* | *Biblical Archaeology Review* |
| *BASOR* | *Bulletin of the American School of Oriental Research* |
| *BZAW* | Beihefte zur Zeitschrift für die alttestamentliche Wissenschaft |
| *CBQ* | *Catholic Biblical Quarterly* |
| *DJD* | *Discoveries in the Judaean Desert (of Jordan)* |
| *GBL* | *Das Grosse Bibellexikon* |
| *JBL* | *Journal of Biblical Literature* |
| *JJS* | *Journal of Jewish Studies* |
| *RB* | *Revue Biblique* |
| *RQ* | *Revue de Qumrân* |
| SBAZ | Studien zur biblischen Archäologie und Zeitgeschichte |
| WMANT | Wissenschaftliche Monographien zum Alten und Neuen Testament |
| WUNT | Wissenschaftliche Untersuchungen zum Neuen Testament |
| *ZDPV* | *Zeitschrift des deutschen Palästina-Vereins* |
| *ZRGG* | *Zeitschrift für Religionswissenschaft und Geistesgeschichte* |

# Notes

### 1. Did the Vatican Suppress the Publication of the Qumran Scrolls?

1. M.Baigent and R.Leigh, *The Dead Sea Scrolls Deception*, London 1991, paperback edition London 1992.
2. *Der Spiegel* 47.1, 4 January 1993, 131.
3. Cf. M.Burrows, *The Dead Sea Scrolls*, London and New York 1955, Chapter 1. There is a later version of the story of their discovery in W.H.Brownlee, 'Muhammad ed-Deeb's Story of His Discovery', *Journal of Near Eastern Studies* 16, 1957, 236-9.
4. Cf. F.de Saulcy, *Voyage autour de la Mer Morte et dans les terres bibliques exécuté de Décembre 1850 à Avril 1851*, Paris I, 164f.; II, 155-67.
5. L.Collins and D.Lapierre, *Oh Jerusalem*, London and New York 1972, is an exciting account of the results, essentially based on reliable information.
6. *The Jerusalem Bible*, London and New York 1968.
7. *Archaeology and the Dead Sea Scrolls*, Schweich Lectures 1959, revised edition London 1973.
8. W.H.Brownlee, 'The Jerusalem Habakkuk Scroll', *BASOR* 112, 1948, 8-18; M.Burrows, 'Variant Readings in the Isaiah Manuscript', *BASOR* 111, 1948, 16-42; J.C.Trever, 'Preliminary Observations on the Jerusalem Scrolls', ibid., 3-16.
9. M.Burrows, J.C.Trever and W.H.Brownlee, *The Dead Sea Scrolls of St Mark's Monastery: I. The Isaiah Manuscript and the Habakkuk Commentary*, New Haven 1950; II.2, *Plates and Transcriptions of the Manual of Discipline*, New Haven 1951.
10. *Ozar ha-megilloth ha-genuzoth she bide ha-universita ha 'ivrit* [Collection of the Hidden Scrolls in the Possession of the Hebrew University of Jerusalem], Jerusalem 1954.
11. *Megilloth Genuzoth*, Jerusalem I, 1948; II, 1950.
12. J.D.Barthélemy and J.T.Milik, *Qumran Cave I*, DJD I, Oxford 1955.
13. J.T.Milik, *Ten Years of Discoveries in the Wilderness of Judaea*, London 1959.
14. M.Baillet, J.T.Milik and R.de Vaux, *Les 'Petites Grottes' de Qumrân:*

*Exploration de la falaise, Les grottes 2Q, 3Q, 5Q, 7Q à 10Q, Le rouleau de cuivre*, DJD III, Oxford 1962.

15. J.A.Sanders, *The Psalms Scroll of Qumran Cave 11 (11QPsᵃ)*, DJD IV, Oxford 1965.

16. J.M.Allegro (with A.A.Anderson), *Qumran Cave 4,I (4Q158-4Q186)*, DJD V, Oxford 1968.

17. J.Strugnell, 'Notes en marge du Volume V des *Discoveries in the Judaean Desert of Jordan', RQ* 7, 1969-71, 163-276.

18. 'Die Handschriften und Editionen der ausserbiblischen Qumranliteratur', in J.Schreiner, *Einführung in die Methoden der biblischen Exegese*, Würzburg 1971, 303-10: 310.

19. J.T.Milik, *Qumrân Grotte 4/II: Tefilim, Mezuzot et Targumim (4Q128-4Q157)*, DJD VI, Oxford 1977; M.Baillet, *Qumrân Grotte 4, III (4Q482-520)*, DJD VII, Oxford 1982.

20. N.Avigad and Y.Yadin, *A Genesis Apocryphon: A Scroll from the Wilderness of Judaea*, Jerusalem 1956.

21. *The Books of Enoch: Aramaic Fragments of Qumran Cave 4*, Oxford 1976.

22. J.P.M.van der Ploeg and A.S.van der Woude (with B.Jongeling), *Le targum de Job de la grotte XII de Qumrân*, Leiden 1971.

23. D.N.Freeman and K.A.Matthews (with R.S.Hanson), *The Paleo-Hebrew Leviticus Scroll (11QpaleoLev)*, Philadelphia 1985.

24. C.Newsom, *Songs of the Sabbath Sacrifice: A Critical Edition*, Atlanta 1985.

25. *Megillat ha-miqdash*, Vols.I-III, Jerusalem 1977 (*The Temple Scroll* I-II, Jerusalem 1983). Y.Yadin reports on the discovery, content and significance of the Temple Scroll in *The Temple Scroll: The Hidden Law of the Dead Sea Sect*, London 1985. How little knowledge one can assume among publisher's readers is evident from the fact that there is also a reference to the forger Edmont B.Székely in the updated bibliography to the German edition (279).

26. Y.Yadin, 'The Temple Scroll – The Longest Dead Sea Scroll', in H.Shanks, *Understanding the Dead Sea Scrolls*, Washington 1992 and London 1993, 87-112; H.Shanks, 'Intrigue and the Scroll', ibid., 116-25.

27. There is a report of all publications of texts up to 1990 in J.A.Fitzmyer, *The Dead Sea Scrolls. Major Publications and Tools for Study*, Atlanta 1990, 9-76.

28. *The Dead Sea Scrolls: Qumran in Perspective*, London 1973, 23f.

29. 'Der Streit um die Rollen von Qumran, Zur Debatte', *Themen der Katholischen Akademie in Bayern* 22/5, 1992, 1-3: 2.

30. Much that experts had already long known was published by S.Rückert, 'Ans Licht der Welt', *Die Zeit* 53, 25 December 1992, 11-14.

31. 'Christus als Pilz', *Der Spiegel* 24/27, 29 June 1970, 138f.; 'Philologischer Pilz', ibid. 25/18, 26 April 1971, 175.

32. J.M.Allegro, *The Sacred Mushroom and the Cross*, London 1970.
33. *BA* 55, 1992, 107.
34. 'Ancient Scrolls Found in Palestine', *The Times*, 12 April 1948, 4.
35. The first of countless articles bore the title 'Scholarship and the Hoax of Recent Discoveries', *Jewish Quarterly Review* 39, 1948/49, 337-63.
36. W.F.Libby, *Radiocarbon Dating*, Chicago 1952, 72.
37. J.L.Teicher, 'Die Schriftrollen vom Toten Meer – Dokumente der jüdisch-christlichen Sekte der Ebioniten', *ZRGG* 3, 1951, 153-209, was a German translation.
38. 'Handelt es sich wirklich um ebionitischen Dokumente?', *ZRGG* 3, 1951, 322-36.
39. *Mehr Klarheit über die Schriftrollen*, Munich 1958, 1.
40. 'A Reporter at Large', *The New Yorker* 31/13, 14 May 1955, 45-121.
41. Edmund Wilson, *The Scrolls from the Dead Sea*, New York 1955.
42. A.Powell Davies, *The Meaning of the Dead Sea Scrolls*, New York 1956.
43. *Bibliographie zu den Handschriften vom Toten Meer*, BZAW 76, Berlin 1957; Volume II, BZAW 89, followed in 1965. Cf. also B.Jongeling, *A Classified Bibliography of the Finds in the Desert of Judah, 1958-1969*, Leiden 1971. At present an ongoing bibliography is appearing in the *Revue de Qumrân*.
44. E.g. K.G.Kuhn, 'Die in Palästina gefundenen hebräischen Texte und das Neue Testament', *Zeitschrift für Theologie und Kirche* 47, 1950, 192-211.
45. J.Daniélou, *Les manuscrits de la Mer Morte et les origines du Christianisme*, Paris 1957.
46. E.Molin, *Die Söhne des Lichtes. Zeit und Stellung der Handschriften vom Toten Meer*, Vienna and Munich 1954.
47. K.Schubert, *Die Gemeinde vom Toten Meer. Ihre Entstehung und ihre Lehren*, Munich and Basel 1958.
48. A.Dupont-Sommer, *Aperçus préliminaires sur les manuscripts de la Mer Morte*, Paris 1950; *Nouveaux aperçus sur les manuscripts de la Mer Morte*, Paris 1953; *The Essene Writings from Qumran*, Oxford 1961.
49. J.M.Allegro, *The Dead Sea Scrolls in English*, Harmondsworth 1956.
50. J.M.Allegro, *The Treasure of the Copper Scroll*, New York and London 1960.
51. *The Dead Sea Scrolls Deception*, 49.
52. 'Die Entlassung', *Der Spiegel* 11, 17 July 1957, 46-8.
53. For what follows see *Der Spiegel* 20, 18 April 1966, 130.
54. *Dead Sea Scrolls Deception*, 167-76.
55. R.H.Eisenman, *Maccabees, Zadokites, Christians and Qumran*, Leiden 1983; *James the Just in the Habakkuk pesher*, Leiden 1986.
56. *JJS* 37, 1986, 130f.

57. 'Scrolls and the Strugnell Antisemitic Mindset', *Jerusalem Post* (International Edition), 23 February 1991, 14.

58. Among others, L.Flaig, 'Die schwierige Brautschau Jesu', *Frankfurter Allgemeine Zeitung* 217, 27 September 1984, 28, tore the book apart.

59. *Dead Sea Scrolls Deception*, 295.

60. Munich and Zurich 1983, 107f.; cf. R.Riesner, 'Neues Evangelium oder altes Gesetz? Zu Franz Alts Friedensbuch', *Schritte* 5, 1984, 15ff.

61. Cf. J.Finger, *Jesus – Essener, Guru, Esoteriker? Neuen Evangelien und Apokryphen auf den Buchstaben gefühlt*, Mainz and Stuttgart 1993, 33-6.

62. *Der wirkliche Jesus. Das total andere Gottesbild* (preface by Franz Alt), Walter Verlag, Olten⁴ 1990, 214-64.

63. K.Herbst, *Jesus, der erste neue Mann*, Munich and Zurich 55-57. Cf. R.Riesner, 'Jesus der Jude zwischen Alt und Anti-Alt', in C.P.Thiede, *Christliche Glaube und Literatur* 5, Wuppertal 1991, 72-9.

64. 'Is the Vatican Suppressing the Dead Sea Scrolls?'. *BARev* 17/6, 1991, 66-71: 68. Reprinted in H.Shanks, *Understanding the Dead Sea Scrolls*, 275-90.

65. *BA* 55, 1992, 107f.

66. *Zur Debatte* 22/5, 1992, 1.

## 2. *Which Qumran Texts are Still Unpublished?*

1. There is a collection of articles from it in H.Shanks, *Understanding the Dead Sea Scrolls. A Reader from the Biblical Archaeology Review*, Washington 1992 and London 1993.

2. Cf. A.Rabinovich, 'MKs [members of Knesset] consider making Scrolls available to All Researchers', *Jerusalem Post* (International Edition), 26 October 1991, 6.

3. The interview appeared on 9 November 1990, the official English version in *BARev* 17.1, 1991, 54-60. Cf. A.Katzman, 'Interview with Chief Scroll Editor John Strugnell', in H.Shanks, *Understanding the Dead Sea Scrolls*, 259-63.

4. B.Schwank, 'Die "Verschlusssache Jesus". Die Qumranrollen und ihr "Geheimnis" ', *Erbe und Auftrag* 68, 1992, 481-91: 484.

5. 'Scrolls Editor Fired for Antisemitism', *Jerusalem Post* (International Edition), 21 December 1990, 6.

6. 'Scroll Editing Speeds up', *Jerusalem Post* (International Edition), 6 April 1991, 6; cf. A.Rabinovich, 'New Wind in the Scrollery', *Jerusalem Post Magazine*, 11 October 1991, 12-15 (also in International Edition, 26 October 1991, 10f.)

7. *A Preliminary Concordance of the Hebrew and Aramaic Fragments from Qumran Caves II to X* (by H.Stegemann, University of Göttingen 1988).

8. O.Betz, *Jesus, der Herr der Kirche. Aufsätze zur Biblischen Theologie*, WUNT 1/52, Tübingen 1990.

9. B.Z.Wacholder and M.G.Abegg, *A Preliminary Edition of the Unpublished Dead Sea Scrolls; The Hebrew and Aramaic Texts from Cave Four*, Vol.I, Washington 1991. In the meantime a second volume has appeared in 1992 (cf. J.A.Fitzmyer, *BA Rev* 19/1, 1993, 62f.).

10. *BA Rev* 18/1, 1992, 70.

11. Cf. J.Siemens, 'Computer entschlüsselt Text der Qumran-Rollen', *Frankfurter Rundschau* 207, 6 September 1991, 28; J. von Uthmann, 'Die Monopolherren werden entthront', *Frankfurter Allgemeine Zeitung* 531, 5 October 1992, 29; B.Z.Wacholder, *Jerusalem Post* (International Edition), 19 October 1992, 22.

12. H.Shanks describes events from his perspective in *Understanding the Dead Sea Scrolls*, XXVIII-XXXIV; A.Rabinovich, 'Dead Sea Fever', *Jerusalem Post* (International Edition), 6 February 1993, 9-11, follows the view of the Israelite Department for Antiquities more closely.

13. J.N.Wilford, 'Monopoly over Dead Sea Scrolls is Ended', *New York Times*, 22 September 1991, 1, 20.

14. 'Israelis und US-Forscher streiten um Copyright an Qumran-Rollen', *epd Zentralausgabe* 184, 14 September 1991, 8f.; 'Zugänglich – Schriftrollen vom Toten Meer', *Frankfurter Allgemeine Zeitung* 224, 26 October 1991, 35; 'Altjüdische Schriftrollen nun jedermann zugänglich', *Frankfurter Rundschau* 251, 29 October 1991, 10.

15. Cf. A.Rabinovich, 'Antiquities Dept Yields on Scrolls', *Jerusalem Post* (International Edition), 5 October 1991, 2; 'Antiquities Dept Denies Giving up Scroll Court Case', ibid., 12 October 1991, 6.

16. N.Hammond, 'Israel Opens Access to Dead Sea Scrolls', *The Times* 64, 29 October 1991, 18; 'Streit um die Schriftrollen vom Toten Meer begraben', *Frankfurter Rundschau* 251, 29 October 1991, 24; 'Israelis geben Qumranrollen zur Erforschung frei', *epd ZA* 208, 29 October 1991, 5f.; 'Schriftrollenfreigabe', *Frankfurter Allgemeine Zeitung* 252, 30 October 1991, 33.

17. Cf. A.Rabinovich, 'Antiquities Dept Allows Access to Scrolls', *Jerusalem Post* (International Edition), 9 November 1991, 6.

18. D.Bar-Illan, 'Scroll Myths and *Times*' Demons', *Jerusalem Post* (International Edition), 19 October 1991, 15.

19. Cf. J.Schachter, 'Last Scrolls Published', *Jerusalem Post* (Inernational Edition), 30 November 1991, 3.

20. *A Facsimile Edition of the Dead Sea Scrolls*, prepared with an Introduction and Index by R.H.Eisenman and J.M.Robinson, I/II, Washington 1991,[2] 1992.

21. Ibid., I, xi.

22. Cf. J.Uthmann, 'Die Monopolherren werden entthront', *FAZ* 231, 5 October 1991, 29.

23. Cf. Z.J.Kapera, *Qumran Chronicle* 1/2-3, 1990/1, 76.
24. Cf. A.Rabinovich, 'Court Stops Sale of Scrolls Book', *Jerusalem Post* (International Edition), 1 February 1992, 24.
25. Cf. A.Rabinovich, 'Scholar sues "Pirates" over Scroll of Righteousness', *Jerusalem Post* (International Edition), 8 February 1992, 16.
26. R.Eisenman, 'Dead Sea Scrolls Lawsuit', *Jerusalem Post* (International Edition), 22 February 1992, 22.
27. Cf. A.Rabinovich, 'Scrolls Case Gets Under Way', *Jerusalem Post* (International Edition), 13 February 1992, 24; 'Scrolls Decipherer awarded NIS 100,000 in Copyright Suit', ibid., 10 April 1993, 24.
28. Cf. H.Shanks, 'Lawsuit Diary', *BARev* 19/3, 1993, 69-71.
29. Cf. A.Rabinovich, 'Combat at the Conference', *Jerusalem Post* (International Edition), 6 February 1993, 11; cf. H.Shanks, 'Blood on the Floor at New York Dead Sea Scroll Conference', *BARev* 19.2, 1993, 63-8.
30. Huntington Library, 1151 Oxford Road, San Marino, CA 91108, USA.
31. *New from Brill* 1992/2, 1.
32. E.Tov, 'The Unpublished Qumran Texts from Caves 4 and 11', *JJS* 43, 1992, 101-36 (also in *BA* 55, 1992, 94-104).
33. S.A.Reed, *Dead Sea Scroll Inventory Project; Lists of Documents, Photographs and Museum Plates*, thus far fascicles 1-14, Ancient Biblical Manuscript Center, Claremont 1991/2.
34. J.H.Charlesworth, *Graphic Concordance to the Dead Sea Scrolls*, Tübingen and Louisville 1991. Further volumes of this Princeton Theological Seminary Dead Sea Scrolls Project under the direction of Charlesworth are announced.
35. We may leave aside here the question whether there are still finds in the hands of Arab discoverers or even in wealthy patrons. There are serious indications that such texts exist. Of course one can only speculate on their extent and character.
36. Shaftesbury, Rockport, Mass. and Brisbane 1992.
37. Ibid., 6.
38. Ibid., 273-81.
39. Cf. A.Rabinovich, 'A Prayer for King Yonatan', *Jerusalem Post Magazine*, also in International Edition, 2 May 1992, 9, 17.
40. 'Brother James's Heirs?', *The Times Literary Supplement*, 4 October 1992, 6f. [He has now changed his mind, *JJS* 1993/2.]
41. *The Dead Sea Scrolls Uncovered*, 1-16.
42. 'Second-rate Scroll Scholars', *Jerusalem Post* (International Edition), 16 November 1991, 22.
43. Cf.H.W.Kuhn, 'Wieder der Messias zu Bestsellern dient', *Die Welt*, 24 December 1992; R.Riesner, 'Im Qumran-Fieber', *Idea Spektrum* 3/1993, 20 January 1993, 15-17; R.Deines, 'Jesus und der "vollkommene Lehrer" ', *Damals* 3, 1993, 24-9; J.C.Greenfield, 'Scrolls Book Shunned

by Well-known Presses', *Jerusalem Post* (International Edition), 20 March 1993, 20: H.Lichtenberger, 'Höhlenausgänge', *Frankfurter Allgemeine Zeitung* 84, 10 April 1993, 29.

44. *A Critical Study of the Temple Scroll from Qumran Cave* 11, Chicago 1990.

45. M.Wise is quite open or unclear about the dating and character of the Qumran writings, 'The Dead Sea Scrolls', in J.B.Green and S.McKnight, *Dictionary of Jesus and the Gospels*, Downers Grove and Leicester 1992, 137-46 (especially 146).

46. Cf. R.N.Ostling, 'Is Jesus in the Dead Sea Scrolls?', *Time Magazine*, 14 September 1993, 11.

47. *Jerusalem Post* (International Edition), 3 February 1993, 11.

48. J.Köhler, 'Die Akte Jesus', *Der Stern*, 1, 1992 (22 December 1991), 28-34.

49. G.Prause, '...und machen Paulus zum Geheimagenten', *Die Zeit* 42, 11 October 1991, literature supplement, 36.

50. M.Hengel, 'Welche Wahrheit bargen die Höhlen?', *Frankfurter Allgemeine Zeitung* 8, 10 January 1992, 29; in expanded form, 'Die Qumranrollen und der Umgang mit der Wahrheit', *Theologische Beiträge* 23, 1992, 233-7.

51. E.Endres, 'Die Machenschaften des Glaubens', *Süddeutsche Zeitung* 283, 9 December 1991, 31.

52. M.Emmerich, 'Wer waren Jesus, Paulus und Jakobus wirklich?', *Frankfurter Rundschau* 297, 22 December 1992, 3.

53. 'Lebte Jesus 200 Jahre früher?, *Samstag* 41/29, 18 July 1992, 3.

54. Ibid., 1.

55. A Krause, 'Warum zensiert der Vatikan die neuesten Forschungen über Jesus?', *TV – Hören und Sehen* 23, 6-12 June 1991, 6.

56. Longer original version, 'Der unbekannte Jesus. Neues vom Sohn Gottes', *Bavaria* 3 on 20 and 27 August 1992.

57. 'Im Gespräch: Jesus und Qumran – keine Versschlusssache', *Bavaria* 3, 11 March 1992.

58. 'Geist aus der Flasche', *Der Spiegel* 46/52, 23 December 1991, 184f.; 'Gold im Grab [Copper Scroll]', ibid. 47/1 (4 January 1993), 120f.

59. Bertelsmann, Munich 1972; from 1974, ro-ro-ro Sachbuch.

60. Joel Carmichael, *The Death of Jesus*, London 1963. Originally this book was merely (as stated in letters as large as the title on the cover of the German edition) '. . .the story of a "king of the Jews" who attempted to seize the temple in Jerusalem by armed force and was condemned to death and executed by the Romans as a rebel'.

61. *Die Zeit* 53, 25 December 1992, 14.

62. Ibid., 11.

63. Gütersloher Verlagshaus, 12 January 1993, 10.

64. *Jesus the Man. A New Interpretation from the Dead Sea Scrolls*, Sydney

and London 1992 (*Jesus and the Riddle of the Dead Sea Scrolls*, San Francisco 1992).

65. 'Did Jesus really die on the Cross?' *BARev* 18/5, 1992, 69f.; reply *BARev* 19/1, 1993, 19.

66. H.Bardtke, *Die Handschriftenfunde am Toten Meer*, East Berlin I,² 1953; II, 1958; G.Molin, *Die Söhne des Lichtes*, Vienna 1954; *Lob Gottes aus der Wüste*, Freiburg and Munich 1957; the German edition of M.Burrows, *More Light on the Dead Sea Scrolls*, London and New York 1958; J.Maier, *Die Texte vom Toten Meer* I/II, Basel 1960.

67. 'Bleibt die Wahrheit unter Verschluss?', *Publik-Forum* 19, 20 September 1991, 19f.; 'War Jesus ein Essener?', ibid. 1, 17 January 1992, 20-3.

68. 'Jesus und die Essener', *Publik-Forum* 2, 19 January 1993, 29f.: 29.

69. *Nachrichten aus Israel*, 3 October 1991, 118.

70. Ibid., 107.

71. R.Sörries, *Deutsches Pfarrer-Blatt* 92/12, 1992, 582-4.

72. E.C.Hirsch, 'Der Skandal blieb aus', *Deutsches Allgemeines Sonntagsblatt* 2, 8 January 1993, 17.

73. *Evangelisches Gemeindeblatt für Württemberg* 10, 8 March 1992, 10.

74. The Landeskirche of Baden is an honourable exception here. In its church magazine it published a whole series and also a critical documentation (H.Maas, 'Wahrheit oder Verwirrung? Die Festung der Frommen im Zwielicht', *Aufbruch* 11-14, 1992, 12). Unfortunately the unhappy discussion over the Dead Sea Scrolls deception was sweepingly identified with the supposed 'Stasi hysteria' (introduction to *Aufbruch* 11, 1992, 12).

75. *Schlagwortverzeichis* 1992/93, A-F, 1500f., O-Z, 4256.

76. Cf. J.Finger, *Jesus – Essener, Guru, Esoteriker? Neuen Evangelien und Apokryphen auf den Buchstaben gefühlt*, Mainz and Stuttgart 1993, 43-6.

77. J.Maier and K.Schubert, *Die Qumran Essener. Texte der Schriftrollen und Lebensbild der Gemeinde*, UTB 224, Munich 1973, ²1991. Originally K.Schubert, *Die Gemeinde vom Toten Meer*, Munich and Basel 1958; J.Maier, *Die Texte vom Toten Meer* I/II, Basel 1960. There is nothing comparable in German to J.A.Fitzmyer, *Responses to 101 Questions on the Dead Sea Scrolls*, New York 1992.

## 3. Were the Qumran Writings composed by Sadducees?

1. The sources are: Philo, *Quod omnis probus liber sit*, 75-91; *Apologia pro Judaeis* 1 (in Eusebius, *Praeparatio Evangelica* VIII, 6-7; Pliny the Elder, *Natural History* V 17.4 (73 CE), and Josephus, *Jewish War* I, 78-80; II, 113, 119-61, 567; III, 11; V, 145 (between 75 and 81 CE); *Jewish Antiquities* XIII 171-2; XV, 371-9; XVIII, 18-20 (93 CE); *Vita* 10-11 (93 CE). There are whole or partial translations of the texts in

C.K.Barrett, *New Testament Background: Selected Documents*, London ²1987; Flavius Josephus, *The Jewish War*, Harmondsworth ²1970 ; *Jewish Antiquities*, Loeb Classical Library 1926ff.

2. The author's most recent account is L.H.Schiffman, 'The Sadducean Origins of the Dead Sea Scrolls Sect', in H.Shanks, *Understanding the Dead Sea Scrolls*, Washington 1992 and London 1993, 35-49. Cf. also Schiffmann's numerous publications on this topic mentioned in n.12 there.

3. Cf. the report by M.Baillet et al., 'Le travail d'édition des fragments manuscripts de QumraMn', *RB* 73, 1956, 49-67, and P.Benoit, 'Editing the Manuscript Fragments from Qumran', *BA* 19, 1956, 75-96. There we learn of the work of the team of editors in Jerusalem and the text fragments from Cave 4.

4. J. Strugnell and E.Qimron, 'An Unpublished Halakhic Letter from Qumran', in A.Biran, *Biblical Archaeology Today*, Jerusalem 1985, 400-5.

5. Z.J.Kapera (ed.), *Qumran Cave 4. Special Report on 4QMMT*, Krakow 1991. This volume has a critical discussion with L.H.Schiffman by Philip R.Davies, Robert H.Eisenman and James C.VanderKam. VanderKam's article, 'The Qumran Residents: Essenes not Sadducees!', ibid., 105-8, is particularly important.

6. According to Eisenman and Wise, *The Dead Sea Scrolls Uncovered*, 182ff., these are two letters, like I and II Corinthians. This division appeals to the term *katabnu elecha* in C 10: 'We wrote to you (before).' But the word *katabnu* has been almost completely supplied, to judge by the text available to us (O.Betz), and is therefore uncertain.

7. Cf. Mishnah, Menahoth 1.3-4; Berakoth 1.1.

8. Cf. Mishnah, Parah 3.7; Targum (Aramaic translation) Pseudo- Jonathan on Num.19.9. The topic of preparing the ashes of the 'red heifer' is discussed in detail in the text 4Q276-7 offered by Eisenman and Wise, *Dead Sea Scrolls Uncovered*, 210-12.

9. Temple Scroll (11QTemple) 47.7-15; Mishnah, Hullin 9.1.

10. Lawrence H.Schiffman's first book bore the title *The Halakhah at Qumran*, Leiden 1975. In it he spoke of a 'halakhic terminology at Qumran' (ibid., 22-7).

11. E.g. in Mishnah, Yadaim 3-4: Tebul Yom; Parah.

12. 'At this time (namely under the first Hasmonaean high priest Jonathan), there were three religious parties among the Jews. . . the Pharisees, the Sadducees, and thirdly the Essenes.'

13. Cf. O.Betz, 'The Eschatological Interpretation of the Sinai Tradition in Qumran and in the New Testament', in *Jesus – Herr der Kirche*, WUNT I/52, Tübingen 1990, 66-87.

14. In his work *Quod omnis probus liber sit* (75), Philo's view is that the Greek name *Essaioi* (= Essenes), the number of whom is over four

thousand, is to be connected with the word 'piety' (*hosiotes*), though this is not etymologically correct in Greek. For Philo these pious are especially good servants of God. .

15. T.S.Beall, *Josephus' Description of the Essenes Illustrated by the Dead Sea Scrolls*, Cambridge 1988, is a detailed comparison with a positive result.

16. C.Newsom, *Songs of the Sabbath Sacrifice: A Critical Edition*, Atlanta 1985.

17. Cf. A.M. Schwemer, 'Gott als König und seine Königsherrschaft in den Sabbatliedern aus Qumran', in M.Hengel and A.M.Schwemer, *Königsherrschaft Gottes und himmlischer Kult im Judentum, Urchristentum und in der hellenistischen Welt*, WUNT I/55, Tübingen 1991, 45-108.

18. B.Z.Wacholder and M.G.Abegg, *A Preliminary Edition of the Unpublished Dead Sea Scrolls*, Fascicle One, Washington 1991.

19. *Documents of Jewish Sectaries. Fragments of a Zadokite Work*, Cambridge 1910.

20. See also the Nahum Commentary (4QpHah 1.6ff.) and Josephus, *Jewish Antiquities* XIII, 380; cf. O.Betz, 'Probleme des Prozesses Jesu', *ANRW* II, 25/1, Berlin and New York 1981, 565-647.

21. Instead of *miqzat ma'aseh ha-torah* (C28f.) it is better to read the plural. These are some regulations ('works') for the right observance of the law.

22. Cf. O.Betz, 'Das Problem des "Kanons" in den Texten von Qumran', in G.Maier, *Der Kanon der Bibel*, Giessen and Wuppertal 1990, 70-82.

## 4. Was Qumran a Fortress or an Essene Monastery?

1. R.de Vaux, *Archaeology and the Dead Sea Scrolls*, Schweich Lectures, revised edition, London 1973; there is an up-to-date synthesis by J.Murphy O'Connor, 'Qumran', in D.N.Freedman, *The Anchor Bible Dictionary* V, New York 1992, 590-4.

2. There are up-to-date discussions of the archaeological questions in P.R.Callaway, *The History of the Qumran Community. An Investigation*, Sheffield 1988, 19-51; M.Broshi, 'The Archaeology of Qumran – A Reconsideration', in D.Dimant and U.Rappaport, *The Dead Sea Scrolls. Forty Years of Research*, Leiden 1992, 103-15.

3. *The Dead Sea Scrolls Deception*, 49.

4. Cf. R.Donceel, 'Reprise des travaux de publication des fouilles au Khirbet Qumran', *RB* 99, 1992, 557-73.

5. 'The Problem of Origin and Identification of the Dead Sea Scrolls', *Proceedings of the American Philosophical Society* 124, 1980, 1-24; 'Who Hid the Dead Sea Scrolls?', *BA* 28, 1978, 68-82; and recently on the discussion of the freeing of the rest of the fragments, 'The Freeing

of the Scrolls and its Aftermath', *The Qumran Chronicle* 2/1, 1992, 3-25.

6. 'Viele Mythen, ein Machwerk und der Schatz der Rebellen', *Die Welt* 36, 12 February 1992, 21; 'Qumran Nowhere?', *The Qumran Chronicle* 2/1, 1992, 31-7; cf. R.Riesner, 'Streit um die Essener', *Die Welt* 26, 24 February 1992, 23.

7. K.H.Rengstorf, *Hirbet Qumran und die Bibliothek vom Toten Meer*, Stuttgart 1960.

8. Cf. E.Tov, 'The Unpublished Qumran Texts from Caves 4 and 11', *JJS* 43, 1992, 101-36: 119.

9. Cf. S.Goranson, 'Further Qumran Archaeology Publications in Progress', *BA* 54, 199, 110f.; 'An Inkwell from Qumran', *Michmanim* (University of Haifa Museum) 6, 1992, 37*-40* [I am grateful to the author for making this inaccessible article available]. For the inkwell from the 'Burnt House' in Jerusalem cf. N.Avigad, *Discovering Jerusalem*, Nashville 1983, 127.

10. The newest interpretation, thought it is still very much in need of critical discussion, sees the pieces of clay as the remains of couches from a private bedroom (Pauline Donceel-Voûte). Cf. Z.J.Kapera, *Qumran Chronicle* 2/2, 1993, 78. There was vigorous criticism of Mme Donceel's theory that Qumran was not an Essene settlement but a country villa at the New York Qumran Congress in December 1992. Cf. H.Shanks, *BARev* 19/2, 1993, 65-8; 19/3, 1993, 62-5. At any rate this view of an archaeologist appointed by the École Biblique which is so opposed to that of de Vaux shows how little one can accuse the Dominicans of a cover-up.

11. Cf. de Vaux, *Archaeology and the Dead Sea Scrolls*, 29-33.

12. Ibid., 103. The potsherd with the alphabet is illustrated in *RB* 61, 1954, plate XXa.

13. For further criticism of Golb's theories cf. F.Garcia Martinez and A.S.van der Woude, 'A "Groningen" Hypothesis of Qumran Origins and Early History', *RQ* 14, 1990, 521-41.

14. *Dead Sea Scrolls Deception*, 237.

15. de Vaux, *Archaeology and the Dead Sea Scrolls*, 28.

16. F.M.Cross, *The Ancient Library of Qumran and Modern Biblical Scholarship*, Grand Rapids ²1980, 77.

17. *Dead Sea Scrolls Deception*, 203.

18. Cf. further G.J.Brooke, 'The Temple Scroll and the Archaeology of Qumran, 'Ain Feshkha and Masada', *RQ* 13, 1988, 225-37.

19. Cf. A.Strobel, 'Die Wasseranlagen der Hirbet Qumran', *ZDPV* 88, 1972, 55-86; B.G.Wood, 'To Dip or to Sprinkle? The Qumran Cisterns in Perspective', *BASOR* 256, 1984, 45-60.

20. Cf. R.Riesner, *Jesus als Lehrer. Eine Untersuchung zum Ursprung der Evangelien-Überlieferung*, WUNT II.7, Tübingen ³1988, 135.

21. de Vaux, *Archaeology and the Dead Sea Scrolls*, 11-14.
22. Cf. R.de Vaux, 'Une hachette Essénienne?', *Vetus Testamentum* 9, 1959, 399-407.
23. Cf. Brooke, 'Temple Scroll' (n.18), 229f.
24. de Vaux, *Archaeology and the Dead Sea Scrolls* 45-8.
25. Cf.M.Broshi, in Dimant and Rappaport, *The Dead Sea Scrolls*, 112.
26. Text in J.Maier, *Die Tempelrolle vom Toten Meer*, UTB 829, Munich 1978, 55.
27. Cf. O.Keel and M.Küchler, *Orte und Landschaften der Bibel* 2, *Der Süden*, Zurich 1982, 451-5.
28. Cf. R.Riesner, 'Begräbnis- und Trauersitten', *GBL* I, Wuppertal and Giessen ²1990, 173-8.
29. P.Benoit, J.T.Milik and R.de Vaux, *Les grottes de Murabba'at*, DJD II, Oxford 1961, 16f.
30. Cf. Keel and Küchler, *Orte und Landschaften der Bibel* 2, 461.
31. Cf. M.Hengel, *Judaism and Hellenism*, London and Philadelphia 1974, I, 218-46.
32. Cf. recently S.Goranson, 'Sectarianism, Geography and the Copper Scroll', *JJS* 43, 1992, 282-7 (with bibliography).
33. Cf. B.Pixner, 'Unravelling the Copper Scroll Code: A Study on the Topography of 3Q15', *RQ* 11, 1983, 323-65; 'Die Kupferrolle von Qumran', in *Wege des Messias und Stätten der Urkirche. Jesus und das Judenchristentum im Licht neuer archäologischer Erkenntnisse*, ed. R.Riesner, SBAZ 2, Giessen 1991, 149-58.
34. Cf. P.R.Callaway, 'Qumran Origins: From the *Doresh* to the *Moreh*', *RQ* 14, 1990, 37-50: 644.
35. Cf. Keel and Küchler, *Orte und Landschaften der Bibel*, 2, 451f.
36. Gaius Plinius Secundus, *Natural History*, V,17,4.
37. G.Jeremias, *Der Lehrer der Gerechtigkeit*, Studien zur Umwelt des Neuen Testaments 2, Göttingen 1963.
38. Cf. J.J.Collins, 'Dead Sea Scrolls', in D.N.Freedman, *The Anchor Bible Dictionary* II, New York 1992, 85-101.
39. 'The Early History of the Qumran Community', in D.N.Freedman and J.C.Greenfield, *New Directions in Biblical Archaeology*, Garden City 1971, 77.
40. 'Implications for the History of Judaism and Christianity', in H.Shanks, *The Dead Sea Scrolls after Forty Years*, Washington 1991, 19-36.
41. J.H.Charlesworth, 'Qumran Scrolls and a Critical Consensus', in *Jesus and the Dead Sea Scrolls*, New York 1993, gives a brief and comprehensive formulation of the Essene consensus.
42. Paris 1988; the German edition was entitled *Ein Mensch namens Jesus*, Munich 1989. There are critical comments by Harmut Rosenau, Hans F.Bayer and Carsten Peter Thiede in C.P.Thiede (ed.), *Christlicher*

*Glaube und Literatur* 5, *Jesus-Interpretationen in der modernen Litera-tur*, Wuppertal 1991.

43. *Ein Mensch namens Jesus*, 708: 'Nevertheless at this point I would like to stress, if only for all those readers who attach importance to work with a scientific foundation, that in this book I have in no way given free rein to my imagination. All the essential statements are based on historical analyses, conclusions and reconstructions. I am certain that many readers would come to similar conclusions if they spent many years struggling with readings of this kind.'

44. *Les manuscripts de la mer Morte et les origines du christianisme*, Paris 1957, [2]1974.

45. *Ein Mensch namens Jesus*, 709.

46. Ibid., 708.

47. Ibid., 712.

48. Cf. R.Riesner, 'Nazareth', *GBL* II, Wuppertal and Giessen [2]1990, 1031-7.

49. *Ein Mensch namens Jesus*, 744.

50. Cf. only J.A.Fitzmyer, 'Aramaic Kepha' and Peter's Name in the New Testament', in *To Advance the Gospel*, New York 1981, 112-4; O.Betz, 'Felsenmann und Felsengemeinde', in *Jesus – Der Messias Israels*, WUNT I/42, Tübingen 1987, 99-126.

51. German edition *Ein Mensch namens Saulus*, Munich 1992, 521.

52. *Dead Sea Scrolls Uncovered*, 65.

53. *Ein Mensch namens Jesus*, 709. The postscript to the French edition in which this statement is made was finished in 1987.

54. *Ein Mensch namens Jesus*, 733.

55. There has been a thorough refutation of Kirsten's Indological fantasies by a scholar who is head of the Oriental Collection of the Bavarian State Library in Munich: G.Grönbold, *Jesus in Indien. Das Ende einer Legende*, Munich 1985.

56. Cf. W.Bulst, *Betrug am Turiner Grabtuch. Der manipulierte Carbontest*, Frankfurt 1990; O.Petrosillo and E.Marinelli, *La Sindone. Un enigma alla prova della scienza*, Milan 1990.

57. Cf. C.Reichel, 'Mr Tite hat seinen Preis', *Die Welt* 272, 21 November 1992, G5.

58. E.R.Gruber, 'Die Geheimnisse von Golgatha', in H.Kersten and E.R.Gruber, *Das Jesus-Komplott. Die Wahrheit über das 'Turiner Grabtuch'*, Munich 1992, 273-329; cf. R.Riesner, *Idee-Spektrum* 47, 1992, 26.

59. Ibid., 287.

60. A.Schweitzer, *The Quest of the Historical Jesus*, London [3]1954, 38ff.

61. S.Wagner, *Die Essener in der wissenschaftlichen Diskussion vom Aus-gang des 18. bis Beginn des 20. Jahrhunderts*, BZAW 79, Berlin 1960.

62. *Das Jesus-Komplott*, 405-8.

63. Circular letter of 20 September 1992.

64. *Das Jesus-Komplott*, 339.

65. Cf. J.Köhler, 'Krise ungeahnten Ausmasses', *Der Stern* 43, 1992, 124f.

66. K.Herbst, *Kriminalfall Golgatha. Der Vatikan, das Turiner Grabtuch und der wirkliche Jesus*, Düsseldorf 1992.

67. 'Lapide kontra Eisenman: Ist Paulus der "Lügenmann"?', *epd* (central edition) 13, 20 January 1993, 6-8.

68. P.Lapide, *Paulus zwischen Damaskus und Qumran. Fehldeutungen und Übersetzungsfehler*, Gütersloher Taschenbücher 1425, 1993. At least a sixth of the book deals with Paul and Qumran.

69. P.Lapide, *Ist die Bibel richtig übersetzt?*, Gütersloher Taschenbücher 1415, 1986. For criticism cf. J.Lange, 'Fehler in der Jesus-Überlieferung?', *bibelreport* 2, 1987, 4-5.

70. Thus P.Lapide, 'Die Nachbarn der Urgemeinde. Erkenntnisse aus der Tempelrolle der Essener von Qumran', *Lutherische Monatshefte* 17, 1978, 273-5, summarizes (in part wrongly) the theory that the Essene quarter and the earliest church were side by side in Jerusalem without mentioning its author, Bargil Pixner. To the uninitiated reader this must give the impression that these are genuine insights of his own.

71. The Catalan Augustinian S.Sabugal, *Anaklisis exegética sobre la conversion de San Pablo*, Barcelona 1976, has provided a basis for this theory; see also 'La mención neotestamentaria de Damasco (Gal.1.17; 2Cor 11,32; Act 9,2-3. 8. 10par.19.22.27par). Ciudad de Siria o región de Qumran?', in M.Baillet, *Qumrân. Sa piété, sa théologie et son milieu*, Paris and Louvain 1978, 403-13. Lapide does not mention this either.

72. Cf. R.Riesner, *Die Frühzeit des Paulus. Studien zur Chronologie, Missionsstrategie und Theologie des Apostels*, Habilitationsschrift Tübingen 1990, 66-79.

73. 'Beim Wort genommen: War Jesus ein Essener?', *Sudwest-Funk* 3, 13 June 1992.

74. '4Q 372 1: A Text about Joseph', *RQ* 14, 1990, 349-65; 'The Psalm of 4Q372 1 Within the Context of Second Temple Prayer', *CBQ* 54, 1992, 67-79.

75. For the question of 'Abba' as an address to God in Judaism cf. J.Jeremias, 'Abba', in *The Prayers of Jesus*, London 1967, 11-65; also *New Testament Theology I, The Proclamation of Jesus*, London and Philadelphia 1971, 61-7.

76. Cf. É.Puech, 'Un hymne essénien en partie retrouvé et les Béatitudes. 1QH V 12- VI 18 (= col.XIII-XIV 7) and 4QBeat', *RQ* 13, 1988, 59-88; '4Q525 et les péricopes des Béatitudes en Ben Sira et Matthieu', *RB* 98, 1991, 80-106.

77. *The Last Three Popes and the Jews*, London 1967.

*5. Does James the Brother of the Lord lie behind the 'Teacher of Righteousness'?*

1. Thus Baigent and Leigh, *The Dead Sea Scrolls Deception*, 22.
2. Eisenman wrote *Eine Studie zum islamischen Recht im Staat Israel*, 1978, and then presented his theories on Qumran and Christianity in *Maccabees, Zadokites, Christians and Qumran*, Leiden 1983; similarly *James the Just in the Habakkuk Pesher*, Cosenza 1984 (Leiden 1986). There is a summary of Eisenman's theory in the article mentioned in n.21.
3. Part III, 'The Dead Sea Scrolls', looks like an addition to the theory about the 'Dead Sea Scrolls Deception' in Parts I and II.
4. Cf. D.Walker and R.H.Eisenman, 'The 1990 Survey of Qumran Caves', *Qumran Chronicle* 2/1, 1992, 45-9.
5. *A Facsimile Edition of the Dead Sea Scrolls*, prepared with an Introduction and Index by Robert H.Eisenman and James M.Robinson, Washington 1991. The title of this book is as misleading as that of the second book produced with M.Wise, *The Dead Sea Scrolls Uncovered*. For these works are not about all the Dead Sea Scrolls generally, 80% of which have long been published; rather, some fragments from Cave 4 are 'published', i.e. presented to the public before their real publication by the scholars to whom they were assigned.
6. R.Eisenman and M.Wise, *The Dead Sea Scrolls Uncovered*, 127.
7. Ibid., 125, 127.
8. Ibid., 126.
9. That is how Eisenman describes his procedure, ibid., 9f.
10. For the Qumran parallels (1QS 8.7f.; 9.3; 1QH 6.25-27) to Matt.16.18f. see O.Betz, *Was wissen wir von Jesus?*, Wuppertal [2]1991, 143 n.83.
11. Cf. O.Betz, 'Kontakte zwischen Christen und Essenern', in B.Mayer, *Christen und Christliches in Qumran*, Regensburg 1992, 157-76, esp. 170f.
12. M.Hengel, *The Zealots*, Edinburgh 1989.
13. C.Roth, *The Historical Background of the Dead Sea Scrolls*, Oxford 1958.
14. G.R.Driver, *The Judaean Scrolls. The Problem and a Solution*, Oxford 1964.
15. *The Dead Sea Scrolls Uncovered*, 10.
16. Cf. O.Betz, 'Der fleischliche Mensch und das geistliche Gesetz', in *Jesus, der Herr der Kirche*, WUNT I/52, Tübingen 1990, 129-96.
17. *The Dead Sea Scrolls Uncovered*, 12; further 'reasons' for this rejection are given in Baigent and Leigh, *Dead Sea Scrolls Deception*, 239-43. The remarks may rightly be claimed to 'confuse the layman'.
18. Cf. G.Bonani, M.Broshi, I Carmi, S.Ivy, J.Strugnell, W.Wölfli, 'Radiocarbon Dating of the Dead Sea Scrolls', *'Atiqot* XX, Jerusalem 1991, 27-

32; cf. further Z.J.Kapera, 'AMS Carbon 14 Dating of the Scrolls', *The Qumran Chronicle* 2/1, 1992, 39-43.

19. *The Dead Sea Scrolls Uncovered*, 13.

20. 'Brother James's Heirs?', *The Times Literary Supplement*, 4 December 1992, 6f.

21. In Z.J.Kapera, *Papers on the Dead Sea Scrolls in Memory of Jean Carmignac*, Krakow 1991, 177-96.

22. This claim sounds strange when one thinks of the attack of his propagandists Baigent and Leigh in *The Dead Sea Scrolls Deception* (Parts I and II): it is directed against the consensus of scholars on the pre-Christian origin of the Essene texts from Qumran which is claimed to have been influenced by the Vatican.

23. What is meant is the comet-like sign of destruction over Jerusalem mentioned by Josephus (*Jewish War*, 288-300), and also the prophecy shaped by Num.24.17 of the rise of the messianic star (i.e. ruler; cf. CD 7; 4QTestimonia) which is also connected with Vespasian by Josephus (ibid., VI, 312f., and Tacitus).

24. Cf. Isaiah 40.3, which is cited in the Community Rule of Qumran (1QS 8.14) and in Mark 1.2f. and parallels (for John the Baptist).

25. It was expected as an eschatological event in Qumran (1QS 4.20-22) and in the circles of John the Baptist (Mark 1.8; Acts 19.1-6).

26. 1QS 9.13 and 10.18ff. are cited for the preparation of the way (8.14 is correct), 1QS 2.1-4.26 (they are mentioned only in 4.21; cf. 8.12ff.).

27. In Z.J.Kapera, *Papers on the Dead Sea Scrolls*, 178.

28. Ibid., 184.

29. *galah* is used in the Damacus Document (CD 7.14f.) with the twofold meaning 'lead away – reveal'. For 'conceal', the Qumran people used the verb *satar, histir*.

30. In Kapera, *Papers on the Dead Sea Scrolls*, 184.

31. Ibid., 181f.

32. Ibid., 184-7.

33. Ibid., 183; Gen.31.23; 35.5 on 1QpHab 9.5. In this way Josephus's Idumaeans (Esau-Edom) are brought into play, but inappropriately; the Idumaeans in fact killed the 'godless priest'!

34. Kapera, *Papers on the Dead Sea Scrolls*, 184, 188, 189, 191. Astonishingly this is rightly opposed by Baigent and Leigh, *Dead Sea Scrolls Deception*, 242f.

35. In this case the third person suffix (-*o*) is to be related to the 'wicked priest': 'his (wicked) court of judgment'.

36. In Kapera, *Papers on the Dead Sea Scrolls*, 187.

37. Ibid., 191.

38. Ibid., 196.

39. Baigent and Leigh, *The Dead Sea Scrolls Deception*, 263.

40. Ibid., 266.

41. Ibid., 286f.
42. Ibid., 320. R.H.Eisenman and M.Wise, *The Dead Sea Scrolls Uncovered*, 273, claim this quite bluntly.
43. Baigent and Leigh, *The Dead Sea Scrolls Deception*, 267.
44. Cf. O.Betz, 'Fleischliche und geistliche Christuserkenntnis nach 2.Korintherbrief 5,16', in *Jesus, der Herr der Kirche*, WUNT I.52, Tübingen 1990, 114-28.
45. Baigent and Leigh, *The Dead Sea Scrolls Deception*, 270-3.
46. M.Hengel, *Acts and the History of Earliest Christianity*, London and Philadelphia 1979; C.J.Thornton, *Der Zeuge des Zeugen. Lukas als Historiker der Paulus-Reisen*, WUNT I.56, Tübingen 1991.

## 6. Does a Qumran Text speak of the Crucified Messiah?

1. *The New York Times International*, 8 November 1991; *The Times*, 9 November 1991.
2. Cf. *Katholische Nachrichten-Agentur* 263, 13 November 1991, 'Announcement of Report of the Execution of Jesus'.
3. Letter of December 1955 (quoted in Baigent and Leigh, *Dead Sea Scrolls Deception*, 84).
4. 'Crucifixion before Christ', *Time Magazine* 67.6, 6 February 1958, 88.
5. R.de Vaux, J.T.Milik, P.Skehan, J.Starcky and J.Strugnell, 'Letter concerning Certain Broadcast Statements of Mr J.Allegro', *The Times*, 16 March 1956, 11.
6. Baigent and Leigh, *Dead Sea Scrolls Deception*, 89.
7. In the concordance it is designated BM 5 (1-6), i.e. it is one of the texts edited by Józef T.Milik. It is among the photographs from the Huntington Library, *A Facsimile Edition of the Dead Sea Scrolls* (ed. R.H.Eisenman and J.M.Robinson), Washington 1991, II, no.1552.
8. 'Kontakte zwischen Christen und Essenern', in B.Mayer, *Christen und christliches in Qumran?*, Eichstätter Studien. NF 32, Regensburg 1992, 157-75: 172.
9. Shaftesbury, Rockport, Mass. and Brisbane 1992, 24-30.
10. One can supplement: '... and the thickets of the forest will be felled by an axe and Lebanon shall fall by a mighty one'. This text, Isaiah 10.34, precedes Isaiah 11. Eisenman presents the text 4 Q285 in *The Dead Sea Scrolls Uncovered*, 24-30.
11. Eisenman's rendering of the Hebrew text and his translation are not completely correct. He speaks of a 'staff from the root (*matt'a*) of Jesse'. However, the text *mig-geza'* (from the stump) of Jesse is correct.
12. The Hebrew expression *nesi' ha'edah* means 'prince of the community', and not 'leader', as Eisenman thinks. It is a distinctive title in the Qumran writings for the Messiah from the house of David, as the Damascus Document (CD 7.20) and the War Scroll (1QM 5.1) show.

13. 'The Oxford Forum for Qumran Research. Seminar on the Rule of War from Cave 4 (4Q285)', *JJS* 43, 1992, 85-94: 88.
14. 'A Slain Messiah in 4Q Serekh Milchamah (4Q285)?', *Tyndale Bulletin* 43/1, 1992, 155-69: 159.
15. Eisenman and Wise, *The Dead Sea Scrolls Uncovered*, 24.
16. Ibid., 29.
17. According to 4 QpIsa (J.M.Allegro, *Qumran Cave Four*, DJD V, Oxford 1968, 13-15), 'the Messiah will rule over all peoples and Magog... and his sword will judge all peoples' (line 202).
18. Eisenman and Wise, *The Dead Sea Scrolls Uncovered*, 27. The usual title for the high priest is *hak-kohen ha-gadol* (the great priest) or *kohen harosh* (the head priest), not *hak-kohen* (thus Eisenman). This determined form only rarely means high priest.
19. Ibid.
20. Cf. O.Betz, 'Die Übersetzungen von Isa 53 (LXX, Targum) und die Theologia Crucis des Paulus', in *Jesus – Der Herr der Kirche*, WUNT I/ 52, Tübingen 1990, 197-216.
21. Cf. W.Grimm, *Die Verkündigung Jesu und Deuterojesaja*, Frankfurt and Bern ²1981.
22. Eisenman and Wise, *The Dead Sea Scrolls Uncovered*, 27.
23. Ibid., 19. The text was originally headed 'On the Resurrection' and the official editors called it a 'Messianic Apocalypse'.
24. Eisenman and Wise, *The Dead Sea Scrolls Uncovered*, 27.
25. Ibid., 20.
26. Similarly M.Wise and J.Tabor, 'The Messiah at Qumran', *BARev* 18/6, 1992, 60f.: like Jesus, he is designated cosmic Messiah.
27. Eisenman and Wise, *The Dead Sea Scrolls Uncovered*, 37-9, have published an Aramaic text (4Q529) which they entitle 'The Words of Michael'. It begins with the ascent of Michael to 'the Highest Heaven' (line 1).
28. Cf. O.Betz, 'Jesus in Nazareth', in *Jesus – Der Messias Israels*, WUNT I/42, Tübingen 1987, 301-17.
29. Cf. O.Betz, 'Jesu Evangelium vom Gottesreich', ibid., 23-54.
30. Eisenman and Wise, *The Dead Sea Scrolls Uncovered*, 68. Formerly the designation 4QPseudo-Daniel was customary.
31. Cf. J.A.Fitzmyer, 'The Contribution of Qumran Aramaic to the Study of the New Testament', *New Testament Studies* 20, 1974, 382-401: 391-4.
32. O.Gillie, *The Independent*, 1 September 1992.
33. 'Fragment d'une Apocalypse en Araméen (4Q246 = pseudo-Dan) et le "Royaume de Dieu"', *RB* 99, 1992, 98-131.
34. This is how G.Vermes, 'Qumran Forum Miscellanea I', *JJS* 43, 1992, 199-305: 301-3, understands the text.
35. F.Garcia Martinez, *Qumran and Apocalyptic. Studies on the Aramaic*

*Tests from Qumran*, Leiden 1992, 162-79, also thinks of an eschatological saving figure. For the connection between Son of Man and Son of God, cf. S.Kim, *The 'Son of Man' as the Son of God*, WUNT I/30, Tübingen 1983.

36. Cf. O.Betz, *Was wissen wir von Jesus?*, Wuppertal ²1991, 101-6, 109-14.
37. Cf. G.J.Brooke, 'The Messiah of Aaron in the Damascus Document', *RQ* 15, 1991, 215-30.

## 7. *Do the Qumran writings Criticize Jesus as the 'Wicked Priest'?*

1. 'Can the Hasmonean Dating of the Teacher of Righteousness be Sustained?' in Z.J.Kapera, *Mogilany 1989. Papers on the Dead Sea Scrolls* II, Krakow 1991, 99-117: 100. The author (O.Betz) heard the lecture which is the basis of this article, given by Barbara Thiering in Mogilany in 1989, as a member of the colloquium.
2. The theory put forward by Jacob L.Teicher of Cambridge in the 1950s that the Dead Sea Scrolls were composed by Jewish Christians comes nearest to Thiering's theory.
3. 'Inner and Outer Cleansing at Qumran as a Background to New Testament Baptism', *New Testament Studies* 26, 1980, 266-77; 'Qumran Initiation and New Testament Baptism', ibid. 27, 1981, 615-31.
4. 'Hatte Jesus drei Kinder, war er geschieden?', *Bild* 169, 22 July 1992, 7.
5. In Kapera, *Papers on the Dead Sea Scrolls* II, 100-8.
6. F.M.Cross, *The Ancient Library of Qumran and Modern Biblical Study*, Grand Rapids ²1980.
7. In Kapera, *Papers on the Dead Sea Scrolls* II, 108.
8. *The Dead Sea Scrolls Uncovered*, 122.
9. In Kapera, *Papers on the Dead Sea Scrolls* II, 108.
10. Cf. M.Delcor, 'Is the Temple Scroll a Source for the Herodian Temple?', in G.J.Brooke, *Temple Scroll Studies*, Sheffield 1989, 67-89.
11. In Kapera, *Papers on the Dead Sea Scrolls* II, 108.
12. The page numbers in brackets in the texts refer to B.Thiering, *Jesus the Man*, London 1992, paperback 1993 (US title *Jesus and the Riddle of the Dead Sea Scrolls*, San Francisco 1992).
13. Cf. O.Betz, 'Kontakte zwischen Essenern und Christen', in B.Mayer, *Christen und Christliches in Qumran?*, Eichstätter Studien NF 32, Regensburg 1992, 157-75: 159-64.
14. According to Thiering, Jesus found the 'twelve apostles' as an already existing body of significant figures in the wilderness community. The most important among them were not Peter and the two sons of Zebedee but Judas Iscariot, Simon the Zealot (who is identical with the Gnostic Simon Magus in Acts 8), Thaddaeus, James the son of Alphaeus, Thomas and Matthew, who are only mentioned in the Gospels in a secondary

way (Thiering, 105). The 'beloved disciple' in the Fourth Gospel must have been John Mark; but Jesus also had a close friendship with Simon Magus, the successor to John the Baptist, who according to Thiering also embodies the poor Lazarus of Luke 16 and the Lazarus in Bethany of John 11. The identification of New Testament figures which can apparently be carried out and justified by *pesher* exegesis gives the reader many surprises.

15. For these trial marriages of Essenes of the second order cf. Josephus, *Jewish War* II, 160f. Marriage is justified by a concern for descendants (*diadoche*). For three years the future wife was on trial to see whether she could bear children; if this proved possible, marriage could follow. 'When conception has taken place intercourse ceases – proof that the object of the marriage was not pleasure but the begetting of children' (Josephus, *War*, II, 161). According to Thiering, Jesus' marriage with Mary Magdalene and that of his father Joseph with Mary belongs in this Essene category (64); that also provides a natural explanation for the Virgin Birth (ibid., 64f.). At her betrothal to Jesus Mary Magdalene is said to have already been well beyond the usual marrying age: perhaps she had already been married once (ibid., 119, 195).

16. Moreover, this construction has long been known and was already used in Lives of Jesus from the Enlightenment on. It has been put forward time and again, e.g. by H.Schonfield, *The Passover Plot*, London 1965, and now also by H.Kersten and E.R.Gruber, *Das Jesus-Komplott*, Munich 1992, 83-5.

17. Paul, the former Pharisee, allowed this second marriage (cf. I Cor.7.15); but it is sharply criticized in the Damascus Rule: 'it is forbidden to take a second wife as long as the first lives' (CD 4.19, 5,6, Thiering 148, 427).

18. L.Star, *The Dead Sea Scrolls. The Riddle Debated*, ABC Enterprises 1991.

19. *Hamburger Abendblatt* 1698, 22 July 1992, 1-2.

20. 'Jesus war nicht der erste Christ', *Quick* 52, 1992, 48-51.

21. *BARev* 18/5, 1992, 69f.: 70.

## 8. Were Manuscripts of the New Testament found in Qumran Cave 7?

1. R.E.Marley, 'Undeciphered Dead Sea Scroll May Reveal Gospel of Luke', *Jerusalem Christian Review* 7/6, 1992, 1.7.

2. *The Dead Sea Scrolls Uncovered*, 68-71.

3. J.A.Fitzmyer, 'Qumran Aramaic Literary Parallels to the New Testament' (1973), in *A Wandering Aramean, Collected Essays*, Missoula 1979, 97-113.

4. Cf. E.Ulrich, 'The Greek Manuscripts of the Pentateuch from Qumran,

including Newly Identified Fragments of Deuteronomy', in A.Pietersma and C.Cox, *De Septuaginta. FS J.W.Wevers*, Leiden 1984, 71-82.

5. For the linguistic situation in Palestine cf. R.Riesner, *Jesus als Lehrer. Eine Untersuchung zum Ursprung der Evangelien*, WUNT II/7, ³1988, 382-7, and now especially also J.A.Lund, 'The Language of Jesus', *Mishkan* 17-18, 1993-3, 139-55 (most recent literature).

6. M.Baillet – J.T.Milik – R.de Vaux, *Discoveries in the Judaean Desert III: Les 'Petites Grottes' de Qumran*, Oxford 1962, 142f.

7. 'Papiros neotestamentarios en la cueva 7 de Qumran?', *Biblica* 53, 1972, 91-100 (authorized English translation by W.L.Holladay as supplement to *JBL* 91.2, 1972, 1-14). His proposals are taken further above all in J.O'Callaghan, *Los papiros griegos de la cueva 7 de Qumran*, Madrid 1974; 'The Identifications of 7Q', *Aegyptus* 56, 1976, 287-94. Further literature in J.A.Fitzmyer, *The Dead Sea Scrolls. Major Publications and Tools for Study*, Atlanta 1990, 168-72.

8. Cf. only the standard work by W.G.Kümmel, *Introduction to the New Testament*, Nashville and London 1975, 185ff., 434.

9. Cf. M.Hengel, 'The Gospel of Mark: Time of Origin and Situation', in *Studies in the Gospel of Mark*, London and Philadelphia 1985, 1-30; R.A.Guelich, *Mark 1-8.26*, Word Biblical Commentary 34 A, Waco, Texas 1989, XXXI-XXXII.

10. C.H.Roberts in DJD III, 144.

11. *Redating the New Testament*, London 1976.

12. *Eternity* 23/6, 1972, 1-14.

13. 'Neue neutestamentliche Papyri III', *NTS* 20, 1974, 357-81: 362f.; 'Über die Möglichkeit der Identifikation kleiner Fragmente neutestamentlicher Handschriften mit Hilfe des Computers', in J.K.Elliott, *Studies in the New Testament Language and Text, FS G.Kilpatrick*, Leiden 1976, 14-38: 21f., reprinted in K.Aland, *Supplementa zu den neutestamentlichen und kirchengeschichtlichen Entwürfen*, ed. B.Köster et al., Berlin and New York 1990, 142-57, 117-41.

14. *Novum Testamentum Graece post Eberhard Nestle et Erwin Nestle communiter ediderunt K.Aland, M.Black, C.M.Martini, B.M.Metzger, A.P.Wikgren*, Stuttgart ²⁶1979.

15. E.g. C.J.Hemer, 'New Testament Fragments at Qumran', *Tyndale Bulletin* 23, 1972, 125-8; G.D.Fee, 'Some Dissenting Notes on 7Q5 = Mark 6.52-53', *JBL* 92, 1973, 109-12.

16. D.Estrada and W.White, *The First New Testament*, Nashville 1978, 93-102; W.N.Pickering, *The Identity of the New Testament Text*, Nashville and New York ²1980, 155-8, 233-4. The last-mentioned author is a supporter of the so-called 'majority text'. In other words, he regards the mediaeval Greek manuscripts as the best form of the New Testament text and earlier manuscripts (including e.g. the fourth-century Codex Sinaiticus discovered by Constantin von Tischendorf) as corrupt copies.

Against his own presuppositions (7Q5 has two variants from the majority text) Pickering accepts the identification.

17. '7Q – Eine Rückkehr zu den neutestamentlichen Papyrusfragmente in der siebten Höhle von Qumran', *Biblica* 65, 1984, 538-59; 66, 1985, 21f.
18. *The Earliest Gospel Manuscript? The Qumran Fragment 7Q5 and its Significance for New Testament Studies*, Exeter 1992.
19. E.g.in B.Schwank, 'Wann wurden die Evangelien abgefasst? Müssen wir umdenken?', *Erbe und Auftrag* 63, 1986, 54-6; H.Burgmann, *Die essenischen Gemeinden von Qumrân und Damaskus in der Zeit der Hasmonäer und Herodier (130 ante 68 post)*, Frankfurt 1988, 429-37; H.Hunger, *Tyche* 2, 1988, 278-80.
20. Above all by H.U.Rosenbaum, 'Cave 7Q5! Gegen die erneute Inanspruchnahme des Qumranfragments 7Q5 als Bruchstück der ältesten Evangelien-Handschrift', *Biblische Zeitschrift* 31, 1987, 189-205.
21. 'Das Qumranfragment 7Q5', *Novum Testamentum* 30, 1988, 97-9.
22. F.Rohrhirsch, *Markus in Qumran? Eine Auseinandersetzung mit den Argumenten für und gegen das Fragment 7Q5 mit Hilfe des methodischen Fallibilismusprinzips*, Wuppertal and Zurich 1990.
23. B.Mayer (ed.), *Christen und Christliches in Qumran?*, Eichstätter Studien, Neue Folge 32, Regensburg 192.
24. C.P.Thiede, 'Bericht über die kriminaltechnische Untersuchung des Fragments 7Q5 in Jerusalem', ibid., 239-45.
25. C.H.Roberts, *An Unpublished Fragment of the Fourth Gospel in the John Rylands Library*, Manchester 1935.
26. Cf. J.O'Callaghan, 'El cambio *dt* en los papiros biblicos', *Biblica* 54, 1973, 41-16; C.P.Thiede in *Christen und Christliches in Qumran?*, 60f.
27. Cf. Thiede, *The Earliest Gospel Manuscript?*, 25f.; id., in *Christen und Christliches in Qumran?*, 71f.
28. There are some more recent advocates in D.J.Moo, *The Letter of James*, Leicester 1985, 34 n.1.
29. 'Die Höhle "7" was kein Einzelfall!', in *Christen und Christliches in Qumran?*, 227-36.
30. Thus especially E.Ruckstuhl, 'Zur Frage einer Essenergemeinde in Jerusalem und zum Fundort von 7Q5', ibid., 1431-7.
31. Letter of 12 November 1991 (ibid., 249).
32. 'Ein neues Bild des Judentums zur Zeit Jesu? Zum gegenwärtigen Stand der Qumran- und Essener-Forschung', *Herder Korrespondenz* 4/1992, 175-80: 180 and letter to R.Riesner of 20 January 1993.
33. G.de Nantes, 'Le "7Q5" fragment de Saint Marc – Don royal de Jésus à son Eglise', *La Contre-Reforme catholique au XXᵉ siècle* 275, 1991, 1-12; 'Die Datierung der Evangelien – Unglaublich, aber wahr?', *Rom-Kurier* 9, 1992, 1-8 (signed 'an exegete'); B.Bonnet-Eymard, 'Ein christlicher Schatz', *SAKA Informationen* 17, 1992, 121-2.

34. '4Q525 et les péricopes des Béatitudes en Ben Sira et Matthieu', *RB* 98, 1991, 80-106: 81.

35. 'Streit um die Rollen von Qumran', *Zur Debatte*, 22 May 1992, 1-3: 2.

36. 'Das Qumranfragment 7Q5 als Beleg einer Frühdatierung des Markus-evangeliums?', *Christophorus* 37, 1992, 117-25: 124.

### 9. What is the Significance of the Qumran Texts for the Understanding of Jesus of Nazareth?

1. Cf. O.Betz, 'Was John the Baptist an Essene?', in H.Shanks, *Understanding the Dead Sea Scrolls*, Washington 1992 and London 1993, 205-16.

2. A report was given to the Qumran Symposium in Mogilany, Poland, by his wife L.N.Gluskina, 'The Teacher of Righteousness in Joseph Amusin's Studies', in Z.J.Kapera, *Mogilany 1989 – Papers on the Dead Sea Scrolls II*, Krakow 1991, 7-22. Cf. also M.Ulman, 'Obituary: Prof. Joseph Amusin', *The Times* 61, 18 July 1984, 12.

3. Cf. M.Hengel, *Judaism and Hellenism*, London and Philadelphia 1974, I, 394-453.

4. The standard collection of Pseudepigrapha is now that by J.H.Charlesworth, *The Old Testament Pseudepigrapha* (two vols), New York and London 1983, 1984. Some scholars, including P.Riessler and A.M.Dupont-Sommer, think that there is strong Essene influence on the Pseudepigrapha.

5. Cf. G.Jeremias, *Der Lehrer der Gerechtigkeit*, Studien zur Umwelt des Neuen Testament 2, Göttingen 1963, 168-267.

6. Cf. Y.Yadin, *The Temple Scroll I: Introduction*, Jerusalem 1983.

7. Cf. R.Riesner, *Jesus als Lehrer. Eine Untersuchung zum Ursprung der Evangelien-Überlieferung*, WUNT II/7, Tübingen ³1988.

8. O.Betz, 'Bergpredigt und Sinaitradition', in *Jesus – der Messias Israels*, WUNT I/42, Tübingen 1987, 333-84; 'The Eschatological Interpretation of the Sinai Tradition in Qumran and in the New Testament', in *Jesus – der Herr der Kirche*, WUNT I/52, Tübingen 1990, 66-87.

9. Cf. O.Betz, 'Jesu Heiliger Krieg', in *Jesus – der Messias Israels*, 77-98.

10. Cf. R.Riesner, 'Formen gemeinsamen Lebens im Neuen Testament und heute', *Theologie und Dienst* 11, Giessen ²1984, 208-18.

11. Cf. B.Pixner, *Wege des Messias und Stätten der Urkirche*, Giessen 1991, 208-18.

12. Cf. O.Betz, 'Kontakte zwischen Essenern und Christen', in *Christen und Christliches in Qumran?*, 157-76: 169-71.

13. The American programme bore the title 'The Saga of the Dead Sea Scrolls'.

14. Cf. O.Betz, 'Das Problem der Gnosis seit der Entdeckung der Texte von Nag Hammadi', in *Jesus – Herr der Kirche*, 361-94.

15. Cf. O.Betz, 'Probleme des Prozesses Jesu', *ANRW* II, 25/1, Berlin

and New York 1982, 566-644; 'Jesus and the Temple Scroll', in
J.H.Charlesworth, *Jesus and the Dead Sea Scrolls*, New York 1993, 75-
103.

16. Cf. O.Betz, *Was wissen wir von Jesus?*, Wuppertal ²1991, 101-6.
17. Cf. further A.Strobel, *Die Stunde der Wahrheit. Untersuchungen zum
    Strafverfahren gegen Jesus*, WUNT I/21, Tübingen 1980; P.Stuhlmacher,
    *Jesus von Nazareth – Christus des Glaubens*, Stuttgart 1988, 47-64.
18. Cf. O.Betz, 'Die Bedeutung der Qumranschriften für die Evangelien des
    Neuen Testaments', in *Jesus – der Messias Israels*, 318-32.
19. *Der sogenannte historische Jesus und der geschichtliche, biblische
    Christ*, Leipzig 1892, English translation Philadelphia 1964.
20. Cf. O.Betz, 'Die Frage nach dem messianischen Bewusstsein Jesu', in
    *Jesus – der Messias Israels*, 140-68.

## 10. *Did the Essenes turn to Jesus as Messiah?*

1. Düsseldorf 1970. For criticism see R.Schackenburg, K.Müller, G.Dautz-
   enberg, *Rabbi J. Eine Auseinandersetzung mit Johannes Lehmanns
   Jesus-Report*, Würzburg ³1970.
2. *The Dead Sea Scrolls Deception*, 197-208.
3. One outstanding example was the Catholic exegete G.Graystone, *The
   Dead Sea Scrolls and the Originality of Christ*, London and New
   York 1956. On the basis of quite different non-apologetic theological
   presuppositions the Protestant H.Braun, *Qumran und das Neue Testament* I/II, Tübigen 1966 (the literature discussed essentially goes up to
   1959) was much more restrained about the similarity.
4. K.Stendhal (ed.), *The Dead Sea Scrolls and the New Testament*, New
   York 1957 (new edition in preparation); J.H.Charlesworth (ed.), *John
   and the Dead Sea Scrolls*, London 1972 (new edition New York 1992);
   M.Black, *The Scrolls and Christian Origins. Studies in the Jewish
   Background of the New Testament*, Chico ²1983; J.Murphy O'Connor
   and J.H.Charlesworth (eds.), *Paul and the Dead Sea Scrolls*, New York
   ²1990; J.H.Charlesworth (ed.), *Jesus and the Dead Sea Scrolls*, New
   York 1993.
5. Protestant: M.Burrows, *The Dead Sea Scrolls*, London and New York
   1955; id., *More Light on the Dead Sea Scrolls*, London and New
   York 1958; F.F.Bruce, *The Dead Sea Scrolls*; H.Bardtke, *Die Handschriftenfunde am Toten Meer: Die Sekte von Qumran*, East Berlin 1958,
   198-211; F.M.Cross, *The Ancient Library of Qumran and Modern
   Biblical Scholarship*, Grand Rapids ²1980. Catholic: G.Nolin, *Die Söhne
   des Lichtes. Zeit und Stellung der Handschriften vom Toten Meer*,
   Vienna and Munich 1954; J.Daniélou, *Qumran und der Ursprung des
   Christentums*, Mainz 1958; R.Mayer and J.Reuss, *Die Qumran Funde
   und die Bibel*, Regensburg 1959; J.van der Ploeg, *Funde in der Wüste*

*Juda. Die Schriftrollen vom Toten Meer und die Bruderschaft vom Qumran*, Cologne 1959; J.Maier and K.Schubert, *Die Qumran-Essener. Texte der Schriftrollen und Lebensbild der Gemeinde*, UTB 224, Munich and Basel ²1991 (1958 or 1960).

6. 'The Dead Sea Scrolls', *Jerusalem Post*, International Edition, 9 November 1991, 22.

7. Cf. R.Riesner, *Jesu als Lehrer. Eine Untersuchung zum Ursprung der Evangelien-Überlieferung*, WUNT II/7, Tübingen ³1988, 126ff., 159f.

8. *Theology and Eschatology*, Oxford 1968.

9. Cf. A.Gelin, *Les pauvres de Yahvé*, Paris ³1945.

10. Cf. H.Stegemann, *Die Enstehung der Qumrangemeinde*, Bonn Dissertation 1970; J.Murphy O'Connor, 'The Essenes and their History', *RB* 81, 1974, 215-44. There is a good summary of the problems in H.Shanks, 'Essene Origins – Palestine or Bablylonia', in *Understanding the Dead Sea Scrolls*, Washington 1992 and London 1993, 79-84.

11. Cf.S.Safrai, 'The Sons of Yehonadav ben Rekhav and the Essenes', *Bar-Ilan Journal* 16-17, 1978, 37-58.

12. Cf. J.Maier, *Zwischen den Testamenten. Geschichte und Religion in der Zeit des Zweiten Tempels*, Würzburg 1990, 260-83.

13. Cf. B.Pixner, 'Wege der Messias und Stätten der Urkirche. Jesus und das Judenchristentum im Licht neuer archäologische Erkenntnisse', *SBAZ* 2, ed. R.Riesner, Giessen 1991, 149-79.

14. Cf. especially also C.H.H.Scobie, *John the Baptist*, London 1964, 32-48.

15. Cf. S.L.Davies, 'John the Baptist and Essene Kashruth', *New Testament Studies* 29, 1983, 569-71.

16. Cf.R.Riesner, 'Bethany Beyond the Jordan (John 1.28). Topography, Theology and History in the Fourth Gospel', *Tyndale Bulletin* 38, 1987, 29-63.

17. Cf. R.E.Brown, 'Die Schriftrollen von Qumran und das Johannesevangelium und die Johannesbriefe', in K.H.Rengstorf, *Johannes und sein Evangelium*, Wege der Forschung 82, Darmstadt 1973, 486-528; and also O.Cullmann, *The Johannine Circle*, London and Philadelphia 1976.

18. Cf. O.Betz, 'Kontakte zwischen Christen und Essenern', in B.Mayer, *Christen und Christliches in Qumran?*, 157-75: 170, and the valuable work by R.J.Bauckham, *Jude and the Relatives of Jesus in the Early Church*, Edinburgh 1990.

19. Cf. R.Riesner, *Prägung und Herkunft der lukanischen Sonderüberlieferung*, Theologische Beiträge 24, 1993.

20. For further instances see J.A.Fitzmyer, 'Peace upon Earth among Men of his Good Will', in *Essays on the Semitic Background of the New Testament*, London 1971, 101-4.

21. Cf. H.Schürmann, *Das Lukasevangelium* I, Herders Theologischer

Kommentar III/1, Freiburg ²1981, 114f.; F.Bovon, *Das Evangelium nach Lukas* I, Evangelisch-katholischer Kommentar III/1, Zürich and Neukirchen-Vluyn 1989, 128f.

22. F.Rienecker, *Lexikon zur Bibel*, Wuppertal 1960, 546.

23. R.Mayer and J.Reuss, *Die Qumran-Funde und die Bibel*, Regensburg 1959, 130.

24. Among the works on this passage, special mention should be made of C.Spicq, 'L'Épître aux Hébreux, Apollos, Jean-Baptiste, les Hellénistes et Qumrân', *RQ* 1, 1958/59, 365-90. Cf. further the authors in Braun, *Qumran und das Neue Testament* I, 153f.

25. The most important witnesses to the tradition are collected in D.Baldi, *Enchiridion Locorum Sanctorum. Documenta S.Evangelii Loca Respicientia*, Jerusalem ³1982, 473ff.

26. Cf.R.E.Riesner, 'Das Jerusalemer Essenerviertel und die Urgemeinde', *ANRW* II 26/2, in preparation.

27. B.Pixner, D.Chen and S.Margalit, 'Mount Zion: The Gate of the Essenes Re-excavated', *Zeitschrift des Deutschen Palästina-Vereins* 105, 1989, 85-95, and plates 6-16; B.Pixner, 'Wege des Messias', 180-207; 'Archäologische Beobachtungen zum Jerusalemer Essener-Viertel und zur Urgemeinde', in Mayer, *Christen und Christliches in Qumran?*, 88-113.

28. J.B.Lightfoot, *Saint Paul's Epistle to the Colossians and to Philemon*, London 1875, 94 n.2.

29. Cf.R.Riesner, 'Essener und Urkirche in Jerusalem', *Bibel und Kirche* 40, 1985, 6-76; 'Das Jerusalemer Essenerviertel – Antwort auf einige Einwände', in Z.J.Kapera, *Intertestamental Essays in Honour of Józef Tadeusz Milik*, Vol.I, Qumranica Mogilanensia 6, Krakow 1992, 179-86; 'Jesus, The Primitive Community and the Essene Quarter of Jerusalem', in J.H.Charlesworth, *Jesus and the Dead Sea Scrolls*, New York 1993, 198-234.

30. Cf. Pixner, 'Wege des Messias', 180-207.

31. Cf. R.de Vaux, *Archaeology and the Dead Sea Scrolls*, London 1973, 21-3.

32. Thus already H.Kosmala, *Hebräer – Essener – Christen. Studien zur Vorgeschichte der christlichen Verkündigung*, Leiden 1959, 297f.

33. C.Grappe, 'A la jonction entre Inter et Nouveau Testament: le récit de la Pentecôte', *Foi et Vie* 89, 1990, 19-27; M.Delcor, 'A propos de l'emplacement de la porte des Esséniens', in Kapera, *Intertestamental Essays* I, 25-44.

34. Cf. R.Riesner, 'Essener und Urgemeinde in Jerusalem', in B.Mayer, *Christen und Christliches in Qumran?*, 139-95.

35. H.J.Schoeps, *Theologie und Geschichte des Judenchristentums*, Tübingen 1949.

36. Cf. O.Cullmann, 'Die neuentdeckten Qumrantexte und das Judenchristentum der Pseudoklementinen', in *Vorträge und Aufsätze 1925-1963*,

Tübingen and Zurich 1966, 241-59 (originally in the 1954 Bultmann Festschrift).
37. Cf. the account in H.Feld, *Der Hebräerbrief*, Erträge der Forschung 228, Darmstadt 1985, 35-8.
38. J.Daniélou, *The Theology of Jewish Christianity*, London and Philadelphia, 1964, 55-64.
39. R.Bultmann, *The History of the Synoptic Tradition*, Oxford and New York 1963.
40. M.Dibelius, *From Tradition to Gospel*, Cambridge 1971.
41. Cf.O.Betz, *Offenbarung und Schriftforschung in der Qumransekte*, WUNT I/6, Tübingen 1960.
42. Cf.J.Schmitt, 'Prédication apostolique', *Dictionnaire biblique*, Supplement VIII, Paris 1972, 246-73; 'Qumran et découvertes au desert de Juda VI D', ibid. IX, Paris 1979, 1011-14.
43. R.Pesch, *Das Evangelium der Urgemeinde*, Herder TB 678, Freiburg 1979.
44. G.Theissen, *Lokalkolorit und Zeitgeschichte in den Evangelien. Ein Beitrag zur Geschichte der synoptischen Tradition*, Fribourg CH and Göttingen 1989.
45. Cf. R.Riesner, 'Jesus as Preacher and Teacher', in H.Wansbrough, *Jesus and the Oral Gospel Tradition*, Sheffield 1991, 183-210: 193-5, 205-7.

# General Index

Acts of the Apostles, 2, 81, 109, 111, 116, 121–2, 136, 139, 147, 155
Aemilius Scaurus, 71
Agrippa I, 57, 64
Agrippa II, 79
Alexander Jannaeus, 28, 99, 101, 103
Allegory, 109, 111–12
American Schools of Oriental Research, 137
Ananus (see Annas II)
Ancient Biblical Manuscript Center, 25–6
Angels, 42–3, 91, 108
Annas II, 78–9
Antigonus, 63
Antiochus, 103
Antipater, 63
Archelaus, 72, 110
Aretas IV, 67
Aristobulus, 109
Asceticism, 48, 105, 109, 144

Babylon, 60, 145
Bannus, 48
Beatitudes, 67, 93
Belial, 43
Bertelsmann Verlag, 32
*Biblical Archaeology Review*, 11, 23, 113, 162
Boethusians, 48

Caiaphas, 105
Celibacy, 41, 59, 104, 127, 130, 136
Christians, 51, 68, 72, 76, 78, 80, 114, 142, 155
Church, earliest, 1–3, 14–16, 18–19, 28–30, 32, 37, 49, 69–73, 81, 109, 147
Community Rule (1QS), 7, 39–43, 99, 127–9, 131–3, 153
Copper Scroll (3Q15), 7, 17, 60, 145
Crucifixion, 45, 83–4, 87, 89, 138

Damascus, 21, 66–7, 77, 81, 104, 144
Damascus Rule, 23, 39, 40, 41, 43, 44, 59–61, 66, 97, 102, 105, 128–9, 145
Daniel, Book of, 90, 92, 94, 96, 104, 111, 143
Demetrius, 103
Diodotus Trypho, 78
*Discoveries in the Judaean Desert*, 10
Droemer Knaur, 32
Dualism, 43, 138

Ebionites, 16, 73, 79, 152
École Biblique, 5, 7, 9–10, 24, 49, 51, 123
Elizabeth, 104–37
En el-juwer, 59
En et-Turabe, 59
En Fesha, 59
Enoch, Book of, 11, 104
Eschatology, 115, 128–9, 131, 134, 136–7
Essene Letter, 35
Essenes, 20–1, 36–7, 39, 41–4, 47–9, 51, 56–62, 64–5, 72–3, 76, 97, 99–101, 103–6, 108–9, 112, 125, 127–8, 130, 135, 137, 141–2, 144–5, 147, 152–3, 155–6, 159–60
  name, 16, 41
  sources, 50, 54
  trial marriages, 59, 107, 136, 145
Eusebius, 81, 139

Form criticism, 153

Gamaliel, 105, 109
Genesis Apocryphon, 10
Gentile Christians, 73–74
Gnosticism, 138
Greek, 41, 123, 129

Habakkuk pesher (1QpHab), 5, 39, 60,

# Index of Modern Authors

# Acknowledgments of maps
# and illustrations

Map 1            Based on a map in the *Einheitsübersetzung*, Katholische Bibelan-
                 stalt, Stuttgart 1980, 1449.
Map 3 and 4      From G. Kroll, *Auf den Spuren Jesu*, Verlag Katholisches Bibel-
                 werk, Stuttgart[10] 1988, 162.
Map 5 and 6      From Othmar Keel and Max Küchler, *Orte und Landschaften
                 der Bibel. Ein Handbuch und Studien Reiseführer zum Heiligen
                 Land 2. Der Süden*, Benziger Verlag AG, Zurich 1982, 463, 469.
Map 7 and 8      From J.H. Charlesworth (ed.), *Jesus and the Dead Sea Scrolls*,
                 Doubleday 1993, 332, after a drawing by David Lind with Frank
                 Blizzard, and 35.
Map 9            From Carsten Peter Thiede, *Die älteste Evangelien-Handschrift?
                 Das Markus-Fragment von Qumran und die Anfänge der schrift-
                 lichen überlieferung des Neuen Testamentes*, Wuppertal and
                 Zurich[3] 1992, 32.
Map 10, 11, 12, 14 From Rainer Riesner (ed.), *Wege des Messias und Stätten der
                 Urkirche*, Giessen 1991, 220, 187, 193, 206–7.